MAKERS OF AMERICAN DIPLOMACY

From BENJAMIN FRANKLIN to ALFRED THAYER MAHAN

MAKERS OF AMERICAN DIPLOMACY

From BENJAMIN FRANKLIN to ALFRED THAYER MAHAN

Edited by
FRANK J. MERLI
and
THEODORE A. WILSON

CHARLES SCRIBNER'S SONS, NEW YORK

Library of Congress Cataloging in Publication Data
Merli, Frank J.   1929–
    Makers of American diplomacy.
    Includes bibliographies.
    CONTENTS: v. 1. From Benjamin Franklin to
Alfred Thayer Mahan.—v. 2. From Theodore
Roosevelt to Henry Kissinger.
    1. Diplomats—United States. 2. United
States—Foreign relations. I. Wilson, Theodore
A., 1940–   joint author. II. Title.
[E183.7.M47]   327.73[B]   73-19866
ISBN 0-684-13786-0
ISBN 0-684-13797-6 Vol I (pbk.)
ISBN 0-684-13798-4 Vol II (pbk.)

1 3 5 7 9 11 13 15 17 19 c/p 20 18 16 14 12 10 8 6 4 2

Printed in the United States of America

To All Our Children

CONTENTS

PREFACE

These biographical essays—all especially commissioned for this collection—encompass a wide range of interpretive viewpoints and represent a significant dimension of the nation's international experience, stretching from the revolutionary war experiences of Benjamin Franklin to the turn-of-the-century naval career of Alfred Thayer Mahan. The figures we have chosen include the obvious presidents and secretaries of state, but to give the reader an idea of the variety and depth of American involvement in foreign affairs, we have also included a representative sample of second-echelon makers of diplomacy. In the selection of contributors we have attempted a balance, geographical as well as generational; but our emphasis has been on the new generation of diplomatic historians trained in the late 1950s and the 1960s. By allowing the contributors the widest possible range of interpretive freedom, encouraging them to find their own ways to illuminate the nature and significance of their subjects, and refraining from any attempt to reconcile opposing interpretations, we intended to avoid the dangers of a facile "consensus" approach and the pitfalls of a "problems" reader. We hope that the collection represents a fair cross section of the debate on the meaning of American diplomacy and the contributions of the men who have molded it.

Because the thrust of this collection is interpretive rather than monographic—and because we hoped to keep the book within manageable bounds—the citations and the scholarly apparatus that a more technical compilation might be expected to contain have been reduced. Omissions should not be difficult to rectify, however; in nearly every case the contributors have derived their essays from works in progress or recently completed in which full documentation can be found.

In the preparation of this volume we received the cooperation of many experts who read the essays for accuracy of information and validity of viewpoint and made helpful, perceptive comments on early drafts. To identify them might imply support for views they do not hold; so we have elected to thank them anonymously but publicly. In addition, Alexander DeConde of the University of California at Santa Barbara, Walter LaFeber of Cornell University, and Richard Leopold of Northwestern University offered helpful suggestions about contributors and the format of the book. Robert Beisner of American University played a key role in the planning stages of the project and has supported it throughout. Without in any way implicating these men in the imperfections this work may contain, we thank them sincerely for the generosity that prompted their responses to our requests for help.

The staff at Scribners, especially Elsie Kearns and Barbara Wood, have been cooperative throughout; their careful attention to detail has saved us from many errors. Mrs. Joan Jander of Dyer, Indiana, compiled the index.

Above all others, one person requires public thanks for his part in bringing this work to fruition. In addition to training both editors and one of the contributors, Robert H. Ferrell of Indiana University has read all the selections, offering incisive criticism. When the mechanics of the project and the difficulty of keeping so many historians in harness threatened to overwhelm us, his calm and judicious advice brought order and a measure of sanity to the operation. At every stage of the project he has been a wise and sympathetic counselor, and for his contributions we are deeply grateful.

The real heroes of the project are the authors, who struggled against an almost impossible deadline, who cooperated so fully in the task of putting the pieces together—and who so cheerfully suffered our sometimes heavy-handed commentary. For the merits of the work they deserve full credit. They have demonstrated that diplomatic history can deal imaginatively with ideas, that it can incorporate and refine new methodological insights from other

branches of history and from other disciplines. Their efforts reveal
that historians of divergent backgrounds, ideological commitments, and convictions can move beyond the partisanship and
acrimony that have so crippled our field in recent years, that they
can meet on common ground and cooperate in the search for a
meaningful, verifiable past.

Thanksgiving Day, 1973   Frank J. Merli
                                                       Theodore A. Wilson

INTRODUCTION

To choose the few men who form the subjects of these essays as pivotal figures—as the "makers of American diplomacy"—from the throng who have influenced the nation's foreign relations is certain to provoke displeasure at the selection of some or the omission of others. To attempt to assign responsibility for any idea or decision in foreign policy to a single individual is an equally thankless task. Even in the early days of the Republic, diplomacy was a product of the actions of numerous persons and groups; as the international responsibilities of the United States expanded, so did the constituencies affecting the conduct of diplomacy. The creation of policy in a democracy derives from a complicated interaction of domestic concerns, political calculations, popular attitudes, seemingly irrational assumptions and beliefs—in short, from assorted, ill-defined, and often contradictory purposes. In such circumstances, designating certain men as personifications of the national will or agents of history may indeed appear a naïve approach to a complex problem.

History, in a sense, remains a composite of innumerable biographies, however, so such a task seemed worth undertaking; but it poses once again the eternal conundrum of free will versus determinism. To what extent, if any, does the act of an individual affect the course of events? Even if responsibility for a decision or a general policy could be clearly attributed to a single person, would not the problem of relating it to subsequent decisions and policies be almost insurmountable? Cause and effect relationships do exist, of course; but normally they are so amorphous and intertwined that attempts to unravel them lead more often to ambiguity than to certitude.

Any attempt to find underlying congruities in the work of American diplomats confronts the problem of contemporary animosity and the biases of historians toward past efforts to manage the nation's affairs. The record suggests, superficially at least, that much of the work of American diplomats has been devoted to tearing down, in word if not in fact, the policies of predecessors. It would appear, therefore, that continuity has not been a dominant feature of United States diplomacy. Further, the special concerns of particular diplomats do not always seem directly related to the larger issues of national policy that transcend presidential administrations, the tenure of a particular secretary of state, or the effective influence of powerful pressure groups.

Such warnings merely restate the obvious: that the contributions of individuals, no matter how many, do not and cannot comprise the total of the American diplomatic experience. The essays in this collection suggest another observation, perhaps also self-evident: that those who have created and conducted America's foreign affairs have often responded to forces outside their control; their decisions have furthered aims and aspirations that they understood little and that interested them less. Statesmen must confront the crises of the moment without leisure to analyze the consequences of their acts. The limits these underlying factors place on the conduct of diplomacy have sometimes been more important than personal initiatives. Whether they know it or not, men are prisoners of the milieu in which they live and function and, with some rare exceptions, are constrained by the dictates of their own experience and the conventional wisdom of their age. Few transcend such limits; fewer still build lastingly or institutionalize their insights.

The following essays suggest at the same time that the participation in diplomacy of human beings, each bringing unique beliefs, patterns of behavior, principles, and ambitions to the common task of directing the country's international business, remains an absolutely essential factor in the diplomatic equation. Men, not abstractions such as Wall Street, the Eastern Establishment, or the United States, "make" diplomacy. These essays treat individuals who are in some ways representative, in some ways atypical, of the men who conducted foreign relations in the first century and a quarter of the nation's history. They suggest the extent to which elements of personality (even idosyncratic behavior and personal foibles) have affected events. Issues of foreign policy and the forces that produce them transcend the purposes and preoccupations of individual statesmen; nevertheless, they can only find expression through the marvelously unpredictable, chaotic realm of human motivation and the decisions of fallible men. "No matter how 'ripe' the time," as David Brion Davis has said so well in another context, "there would be no coalescing of . . . opinion until specific decisions and commitments were taken by individual men. . . . Yet when all allowances are made for . . . trends and climates of opinion, one must ultimately come down to the men who precipitated change." [1] Understanding this fact, so obvious yet so often ignored, is a necessary beginning to any re-creation of the context of American diplomacy.

These essays on men who in some way contributed to the making or implementation of American diplomacy were originally envisioned as informative but disparate pieces that would form a gallery of diplomatic portraits, reflecting internal meaning but perhaps offering little to assist the reader's grasp of the relationships that cut across eras and styles of diplomacy. Surprisingly, a process of selection that because of circumstance contained an element of randomness and guidelines that offered the contributors considerable flexibility produced something more than a mere "collection." The result demonstrates far greater continuity in the outlooks and actions of these diplomats than anyone had anticipated.

Time wrought amazingly few changes in the essentials of foreign affairs—a surprising statement unless one reflects on the basic components of the world views of Alexander Hamilton or

1. David Brion Davis, *The Problem of Slavery in Western Culture* (Ithaca, 1966), p. 489. Professor Davis is discussing the rise of antislavery sentiment and John Woolman's part in precipitating it; but his point about individual responsibility applies as well to the diplomatic realm.

James G. Blaine. Survival in a hostile international environment remained the touchstone, and the options by which survival was to be ensured appeared to be as restricted and fraught with peril in 1900 as they were in the nation's formative years. Power—its definition, articulation, and believability—stands at the center of the agonizing choices with which all American diplomats have struggled.

Certainly the problems that beset the Committee of Correspondence of the Continental Congress differed in degree, and to some extent in kind, from the issues the Department of State faced at the end of the nineteenth century when the United States emerged as a great power. Still, the common themes—from the search of Franklin, Hamilton, Jefferson, Madison, and their peers for a diplomatic strategy that would protect the national interest, assure independence, ward off threats to domestic stability, provide for expansion, and ensure a maximum of commercial opportunity in world markets, and to do all these things while satisfying deep-seated convictions about America's moral superiority, to the formulation of similar goals by Fish, Blaine, and Mahan—are notable and amazingly consistent. The imprint of the early lessons of the 1790s has proved remarkably durable. The international arena at the nation's birth reeked of violence, corruption, and hostility toward the innovative (and therefore threatening) institutions and ideas fostered by the American experiment. That arena, however, was also a marketplace in which commodities, both actual and abstract, necessary for America's survival and growth were traded. Thus, from its inception, American involvement in the world remained ambivalent: diplomatic engagements were restricted to matters that were essential to the nation's well-being and safety; but on the other hand, it was considered permissible, even desirable, to exploit opportunities offered by Old World conflicts and by the disintegration of its political and economic systems. The means by which American objectives were to be realized—isolation (in its peculiar nineteenth-century sense), neutrality, hemispheric domination, reliance on a higher law, exploitation of Manifest Destiny, territorial and commercial expansion, and a quite remarkable talent for fishing in troubled waters—remained constant in importance throughout the nineteenth century.

Although the Founding Fathers might have been surprised by the transformation, over the course of the nineteenth century, of some of these diplomatic techniques (such as isolation and neutrality) into goals in themselves, they shared with later generations of American leaders certain convictions about an appropriate "style" for the nation's diplomacy. The circumstances in which the United States became ensnared varied greatly during this period, but the manner and overall direction of diplomacy changed little. These essays reveal much about such matters as the responsiveness to public opinion of those who made foreign policy, the impact of pressure groups and elites, and assumptions about America's role in the world; indeed, they suggest that a broader definition of diplomacy is needed. Throughout these assessments of public careers winds the theme of the American people's preoccupation with internal growth, with a consequent influence on diplomacy. Deeply intertwined with this theme is another major one, that of America's mission: the belief in the United States as the agent of providential purpose, the repository of a sacred trust, the New Jerusalem. Those who sought to guide the nation's destiny believed that it should teach right precepts, the virtues of liberty and of republican government, to less enlightened peoples. Much of the proselytizing was rhetorical and remained so; but there was an almost irresistible pressure to convert rhetoric into reality, and on an ever larger scale. Whether or not the new diplomacy of Seward, Fish, Blaine, and Mahan constituted a break with tradition remains a moot point. After all, America began its national existence with an attempt to implement a new order of things—a new order, it should be noted, of universal applicability. The empire of liberty was by definition expansionist; creation of that empire surely constituted a key concern of the makers of American diplomacy in the nineteenth century.

Benjamin Franklin by Joseph Sifrede
Duplessis, Henry E. Huntington Library
and Art Gallery. Photo courtesy of
Robert Merli

BEN
FRANKLIN

in France:
A Maker of American Diplomacy

Cecil B. Currey

Had someone inquired of Ben Franklin, during his service to the Continental Congress in 1775 and 1776, the number of jobs, requests, and committees to which he gave his time, surely the old man's memory would have failed him. The period between his return from England on 5 May 1775 and his departure for France on 25 October 1776 was undoubtedly the busiest of Franklin's public life. Committee meetings filled his days; dozens of official and semiofficial tasks faced him as he served both the nation and Pennsylvania, kept up a heavy correspondence on public and private matters, and met with an endless stream of callers.

It was no wonder that Franklin was usually tired and often sick. Sixty-nine years old when the Pennsylvania House of Assembly chose him as a delegate to the Second Continental Congress, Franklin was both one of the older and one of the better-known men in that body. He was one of the few living Americans with a

1

thoroughly established international reputation, achieved in part because of his prominent service as colonial agent in Britain for four colonies before the war.

Franklin, having spent all the years since 9 December 1764 in England, had sailed from the mother country in late March, and arrived in the American colonies on 5 May 1775. While his ship tossed at sea, the smoking firebrands of discontent, resentment, and resistance finally flared into open war and rebellion. The monumental event began before Franklin landed at Philadelphia. John Pitcairn, major in His Majesty's Royal Army, was ordered to lead a column to Lexington and Concord to seize John Hancock, Sam Adams, and hidden stores of munitions. There a Massachusetts militia captain, John Parker, and his sixty men confronted the British. The militia had earlier heard Parker tell them, "Do not fire unless fired upon, but if they mean to have a war, let it begin here!" Shots rang out and rebellion began. Delegates to the Second Continental Congress hastily assembled in Philadelphia where Franklin joined his colleagues five days after his return from abroad.

It was proper that Benjamin Franklin should sit among the members of America's nascent government. Born in obscurity, he had carefully nurtured his native talents to their utmost. He had taken a faltering newspaper and made it one of the best known in the colonies and the most lucrative. Although lacking family and status he had become acceptable to even the highest levels of society. His business made him rich but it was his mind that made him well known. He mastered several languages and many of the major sciences of his day, and he became one of the most innovative men of his time. Glorying in relationships with other men, Franklin entered Pennsylvania politics and by the mid-1750s was an acknowledged leader of the legislature. In 1756 and again in 1764, his province chose him as a colonial agent, or lobbyist, before the official boards and agencies of the mother country. As agent, he represented the interests of Pennsylvania on matters of trade, Indian affairs, and various legal issues. He sought to promote in every way possible the well-being of his colony. His adept handling of issues prompted Georgia to commission him as agent in 1768; New Jersey sought him in 1769 and the lower house of the Massachusetts legislature appointed him in 1770. Many colonists regarded him as the most important American in England; the time came when Franklin himself succumbed to that notion.

In later years, Franklin liked to believe that his testimony before the Commons in 1766 had been instrumental in securing repeal of the Stamp Act. In the years after repeal, he was often in the forefront of those counseling resistance to the policies of the mother country. In the vanguard of radical action, he usually held political opinions more advanced than those of many of his countrymen, although in 1765 and 1766, when the colonies adopted nonimportation as a weapon against England, Franklin's letters were generally quiet on the matter. By 1768, however, he also had adopted that policy as the best available economic tool against British taxing programs. In 1767, when he learned of the new Townshend system of excises planned for the colonies, he began a quiet little game with some people that was, in its own way, significant. As deputy assistant postmaster general, it was his privilege to frank his letters. His usual mark was "Free. B. Franklin." Tongue in cheek, he changed it to "B. Free Franklin."

How much colonial resistance Franklin's advice inspired remains a matter of conjecture. Yet General Thomas Cadwalader, Alexander Colden, and General Thomas Gage agreed that his intervention sustained and prolonged American nonimportation during the late 1760s. Franklin's advice to the colonies, however, caused him to lose favor with many members of the imperial government. In earlier years a friend described him as "forever with one Member of Parliament or other." Radical advice, quarrels with cabinet members, and other questionable activities so changed attitudes that a friend later wrote Franklin's son that his father was not only on "bad terms with Lord Hillsborough [but with] the Ministry in General." By the early 1770s, Franklin had acquired several nicknames, including the "Hoary Old Sinner," the "Judas of Craven Street," and "Old Traitor Franklin." He was considered even more a *persona non grata* among British official-dom when he sent to the governor's opponents in the legislature some potentially damaging letters written by Governor Thomas Hutchinson of Massachusetts. Sam Adams got them, edited them to seem much worse than they actually were, and printed them in the newspapers. Many called for the removal of the governor. The British Ministry, taking a dim view of the episode, shortly thereafter dismissed Franklin from his postmaster's position.

Part of the reason for Franklin's headstrong prewar attitudes toward the British government may be found in his long-standing hope of acquiring huge tracts of land in western America. When Franklin retired from business in 1748 he had become convinced that immense riches were to be had through western land investments, and he participated in a number of abortive attempts to exploit land in the West. At the same time, Franklin led a Pennsylvania political movement urging the crown to withdraw proprietary rights from the Penn family. In public he argued against the wisdom of proprietary holdings; privately he sought them for himself.

The Proclamation Act of 1763 prohibited further western settlements. While planning ways to get around the provisions of this law, Franklin bought acreage in Quebec and Nova Scotia and joined a group of speculators, including his Philadelphia friend Samuel Wharton, who thought they could make money in the West in spite of the 1763 law. For two years Franklin and his associates sought permission from the crown for a land grant on the Illinois River. As a result of their efforts, the crown almost issued a charter to the group, but the plan failed when colonial affairs came under the control of the new secretary of state for the American colonies, Lord Hillsborough, who refused to approve a new establishment. Franklin's goal of an Illinois colony was seen to be hopeless early in 1768, so he and his partners abandoned the effort. They then organized the Indiana Company to seek a tract of land near present-day Pittsburgh. This effort also failed.

Samuel Wharton voyaged to England in 1769, and, with Ben Franklin and Thomas Walpole, an English banker, established still another speculative group, which included large numbers of British officials of all ranks and degrees of influence. This enterprise, the Walpole Associates, was established early in 1769 but was soon reorganized as the Grand Ohio Company, which sought a vast charter grant in the vicinity of the present state of West Virginia to be called Vandalia. Franklin and other leaders of the company used many questionable methods in pursuit of their western colony: falsified petitions, secret memberships, code names (Franklin was known as "Moses"), and even lies. Such tactics worked sufficiently well so that by 1773 it appeared that

Franklin and his confederates would soon be proprietors of an American colony; but it was not to be. The Hutchinson letters scandal, the Boston Tea Party, the rapidly disintegrating colonial situation, and Franklin's part in it brought governmental reappraisals, and the ministry shelved the project. To get it moving again, Franklin publicly resigned from the Grand Ohio Company early in 1774 while privately retaining full membership and all his stock shares. The ruse was ineffective; the project was still stalled when Franklin returned to America in 1775.

Now all this was in the past—but not the dead past, for Franklin still hoped to become a member of the landed rich. Instead of asking permission for the western colony from the crown, he and his partners (including the British ones) turned to the Continental Congress. Again the speculators reorganized. As Samuel Wharton put it, they should "take into the Partnership . . Members of the Congress" which would create a "Thousand political Reasons" why that body should grant them lands across the mountains. Not willing to wait for official approval the partners met for business in March 1776 at the Indian Queen Tavern in Philadelphia, with Franklin chairing the session. His son, a prominent Tory, who had been a longtime member of these enterprises, was not present, for he was under house arrest at his home in Perth Amboy. Politically divorced from his son, Ben still looked out for his economic interests and that day voted not only his own shares of stock, but his son's as well. After electing officers, the organization authorized the sale of four-hundred-acre tracts of land to all comers. Advertisements appeared in Franklin's old newspaper, the *Pennsylvania Gazette*. It is not clear whether the speculators discussed the fact that they had neither legal title to those lands nor the right to sell even one acre.

In spite of Franklin's best efforts, he gained nothing concrete toward his real estate goal during 1775 and 1776. He had too little time in which to concentrate on his own personal ambitions because of other duties. There were letters to write, people to interview, foreign visitors with whom to talk, committee meetings to attend, including the most Important committee on which he sat, the forerunner of our present Department of State, the Secret Committee of Correspondence.

Ben Franklin became chairman of this committee and took an active part in the early diplomacy of the revolutionary war. The committee gathered information from Europe and sent agents there to contact foreign governments and to procure aid, assistance, trade agreements, and military alliances. The day after Franklin's appointment, 29 November 1775, the committee chose its first European agent, a Virginian residing in London named Arthur Lee. Lee and Franklin had been acquainted for years, Lee having for a time served as under-agent for Massachusetts, and the two already disliked each other. The following March of 1776, the Committee of Secret Correspondence sent its first agent to Europe to negotiate with the French government: Silas Deane, who went to France knowing nothing of diplomacy and less of the French language.

By mid-1776, after Franklin's return from a futile effort to persuade the French colonists in Canada to join the American cause, he began considering ways to extricate himself from the complexities and inconveniences of the North American scene. When the Continental Congress decided to send another man to Europe to help Deane, Franklin made the right suggestions and succeeded in being named a commissioner to France. There would now be three men there: Arthur Lee, Silas Deane, and Benjamin Franklin, appointed as coequal members of the American mission. Congress's fetish for committees would nearly prove the undoing of the American cause because of the squabbles, self-seeking, and accusations that would emanate from the scandal-ridden American mission in Paris.

On the basis of recent research, it is at least doubtful whether Franklin decided to go to France so much from a desire to serve the new United States of America as from a need for a more restful and less dangerous environment. France would surely be less hectic, more cosmopolitan and cultured than Philadelphia. In the City of Lights he might be able to return to the leisurely life-style he had earlier pursued in London. Already elderly, he resented the necessarily long hours demanded of him in America that put an undue burden upon his health. In the New World, he was in any case somewhat out of his element. He had been away from the colonies almost continuously since 1757, a total of nineteen years. More oriented toward Europe than America by his long absence, Franklin was a true cosmopolite. As an agent of the Continental Congress, he would have in Paris the prestige that would come

with that title. Living abroad, he would share none of the blame if
the uprising in the colonies failed. In that eventuality he would be
far safer from imperial retribution in France than in the United
States. If France joined the war effort in behalf of America,
Franklin knew that much of the credit would be his. Yet had he
foreseen the troubles ahead of him in France—the ugly rumors
that would circulate about him, the near ruin of his reputation and
career—he might have changed his mind; for the American
mission would become an unequal troika, each of the three
pulling in different directions, marching each to the sound of his
own drummer.

Paeans of praise have come from Franklin's biographers as
they have told of his wartime diplomatic service. Charles Evans
Hughes, an ex-secretary of state and chief justice of the Supreme
Court, wrote that Franklin had "for all time set the standards for
American diplomacy" and added that he was "the greatest of all
the diplomatic representatives of this country and has no superior
among those of any time or of other nations." Popularizing
historian Helen Augur contended that Franklin became "the most
dazzling diplomat in the country's history." Another author has
insisted that "due largely to Franklin's adroit diplomacy, the treaty
with France was signed." Still another, unaware of Franklin's
warning, often repeated, that virgin America should not go
suitoring to Europe in search of wartime aid, portrayed Franklin as
one of the leading Americans to urge the French toward an
alliance with America, repudiating others who were "fearful of sly
courtiers and suspicious of alliances." From such authors, a reader
would never learn of certain shadowy phases of Franklin's life in
Paris that mark heavily the life and career of the oldest of our
Founding Fathers during the years he spent abroad in the service
of the American Congress.

Even while serving as chairman of the Secret Committee of
Correspondence, Franklin had urged Silas Deane to contact
Edward Bancroft once he got to France. Bancroft was a British spy
who rifled Deane's files at will and who eventually recruited him
into membership in the British Secret Service. When Franklin
arrived in Paris, he continued to employ Bancroft, defending him
from all charges brought against him, including those of Arthur

Lee who quickly identified him as a British spy. Franklin furthermore hired other spies for various positions at the American
mission, such as William Carmichael (alias Pierre Le Maître) and
Jacobus Van Zandt (code name George Lupton). Franklin repeatedly met with agents sent by the English ministry who sought to
disentangle him from his loyalties to America. One was his old
comrade from prewar days, the Moravian pastor John Hutton;
another was a Franklin acquaintance, Benjamin Vaughan. The
chief of the British Secret Service network in France, Paul
Wentworth, visited Franklin more than once and offered him huge
bribes to change sides. A member of Parliament, William Pulteney,
saw Franklin twice in Paris, and his old friend Thomas Walpole
sought credentials as an agent of the ministry of Lord North.
Refused such legitimacy, he journeyed to Paris anyway. If Beaumarchais's information was correct, this listing does not begin to
exhaust the names of those from the British Secret Service with
whom Franklin met during 1777, let alone in subsequent years.

     Franklin had been in France for but a short time when, with
his landlord Chaumont, Robert Morris, the congressional secretary
of finance, Silas Deane, and others, he became involved with
American merchants in exploiting the rich trade in scarce commercial goods. Franklin and Deane named the former's grandnephew, Jonathan Williams, Jr., as head of the American commercial agency at Nantes in order to control the trade at that port city
and to profit from the sale of prize ships auctioned there. Williams
sold such vessels short, repurchased them, and resold them at a
tidy profit, all despite Congress's appointment of William Lee as its
agent there! Franklin and Deane worked hard to keep Williams in
Nantes and Lee away from it.

     In another moneymaking effort, Ben's fellow commissioner
Silas Deane, his old speculative partner Samuel Wharton, who was
still in London, and Edward Bancroft, secretary for the mission,
joined forces to use inside information on war news to play the
British stock market. Franklin, who would have had to know what
was going on, saw fit to close his eyes.

     Franklin's security over personal and state papers was slip-
shod. His controls would have made a modern security officer
blanch and even in the eighteenth century were something of a
scandal. It is difficult to justify such carelessness. He knew the
realities of international intrigue as well as anyone. His knowledge
was honed during his congressional service from May 1775 to

October 1776. Work on the Secret Committee of Correspondence and the Committee of Secret Correspondence put him in touch with many kinds of intelligence activities. He had appointed secret agents of the United States and had parleyed with French agents sent to contact the American government. He discussed with his colleagues various procedures to follow in obtaining intelligence data. There is little doubt of Franklin's thorough acquaintance with clandestine purposes and methods and of his knowledge of the need for constant security measures to forestall intelligence leaks to the British. He had long used mail drops, ciphers, pen names, false information to mislead others, and other methods of clandestine warfare. Experience in these methods made him as well fitted as any living American for the intrigues of European diplomacy. There are simply no records available, however, to indicate that he ever paid the slightest attention to security measures.

The nature of the assignment given Franklin by Congress necessitated a meticulous regard for security, for some of his duties simply could not be made public nor disseminated on other than a need-to-know basis. Yet when friends faulted him for leaving papers exposed, he laughed at or ignored them. Reminders that he was "surrounded by spies" and advice to keep his papers away from any "prying eye" made little impact.

If Franklin was an astute man, reputed by all who knew him to be keenly aware of what went on about him, he must have known of the duplicity of his associates. Others knew that his headquarters was riddled with security leaks; why did not he? If he did not know his staff was sending information to England, he was less capable than he has been represented by his biographers; if he did know, he was more culpable.

Sent to France to procure military aid and, hopefully, an open alliance, Franklin told his colleague Arthur Lee that "I have never yet chang'd the Opinion I gave in Congress, that a Virgin State should preserve the Virgin Character, and not go about suitoring for Alliances. . . ." Much later, to Arthur's brother, William, "the Doctor replyed that it was a matter to be considered whether it was worth our while to ask any of the Courts of Europe to acknowledge our Independence." William Lee noted that "this, I confess, astonished me greatly." Franklin's lukewarm support of American Independence may be seen in the report of Paul Wentworth, the French bureau chief, to William Eden, head of the

British Secret Service. Wentworth and Franklin met for discussions late in 1777 and early in 1778. Wentworth then reported to Eden that "72"—the code number for Franklin—"most particularly Commanded [his affection for England] to be mentioned, & his wishes to stop the progress of war in America." He continued that Franklin hoped "the acknowledgement of the Independency should not be made. . . ." William Carmichael, in a report to England, agreed with Wentworth. He wrote that "our leading man" trembled at the thought that France might soon join America in its war effort. "He wishes no European connection," said Carmichael.

Franklin and Deane both listened to blandishments promising rich rewards if they would help reconcile America and England: governorships, principal secretariats of the cabinet, holders of the privy seal, knighthoods, and baronetcies. Another British agent, William Pulteney, called upon Franklin. Pulteney's brother, George Johnstone, soon to be a member of the ill-fated British Carlisle Peace Commission, later claimed he had information based on those meetings of Pulteney and Franklin. Johnstone asserted that Franklin had suggested that the members of the Carlisle commission offer American leaders seats in Parliament as an inducement for abandoning the war effort. Such a bribe "would be more alluring than any other," Franklin had reputedly said. When the statement was attributed to him he wisely and vehemently denied it, as one would expect him to do; but the claim is still interesting in light of other more demonstrable shadows within which he moved while in Europe.

Franklin met with so many secret visitors from England, many of them members of the British intelligence apparatus, that Beaumarchais warned Vergennes "that secret advances are being made by England to Mr. Franklin, which you are doubtless unaware of. . . ." Between his arrival in France and the end of 1778, Franklin reputedly received no less than twenty English visitors with whom he met secretly. One rendezvous point was an old barge, *Le Pot de Vin,* which had been converted into a bathhouse and was anchored in the Seine not far from Franklin's home at Passy. There, amidst obscuring vapors of steam, an old, balding "Englishman" with long hair who was an excellent swimmer occasionally met unidentified persons. No, the attendants did not know his name, for he had not given it to them, but it is known that Franklin took almost daily swims in the Seine for exercise.

Shortly after Franklin arrived in Europe, he prevailed upon Arthur Lee to undertake a diplomatic mission to Spain in his stead. Lee did so and was successful in gaining some Spanish aid for America. When he returned to Paris, however, he was puzzled to notice that both Franklin and Deane ignored him. They did not inform him of business they had conducted in his absence, nor did they allow him to have keys to locked files, although he was equally credentialed with the other two. Meetings were held, decisions made, and money spent without consulting him. Soon, on Franklin's request, Lee was sent off to Berlin to arrange a treaty with the Prussians. One of the spies in the American headquarters noted the reason for the trip in a letter to England: "There is really some Business, but his Absence is also wanted. We shall now have a clear stage."

After Lee returned from the fruitless trip to Berlin, where his papers had been stolen, copied, and then returned by British agents, he began his first open criticisms of Franklin when he learned that the two colleagues had spent more than five million livres of public money and claimed to owe still more; yet they had no vouchers, receipts, or account books to explain the expenditures. Worried about Lee's suspicions, Franklin tried to weaken any future testimony the Virginian might give by spreading rumors that he was mentally ill. He spoke of Lee's "Sick Mind" full of "Jealousies, Suspicions & Fancies" which were the "Symptomatick Forerunner" of insanity. Deane also took up the cudgels against Lee and the two were so effective that one embassy employee later wrote, "I have heard Dr. Franklin say he thought Arthur Lee was crazy, and I am sure it was current enough at Nantes."

Then Franklin deftly administered the *coup de grâce*. When he learned that Lee needed a private secretary, he recommended a recent arrival from England, John Thornton, whom Lee hired, not knowing he was an army major and a British spy. Franklin reported to Vergennes that the Virginian now had a known British spy working for him and that such naïveté could not be countenanced. Vergennes reported this matter to the French chargé in America, Conrad Alexander Gérard de Rayneval, and at his request the United States Congress recalled the thoroughly burned Lee.

Franklin was also on dangerous ground in his support of a

Maryland sea captain, Joseph Hynson, who had been suborned by the British Secret Service. Franklin and Deane kept Hynson in France on the American subsidy list for many months until he finally had the chance he had been awaiting. Hynson's English superiors had instructed him to steal American diplomatic dispatches. He did so, substituting blank paper for the original reports and letters. He thus made off with most of the confidential correspondence between the French government and the American commissioners from 12 March to 7 October 1777, a real coup for the British. It was during this period, one author has claimed, that Franklin came "nearer than ever before in his life to sinking his fame in an infamy of corruption."

An American Congress made suspicious by the rumors it was hearing from abroad recalled Silas Deane and replaced him with John Adams. It did not take Adams long to detect the abysmal defects in Franklin's financial system. Huge sums had been spent carelessly, Adams claimed, but no one could remember how. Large debts remained unpaid, yet no records could be produced to justify them. Franklin, pressed for an audit of expenditures, called in Samuel Wharton and Edward Bancroft to review and certify the accounts. Strangely enough, they found them to be proper and in order.

Deane returned to Paris from the United States in 1780 and moved in with Franklin. The two had once calumniated Lee by describing him as insane. Since John Adams now watched both of them carefully, they again tried the same tactic; Franklin, Deane, and Bancroft all claimed Adams to be "actually mad."

Deane wrote a series of letters for the British Secret Service calling for reconciliation with England. They were later sent to America and published in New York by James Rivington, a Tory printer. The incident irrevocably finished Deane's career. Franklin never condemned him; instead, he loaned money to him and corresponded with him. Deane continued to use Franklin's home as a mail drop. As late as 1782, Franklin wrote a certificate of probity for his ex-colleague, asserting that he had always been honest and upright in the public service. William Lee claimed that Franklin had done so for fear that if he did not it might be learned that he had been as crooked as Deane.

During the negotiations for peace with Britain after 1781, John Jay and John Adams, the other two principal negotiators with Ben Franklin, were not terribly impressed with the old gentleman's help. For a time Franklin supported a peace that would not require Britain's recognition of America's independence. According to some, he seemed to be willing to allow Spain and France to "coop us up within the Allegheny Mountains." He urged his fellow negotiators to accept certain French diplomatic moves inimical to the United States. Far from being the most "dazzling diplomat in America's history," Franklin's colleagues often regarded him quite literally as a "pain in the neck." A rumor then circulated that Franklin "worked secretly against the treaty." Jay, of course, denied it and defended Franklin's role in the negotiations; but the mood around Franklin and attitudes at home led him to ask Jay for a testimonial to his service in behalf of the American cause. Jay gladly complied, thus helping Franklin in his expressed wish to carry his reputation with him intact, at least to the grave.

Until recently it would have been impossible for a reader to have learned of these darker phases of Franklin's overseas career, for no book or article has discussed them in any detail. When the evidence is in, will our assessment of Franklin's role as a maker of American diplomatic history be affected? In spite of blemishes upon Franklin's career, the traditional picture extolling his service in France is not completely wrong; it is incorrect only in the details from which older, and essentially proper, conclusions have been drawn.

The treaties of 1778 are but one example. The French were not moved to make an alliance with the United States because of America's military victory at Saratoga in 1777 as some have believed. Still less did the government of Louis XVI and Vergennes act because the brilliant, personal diplomacy and argumentation of Ben Franklin persuaded them that the time had come to act. The French ministry decided upon its course of action only when there seemed to be a real possibility of renewed British-American accommodation. On such matters they were remarkably well informed. By late 1777, worried about the possibility of Anglo-American rapprochement, the French ministry announced its intention to sign a treaty with America. It is possible that Franklin may well have had this in mind when he met with emissaries of the English Secret Service; some authors have long thought so. Whether that was or was not his own purpose, the result was the same: France would ally itself with the hard-pressed Americans. The tide of war turned, and Franklin, knowingly or unwittingly, was partly responsible.

In spite of his links with the British Secret Service that would have besmirched his record had they become known to his constituents at home, Franklin made important contributions to the American cause. Perhaps his help came not so much through what he did in France in an official way, for he was often lackadaisical, distracted, diffident, and unwilling to try to push the Vergennes government to an early decision regarding an alliance. This attitude exasperated the younger and more energetic Arthur Lee; yet Franklin was not deterred. He presented his credentials and then turned to other activities, content to wait for the monolithic French regime to act in its own way and time. Until that moment came, Franklin felt free to amuse himself as he pleased. His aplomb in doing nothing captivated the French. They sensed his love of *la dolce vita* and *feminae blandissima*. It was obvious to them that he relished life in France, enjoyed its people, and was taken with their culture and ways. His fascination was infectious and the French gladly returned his interest.

For the French, Franklin was more than simply another diplomat; he was a symbol of all they found fascinating in the New World. He dressed simply, spoke frugally and sparely, but his thoughts came from a mind tempered like steel. For them he was the American Quaker, the constitution maker. It was Franklin who had "snatched the lightning from the heavens and the sceptre from the hands of tyrants." When he met Voltaire at a public theater the two embraced and those who watched cried out that *"Solon et Sophocles"* had met. Courtiers and commoners alike enjoyed Franklin's wit and listened avidly for his latest bon mot. Franklin loved the ladies—so many of them—from his wife, Deborah Read Rogers Franklin in the 1740s, Katherine Ray Greene in the 1750s, his landlady in London, Mrs. Margaret Stevenson, in the 1760s, to the fullness of the 1770s and 1780s in France: Countess d'Houdetot, Madame Brillon de Jouy, and Anne-Catherine de Ligniville Helvétius. This was a trait Frenchmen could understand and they were entranced at the attraction this elderly man had for their womenfolk. They relished gossiping about his latest love interest and drew him to their breast.

Everything that Franklin did became grist for the French mill, whether it was his invention of a new word, *stormonter,* meaning

Benjamin Franklin's reception at the Court of France (1778)

"to lie" and derived from the name of the English ambassador, Lord Stormont, or his latest attack of the gout, or a new broadside from his private printing press in his home at Passy, L'Hôtel des Valentinois. Statuettes of Franklin, called miniatures, were struck by the thousands and Frenchmen, high and low, were not content until they owned one.

This love affair between *le pauvre Richard* and the French nation had repercussions across the Atlantic. For decades France had been the sworn enemy of Americans. Its autocratic monarchy, its Roman Catholicism, its foreign tongue that filled so awkwardly the mouths of Americans trying to speak it, its competing New World colonies, its invading armies and naval dreadnoughts—all had threatened Americans who long before had come to despise the French. England and its New World colonies had fought war after war against that European power. Now in only a few months the Americans' long-formed and time-hardened attitudes began to change; France had opened its arms to one of their own. Suspicions softened—from obvious necessity due to the importance of securing arms from that nation and because of the importance of gaining avowed allies in the struggle with Britain, and because of Old Ben's thorough enjoyment of that Catholic land and its strange people. Franklin was not purposely trying to change the hundred-year-old attitudes of his fellow Americans; he was simply having a good time as only he knew how to do, but his fun had wondrous side effects two thousand miles away. As much as anyone who could be named, Franklin's personal influence helped turn the new United States to a more open attitude toward France.

Elsewhere in this book, Lawrence Kaplan examines what Thomas Jefferson wanted for America. He analyzes with clarity the goals and accomplishments of the nation's third president within that framework. It would be difficult to fit Franklin's contributions within a similar frame. He was too free a spirit, too unwilling to accept the limitations that bound other men. An example might be his attitude toward money. Whereas Arthur Lee kept careful account of his expenditures in France, and Silas Deane deliberately obscured the dubious ways in which he spent money, Franklin chose a different path. He refused to commit himself to either of his colleagues' methods; as legend would have it, a curious congressional committee questioned his spending when he returned to the United States. The particular question was a mission account deficit of approximately one hundred thousand pounds. Asked of its whereabouts, Franklin loftily replied, "I was taught when a boy to read the scriptures and to attend to them, and it is there said: muzzle not the ox that treadeth out his master's grain." His meaning was clear. Benefits had come to the United States through his service in France; if this service cost America something, if Franklin benefited from that service, then Congress should simply accept that fact and not bother him with mundane accountings.

For Franklin, then, his single-mindedness, his diplomacy—whether in England before the war or in France during the conflict—was devoted to his own purposes rather than to the Revolution. When both interests coincided, he was quite willing to lend his talents to the American cause; when they diverged, he begrudged demands upon him and followed his own inclinations. Today his attitude would be described as "doing his own thing"; that was Franklin's forte. Perhaps more than any other Founding Father, Benjamin Franklin, because of his long stay in England, was aware of the benefits of British government and culture to America. Yet his own temperament was such that in the prewar years, in order to forward his own private goals, he was willing to sacrifice those benefits and work with men seeking independence. In those years some in America suspected Franklin of being willing to ignore their interests for his own; but at least as many thought him to be their voice in the mother country and learned to look to him for the views that would fix and justify their own. Because of overlapping interests, Franklin's personal power struggle coincidentally bolstered colonial seekers of independence and they took him to their bosoms unknowing or uncaring that he was only a practical man working for his own ends and not totally committed, as were they, to the "cause." The question that must be asked about this man is simply, "What did Franklin want for Franklin?"

Examination of Franklin's life reveals a streak of selfishness that guided him and kept him ever mindful of his own goals and purposes no matter what face he showed to the world. His positions were often variable, shifting as the winds, and it is often difficult to know exactly where his sympathies really lay during the war, or how firm was his commitment to the colonial cause.

Perhaps no one will ever know what kind of person was this doughty old man. He was at least far more European than American. His parochial views as a colonist had been tempered in his contacts with the scientists, the literati, the raconteurs of England and the Continent. He received the accolades and memberships of learned societies across Europe. Wherever he traveled, he encountered those who already knew him by reputation and who avidly sought to learn from him. His own views, tempered by acquaintance with European statesmen, scientists, and philosophers, allowed little localism to remain in his ideas. Whether colonist or cosmopolite, he worked first and foremost for Benjamin Franklin. Perhaps this is of little moment; Franklin was no mere mortal even in his own lifetime, and perhaps he who had seen so much and accomplished such great things should not be expected to adhere to the same codes of living that bound lesser men.

Minutiae never fascinated Franklin. He disdained, for the most part, the details of diplomacy; his correspondence was often answered reluctantly and late; papers signifying unfinished work inevitably fouled his desk; his appointment calendar was too seldom clear and was usually a snare dotted with the names of little men waiting to see him about small matters. Such tasks left him drained and bored. His forte was rather the grand display: standing undaunted before the House of Commons in 1766 testifying for the needed repeal of the Stamp Act, a state dinner as guest of George III, suffering in silence before the righteous thunder of Wedderburn in 1774 in the halls of the Privy Council, riotous homecoming to Philadelphia in 1775, festive crowds joyously celebrating his arrival in and procession through France on his way to Paris in 1776, signing of the French treaties as commissioner for America in 1778, presentation to Louis XVI. All such things were the victories upon which Franklin doted and which made lesser things possible to bear.

In his own free time, he sought amusing occupations. He much preferred sitting in England at the Honest Whig Coffee House talking with Burke or Priestley or Canton, or coming home from a party with a "thickened head," or publishing the *Craven Street Gazette* to entertain little Polly Stevenson, or engaging in double entendres in Paris with his favorite lady friends than in pursuing the humdrum but necessary routine of diplomacy. It is not that business was never done so much as that it was done late and without enthusiasm.

Franklin stood in bold relief to his two colleagues in France. Silas Deane, corrupt to the core, concentrated on enriching himself by selling his soul to Robert Morris, Beaumarchais, and the British Secret Service. Arthur Lee, desperate to aid the new nation, agitated himself frenetically and frantically. He traveled to Spain, to Prussia, palavered with his brothers, and sought evidence of corruption to substantiate his suspicions of his two colleagues.

Franklin, only five feet eight inches tall, stood head and shoulders above his co-workers. By pursuing his own ends he provided bountiful but coincidental benefits for America. Old and wise, he knew all there was to know about corruption. He may even have delicately participated in it when he wished, without staining his fingers. Perhaps he made a few dollars. Franklin occasionally flirted with British agents while he pondered the relative advantages of loyalty to America or noble rank in England. Laughing at them all, using them when he could, he turned to his real loves in Paris: printing, chess, jokes, weighty conversations, women, good companions, and better food. When one has recorded the blemishes and acknowledged the peccadilloes, what then may be said of Franklin's service to the nation?

The coincidental benefits or contributions of Franklin to America include the symbol he became for many Americans, the part he played in bringing Americans and Frenchmen to change their minds about one another; he may well have been instrumental in causing the French government to move toward an American alliance more quickly when it learned through its spies that Franklin was talking rapprochement with British emissaries. These diplomatic victories were real enough even if the thought of them was not always uppermost in Franklin's mind. Yet these coincidental contributions form the base of his historical reputation.

This Talleyrand of the West did not fit conventional molds. He was entirely capable of simultaneously handling and manipulating his own divergent interests and those of the British, the French, and the Americans. One must distinguish between what he really wanted and what he merely talked about, between what he said and what he did, between what he only speculated upon and what he committed himself to accomplish. Gerald Stourzh's remarkable monograph, *Benjamin Franklin and American Foreign Policy*, misses much of that essential nuance. Stourzh did not fully separate what Franklin proposed from what he actively sought, nor was he sufficiently aware of his subject's shortcomings. Consequently Stourzh adopted a too uncritical view of Franklin. His book remains required reading, however, for he properly noted many of the wide-ranging considerations in diplomacy and foreign policy that flowed from Franklin's talented mind. Those ideas usually had to be accepted and acted upon by others, for Franklin, after conceiving them, often turned to new and different matters. It may be that Benjamin Franklin's great contribution in the field of diplomacy was in the realm of ideas rather than on the field of action—not what he did so much as what he suggested. His value lay in his interpretation for others of doctrines already available and in his proposing new concepts in such moderate language that they became persuasive to others. His deeds were often narrow and self-centered; his thoughts, on the other hand, sparked concentrated action by others, and so often became part of the foundation of American foreign policy. No student of nineteenth-century diplomacy should ignore this fact. It is possible that historians, in stressing the virtuosity of Franklin's performance, have missed an important theorist of American diplomacy.

In this respect, we might remember Franklin's advice that new states ought not to go suitoring after alliances, or ponder his warnings against European connections unsupported by mutual interests. Washington's Farewell Address echoes such sentiments, and the first president's "great rule of conduct" in international affairs advised Americans to have "as little *political* connection as possible" with foreign nations. The ideas of John Quincy Adams, as given by James Monroe in his famous message of 1823, also have a Franklinesque ring: the "true policy" of the United States was to abstain from European affairs in the hope that Europe would reciprocate. Even the campaign posters of 1916, proclaiming that Wilson had "kept us out of war," or Franklin Delano Roosevelt who, in September 1940, declared that he had said again and again to the mothers and fathers of America that their sons would not be sent to fight in any European war, are reminiscent of Franklin. Isolation, surely one of the most persistent themes in American foreign policy, extends back to Franklin's attitudes toward entangling alliances; yet historians have seldom connected his name with that theme.

Within that position of isolation and distrust, another strong theme remained, which may well have arisen from Franklin's attitudes regarding Franco-American ties and friendships. From the time of the Sage of Passy's joyful life with his French friends during the Revolution to John J. Pershing's cry of "Lafayette, we are here!" to the GIs of World War II who believed their battles to free France were repayment of an old debt, Americans have held France in particularly high esteem among European nations, for it was France that came to their aid during the War of Independence when America desperately needed help. Thus the "common wisdom" has assessed the historical past.

Franklin conceived another persistent idea in the American approach to foreign affairs: "superparliaments" that might promote harmony and ensure peace. He set forth his Albany Plan of Union as early as 1754 in an effort to establish a new imperial body to oversee affairs of common concern to both the English people and their American colonies. His view has become part of the American Dream and may be seen in the sporadic support of America for justice among its own states, for various European unification efforts, in Wilson's hopes for the League of Nations, in participation in the United Nations, and in support for such partial unions as the European Economic Community. Although by 1775 Franklin opposed a "united nations organization" for the British Empire, he continued to think highly of the concept itself as an answer to many of the ills of warring nations. In 1787, still enthusiastic about the just-completed American Constitutional Convention in Philadelphia, Franklin wrote an old friend, Ferdinand Grant, that Europe should also unite. "I do not see why you might not in Europe carry the Project of good Henry the 4th into Execution, by forming a Federal Union and One Grand Republick of all its different States and Kingdoms, by means of a like Convention, for we had many Interests to reconcile."

Benjamin Franklin could be scathing in his denunciation of the actions of nations that were not bound by concepts of law and justice. To Richard Price, Franklin spoke of his hopes for "the Discovery of a Plan, that would induce & oblige Nations to settle their Disputes without first Cutting one another's Throats." John Baynes reported that Franklin "observed that nothing could be more disgraceful than the scandalous inattention to treaties" demonstrated by various nations. He did, however, think "the world would grow wiser, and wars become less frequent." Most plans to speed that process along were impracticable, Franklin said, for "they supposed a general agreement among the sovereigns of Europe to send delegates to a particular place. Now, though perhaps two or three of them might be willing to come into this measure, it is improbable and next to impossible that all, or even a majority of them would do it." A century or two might allow enough time for all Europe to "agree upon an alliance against all aggressors, and agree to refer all disputes between each other to some third person, or set of men, or power." Such a development was truly important, thought Franklin, because neighboring states required justice as much as neighboring citizens. In his view a robber who plundered in a gang was as despicable as one who acted alone, and a nation that made an unjust war was "only a great Gang." Thus Franklin spoke of this concern, basing his case as was his wont upon pragmatic, practical concerns rather than upon some idealistic concern for liberty or freedom.

During Franklin's term in the Continental Congress he counseled his fellows on two other matters. The first related to American expansion into the trans-Allegheny West and the absorption of Canada, and was born of his hopes for profit in land speculation. This long-standing dedication, when transposed into political terms, became a justification for expansionism for the young nation. Part of his interest in western land stemmed from what has been called "defensive imperialism," the need to oust foreign powers in order to create what Jefferson would call an empire of liberty in the New World. Franklin was as ardent an expansionist as any of the Founding Fathers, and his writings, whether in 1760 or 1776 or 1785, provided a sound rationale for acquiring as much of the West as possible. The American hunger for land broadened with the peace treaty of 1783; that stream became a river with the acquisition of Louisiana in 1803. With Manifest Destiny in the 1840s it became a raging torrent, and the "white man's burden" and overseas involvement changed it into a veritable flood tide of American diplomacy by the 1890s.

Franklin also tried in Congress to broaden the definitions of international law. He hoped that warring nations might ultimately be made to limit their actions to military objectives and to avoid harming neutral nations or individuals engaged in peaceful pursuits of agriculture and trade among enemy populations. Franklin failed to accomplish his goal, but his view of the pacific character of commerce was embodied in the American Plan of 1776 which stated that "free ships make free goods." This doctrine became the cornerstone of the American definition of neutral rights in the nineteenth century and was incorporated into the Treaty of Amity and Commerce signed with France in February 1778.

Two years later, Franklin explained how his idea was gaining currency in Europe: "All the neutral states of Europe seem at present disposed to change what had never before been deemed the law of nations, to wit, that an enemy's property may be taken wherever found, and to establish a rule that free ships shall make free goods. The rule is in itself so reasonable, and of nature so beneficial to mankind, that I can not but wish it may become general." That view did not prevail, and the United States, having fought one war with the mother country to achieve independence, found itself embroiled thirty-four years later in another to maintain it. Mindful of Franklin's contribution to his country's definition of neutral rights, President James Madison said in 1814 that the United States would not continue to honor the doctrine of "free ships, free goods" unless a refinement, almost a new principle, was also observed, "namely, that unarmed merchant vessels, like wagons or ploughs, the property of one belligerent, should be unmolested by the. other." That doctrine, he proudly asserted, had "an undisputed American father in Doctor Franklin."

An examination of the extraordinary ideas of Benjamin Franklin remains crucial for an understanding of the development, formulation, and implementation of American foreign policy. Franklin remains one of the chief figures in America's pantheon of greatness, for his ideas, taken up and built upon by others, have become pervasively influential melodies in the hymnody of United States diplomacy.

BIBLIOGRAPHIC NOTE

Extensive documentation for the views expressed in Professor Currey's essay may be found in his two books, *Road to Revolution: Benjamin Franklin in England, 1765–1775* (New York, 1968) and *Code Number 72: Ben Franklin, Patriot or Spy* (Englewood Cliffs, N.J., 1972). To date the best one-volume biography of this distinguished American remains Carl Van Doren's *Benjamin Franklin* (New York, 1938); in some two hundred pages

Verner W. Crane has compressed a wealth of information and shrewd analysis, *Benjamin Franklin and a Rising People* (Boston, 1954), a volume in Oscar Handlin's American Biography series. Both of these biographies are somewhat dated and no doubt as the voluminous Franklin papers are published new biographies will appear. For a firsthand look at Franklin's varied activities the reader should consult Leonard W. Labaree et al., eds., *The Papers of Benjamin Franklin* (New Haven, 1959–), and Labaree's annotated edition of the *Autobiography of Benjamin Franklin* (New Haven, 1964).

Gerald Stourzh's *Benjamin Franklin and American Foreign Policy* (Chicago, 1954) remains a pioneering and indispensable appraisal of Franklin's approach to problems of diplomacy and foreign affairs. It provides, in the words of one reviewer, the first "balanced interpretation of Franklin's ideas in the field of foreign policy."

For extended coverage of the colonial background of the Revolution see the magisterial work by Lawrence H. Gipson, *The British Empire before the American Revolution*, 14 vols. (New York, 1958–69), an impressive monument of American scholarship. See also the same author's volume in the New American Nation series, *The Coming of the Revolution, 1763–1775* (New York, 1954). For the intellectual background of the war one must consult Bernard Bailyn, *The Ideological Origins of the American Revolution* (Cambridge, Mass., 1967).

For the foundations of American statecraft and the colonial experience in international affairs, the book to consult is Max Savelle, *The Origins of American Diplomacy: The International History of Anglo-America, 1492–1763* (New York, 1967), the first volume in the American Diplomatic History series under the general editorship of Armin Rappaport. Also worth consulting are Savelle's "The American Balance of Power and European Diplomacy, 1713–1778," in Richard B. Morris, ed., *The Era of the American Revolution* (New York, 1939); "Colonial Origins of American Diplomatic Principles," in the *Pacific Historical Review* 3 (September 1934), 334–50; and "The Appearance of an American Attitude toward External Affairs, 1750–1775," *American Historical Review* 52 (July 1947), 655–66.

Two recent works that include the nation's early experience with international affairs are Felix Gilbert, *To the Farewell Address: Ideas of Early American Foreign Policy* (Princeton, 1961), and Paul Varg, *Foreign Policies of the Founding Fathers* (East Lansing, Mich., 1963). Both are model studies.

The classic account of revolutionary diplomacy remains Samuel Flagg Bemis, *The Diplomacy of the American Revolution* (New York, 1935), the one book on its subject against which all others are measured. A masterly account of the negotiations for peace at Paris is Richard B. Morris, *The Peacemakers* (New York, 1965); Morris also examines some of the mythology and misunderstanding surrounding the work of American diplomats at Paris in "The Diplomats and the Mythmakers," a chapter in *The American Revolution Reconsidered* (New York, 1968). For an attempt to see the events of the revolutionary era as part of the developing storm in Europe, see Richard Van Alstyne's *Empire and Independence: The International History of the American Revolution* (New York, 1965), a volume in Robert Divine's America in Crisis series. For a provocative and wide-ranging assessment of some of the larger issues of the era see Robert R. Palmer, *The Age of the Democratic Revolution: A Political History of Europe and America, 1760–1800*, 2 vols. (Princeton, 1959–64). William Stinchcombe's *The American Revolution and the French Alliance* (Syracuse, 1969) traces the impact of congressional involvement in foreign affairs and the fate of the alliance in America. For a pioneering effort still worth reading see Edward S. Corwin, *French Policy and the American Alliance of 1778* (Princeton, 1916).

ALEXANDER HAMILTON

and the Diplomacy of Influence

Ian Mugridge

It is presumably no accident that one of the major modern biographies of Alexander Hamilton is subtitled *Portrait in Paradox* or that his reputation, unlike that of some of the other principal American leaders of his time, has undergone great changes since his death in 1804. Hamilton's actions, perhaps more than those of some of his better-known contemporaries, have been subject to widely differing interpretations. Unlike his mentor, George Washington, or his rival, Thomas Jefferson—men apparently blessed with a basic internal consistency and confidence in themselves and their place in society which enabled them to meet challenges and vicissitudes with equanimity and confidence—Hamilton was hardly cast in a heroic mold. Intellectually, of course, he was the

The author gratefully acknowledges a President's Research Grant from Simon Fraser University which facilitated his work on this essay.

undoubted superior of Washington and at least the equal of
Jefferson; but there seemed to be something lacking in him, what
Adrienne Koch has called "a basic defect of character," which
ultimately diminished his standing as a statesman and a national
leader. Professor Koch has also noted that recent interpretations
have been too kind to Hamilton.

It would be an exaggeration to blame Hamilton's origins and
upbringing for his deficiencies, though perhaps the former reinforced the latter. He was born in or about 1757 on the West Indian
island of Nevis, "the bastard brat of a Scotch pedlar" as the much
provoked John Adams once put it, and brought up by his mother
until her death when he was twelve years old. Soon afterward he
set out to make his way in the world. He was blessed with three
basic ingredients for success in that endeavor: brains, ability, and
benefactors, a combination that took him through years of
struggle and hardship until he left for the American mainland in
1772 to embark upon a university career.

In eighteenth-century terms, such origins were dubious;
Hamilton never cared to advertise them, though he never entirely
severed connections with his father and other members of his
family. Other men, however, have come from equally unfavorable
backgrounds and have not exhibited the character traits that
Hamilton repeatedly demonstrated. His background did give him
an almost frantic determination to succeed, to advance to what he
considered his proper place in society, and an equally fierce pride
in his achievements. That these qualities later degenerated into
mere snobbishness, contempt for the lower orders, and a querulous self-defensiveness flowed at least as much from defects in
Hamilton's character as from boyhood deprivations.

When Hamilton arrived in New York City, the series of events
that led to the Revolution and the War of Independence was
already well advanced. He began his studies at King's College,
entering the path that led him to a position of power and authority
in postwar American society. He advanced from a young and
eloquent orator and pamphleteer to an influential and dashing
aide-de-camp to General Washington so that, by the time of the
peace settlement in 1783, he was no longer an obscure and
struggling student, dependent for his survival largely on his own
wits and the generosity of his benefactors. He finished the war as a
colonel, with the friendship and esteem of Washington and a
reputation for dashing if somewhat irresponsible bravery. He then

became, for a short time, a member of the Continental Congress and a lawyer of growing reputation and affluence. Finally, through marriage to Elizabeth Schuyler in which, to quote John C. Miller, "love, money, social prestige and ambition met in happy conjunction," his social and financial status in New York had become secure.

From 1783, until his death over twenty years later, Hamilton remained a major force in American politics, both nationally and locally. His participation in the movement for constitutional reform and in the drafting and adoption of the new Constitution was of undoubted and overwhelming importance. Equally, his work as secretary of the treasury in Washington's two administrations made an enormous contribution to the financial and administrative structure of the new nation as well as to the directions the government took in domestic and foreign policy. After Washington's retirement he remained an acknowledged leader of the Federalist party both in New York and at the national level and was frequently able to affect the policies of the Adams administration. These years, however, were less happy and far less successful; they served as an example of something against which Hamilton warned his countrymen in the *Federalist*: the corrupting influence of being out of power. Alexander Hamilton was then at his worst. Deprived of national office, he used his considerable influence and talent for intrigue to subvert the authority of John Adams whose office he almost certainly wanted for himself. This led to a widening breach with the president, finally made irreparable by the peevish, pointless, and inexcusable attack on him that Hamilton published a month before the election of 1799. His behavior also widened the gap between himself and Jefferson, vice-president under a president with whom he often disagreed and ultimately defeated, but whom he respected and showed no inclination to undermine as Hamilton did. Finally, having fought against the reelection of Adams and against his replacement by Jefferson, Hamilton found himself on the outside, unable to influence in any substantial way the direction of the government, an increasingly querulous and ineffective voice in the political wilderness. Soon afterward, he died as the result of a foolish duel, a ridiculous climax to a fifteen-year feud with a man who was Hamilton's equal only in the enormity of his pretensions.

Hamilton did possess considerable intellectual ability, and he supplemented this with an equal talent for administration. His attention to and grasp of the problems and details of his tasks as an officer in Washington's command, as a lawyer and legislator, and as secretary of the treasury are truly impressive. His talents frequently became liabilities, for he often appeared unable to decide what affairs did not concern him and when he should take no part in them. He tended to make all the business of government, from whatever department, his province; his desire to interfere often helped to negate the constructive nature and good influence of his work. His removal from power only exaggerated this tendency and converted it into plots to influence the Adams cabinet. Later, it led him to play a role in the destruction of the opposition as well as the demise of his own party.

One must add to this catalog of defects an apparently overwhelming desire for self-justification, charitably termed "frankness" by one biographer, which appeared again and again in Hamilton's writings, even during his years of power and influence. Probably his disputes with George Clinton and Thomas Jefferson showed him at his worst in this respect. Writing to Washington about his clashes with Jefferson and Madison, Hamilton loudly justified his own questionable activities by claiming purity of intention and by denouncing what he saw as the sinister machinations of his enemies.

The roots of these many failings were within Hamilton himself. While his background had supplied him with a yearning to advance his status in society, it also narrowed his perspective and restricted effective use of his abilities. Hamilton's times offered challenging opportunities and brought him into contact with unusual men and events, but in the end, despite his intellect and talent, his apparent smoothness and cultivation, he could not survive and flourish in such circumstances. He had not the depth, the confidence, or the grace of, say, Jefferson, who represented much that Hamilton wanted desperately to be and whom, not surprisingly, he grew to dislike intensely. He had not the steadfastness, the soundness, or the assurance of Washington, who dominated the revolutionary and postwar periods. In power, Hamilton achieved much and contributed much of value to the growth of his country; out of power, he lapsed into intrigue and pettiness, and perhaps only an untimely death prevented the ultimate destruction of his career and reputation.

Throughout his public career, between the end of the War of Independence and the end of Washington's second administration, one of Hamilton's prime concerns, if not his principal objective, became the establishment of the United States as a strong and united nation, prepared and equipped to take its place among the great nations of the world. On this question, little disagreement emerged between Hamilton and his most prominent contemporaries during the late eighties and early nineties. Substantial agreement existed between the leaders of the movement for constitutional reform and the new federal government that all energies had to be channeled in the direction of creating a nation that could command respect in the international arena. This was the case even among those who, like Jefferson, Madison, and Hamilton, quarreled so bitterly in later years.

Where Hamilton parted company with his contemporaries— or perhaps merely carried certain ideas further than they—was in the role he assigned to foreign policy in relation to the growth of the nation. Hamilton believed that there could be no realistic division between foreign and domestic policies, for the one supported and augmented the other and both had to be used to move the nation toward self-sufficiency and international influence. If one of these had to be paramount in the national concern, it was foreign relations: the future of the United States as an industrial and commercial power depended largely on the way in which the rest of the world regarded the new nation.[1]

The great English philosopher F. H. Bradley once rather lightheartedly described metaphysics as "the finding of bad reasons for what we believe upon instinct." In this sense, there was something of the metaphysical in Hamilton's approach to questions of national policy. As a poor, ambitious social climber, he had always recognized that the path to success lay in the establishment of his position. As one of the leaders of a poor, divided, and ambitious nation, instinct told him the same thing: that the way to international prominence and respectability lay in establishment of the new nation as honest, fiscally dependable, and firm. In the pursuit of such objectives, the final goal had to be kept clearly in sight and extraneous considerations cast aside.

1. Gerald Stourzh, *Alexander Hamilton and the Idea of Republican Government* (Stanford, 1970), pp. 126–70. See also the essay on Thomas Jefferson in this volume.

National policy had to be designed to ensure domestic unity and strength; then a strong, unified nation might turn its attention to enhancing its prestige abroad. Such was the essence of the Hamiltonian message; it was a theme he repeated throughout his public career.

Although Hamilton's public statements repeatedly expressed faith in the potential of the new nation, he was equally sure that this could only be realized under a form of government different from that of the feeble, nearly impotent Articles of Confederation. Survival in a world filled with actual or potential competitors and on a continent crowded with powerful and potentially hostile neighbors required a government that could give the United States the order, stability, and, through them, the strength and authority to stand confidently on independent ground. Such advantages, such necessities, could never be gained from a government national in name only, whose regulatory power was hopelessly dissipated among thirteen states, whose cohesion in wartime had been precarious and in peacetime virtually nonexistent.

In spite of the progress made by the United States during the 1780s, Hamilton and a growing number of his contemporaries became convinced of the need to jettison the Articles in favor of a stronger constitution. His views of government and national policy, expressed with cogency and consistency in the years between the Treaty of Paris and the Constitutional Convention, later appeared in their most comprehensive form in the *Federalist*, one of the most remarkable exercises in political theory ever produced in the United States. Neither the views of American foreign policy expressed in these papers and the functions of government in formulating and carrying them out, nor Hamilton's work in gaining support for constitutional reform by stressing the baneful effects of America's impotence abroad, have been properly appreciated.

The basic purpose of the *Federalist* was to persuade the people of New York of the virtues of the proposed federal Constitution. Even though these papers were subject to the limitations of propaganda, the evidence of Hamilton's earlier writings as well as of his subsequent words and actions suggests that the opinions presented in the *Federalist* reflected deeply held convictions on these subjects, so that they may therefore be taken as a reasonably accurate guide to his view of the world.

Hamilton believed that the United States, divided and weak,

had cut such a poor figure in the world that even after five years the peace treaty had not yet been fully implemented. This had been the fault partly of Great Britain and partly of individual states. It was also partly the fault of the "nation," for the government of the Articles possessed neither the power nor the authority to compel recalcitrant states to meet their obligations or to ensure that foreign powers met theirs. Congress and its officers were helpless when states, allies, or enemies could not be brought into line. Frequently, requests or representations made to the American government had not been refused; they were simply ignored. In addition to problems over the treaty, all the other major international problems faced by the United States during the eighties remained unresolved: the West remained tenuously attached to the nation; the British still held the western posts; the Spaniards adopted an equivocal attitude toward American rights on the Mississippi River; attempts to enter into a commercial treaty with Great Britain floundered; and efforts to extend American overseas commerce had failed miserably.

To Hamilton, as to his collaborators, a country so threatened and so much at the mercy of external forces could not long survive. John Jay argued that "among the objects to which a wise and free people find it necessary to direct their attention, that of providing for their *safety* seems to be the first." "A cordial Union under an efficient national Government" could best achieve such safety. Hamilton agreed with his colleague that "safety from external danger is the most powerful director of national conduct," and he claimed that the first object of government must be to guarantee such safety, even at the cost of decreased freedom for the people. It followed from these assumptions that a government like that under the Articles, deprived of effective powers of taxation and of ability to act in a unified way at home or abroad, could not—indeed should not—long survive as an independent state. The depressing experience of the postwar period had confirmed the truth of these observations.

Such a situation could not continue under the proposed Constitution, which would give the central government the power, and thus hopefully the effectiveness, denied it by the Articles. Power over taxation, interstate commerce, foreign relations (through the right to make treaties and to undertake direct control over foreign policy), and the army and navy would belong to the federal government rather than to the individual states with

their lamentably particularist record. This newly acquired authority would be the basis for the growth of the United States into the
great nation in which Hamilton had always believed. To him,
power comprised the central fact of political life at any level.
Without it, any kind of government would become ineffective;
with it, the development of a nation to its highest potential could
become a reality.

Such views Hamilton made explicit in his sections of the
Federalist. Later when ideas could be translated into action, when
theories had to stand the test of implementation, the depth of
Hamilton's commitment to such positions became apparent. The
remarkable consistency of his views on the importance of foreign
policy, on the primacy of national strength and security, and on
the necessity for government authority is impressive. Although
specific examples of the ineffectiveness of the Articles, the debility
of the Congress, or the humiliations of the national government
had doubtless reinforced Hamilton's opinions expressed in the
Federalist, he could have written the theoretical sections at almost
any time after 1775.

Hamilton and his collaborators had sought to persuade the
people of New York that the government under the new Constitution would cure the Confederation's ills and would provide the
impetus necessary to push the United States toward greatness; but
in 1789, at President Washington's first inauguration, nothing
changed except the government. The test of theories expounded
in the federal Constitution, in the *Federalist*, and in all that had
been written and spoken about the new government lay in the
future. As in all such cases, the trial of men and their attitudes
toward government and power consisted not in what they said
about them but in what they did with them.

Any study of the new nation's foreign affairs necessarily
focuses on a consideration of the foreign policy views that
Hamilton recommended to the Washington administrations. The
first president's foreign policy between 1789 and 1796 was, to all
intents and purposes, that of his secretary of the treasury. So
strong was Hamilton's influence, often far exceeding that of the
secretary of state, that he played a key role in determining the
initial American response to the external world. Hamilton's in-

fluence was significant in the Nootka Sound crisis of 1790, the Neutrality Proclamation of 1793, and Jay's Treaty and the debate over its ratification in 1794–95. Moreover, the most characteristic expression of Washington's approach to foreign affairs, the Farewell Address, bears the strong imprint of Hamilton's thinking.

His attitudes toward the foreign relations of the United States from 1789 to 1796 are completely consistent. His words and actions form a remarkable, unified whole, bringing together both his experiences in nation building and his reflections on the nature and uses of national power. His assessment of the position of the United States and his estimate of its future led him to firm conclusions and precise objectives in the international arena that became the goals of his years in power. Felix Gilbert has noted: "Although many Americans looked upon the prospect of participating in power politics only with horror or acknowledged the necessity of such a thing only with reservations and hesitation, eighteenth century power politics had an effective advocate on the American continent. It spoke authoritatively through the voice of Alexander Hamilton."[2]

Convinced that European conceptions about the nature of international relations were accurate and applicable to the New World, Hamilton reasoned that, whether or not the United States wished to withdraw from contact with other nations or to change the nature of international relations, whether or not it wished to impose on the Old World some new order of its own devising, such a course would be impossible until the nation had first established a position of influence among European powers. To move the country toward that goal, the new government first had to strengthen the nation at home by establishing firm control over the country, by placing public credit and national finances on a sound footing, by fostering American industry, and by expanding its commerce. The government might then maneuver more effectively in the international sphere. Hamilton, of course, was keenly aware of the relationship between domestic and international affairs.

Moving the nation to its rightful place in the world arena was a task both delicate and hazardous. The creation of constitutional

---

2. Felix Gilbert, *To the Farewell Address: Ideas of Early American Foreign Policy* (Princeton, 1961), p. 111.

government in America did not automatically resolve diplomatic problems. Great Britain, while not exactly hostile, was certainly not friendly, and it retained control of the northern frontier of the United States as well as much of the back country in the old Northwest. By refusing to surrender their forts in that region, the British technically contravened the 1783 treaty, but they cited American noncompliance with other terms of the treaty as justification for their violation. Spain, though weak, clung stubbornly to its control of the Mississippi River and New Orleans, thus contributing to dissension in the trans-Allegheny West among Americans who were thereby cut off from a much needed outlet to the sea. The Atlantic remained effectively under British control, and the government at Whitehall, under the influence of men like Hawkesbury and Sheffield, had shown no inclination to liberalize its commercial policies to give American merchants greater access to British ports either at home or in the West Indies. Attempts to open other markets in Europe had been largely unsuccessful, and while American commerce was not foundering, neither was it expanding. In sum, when Washington took office the international situation contained little that was encouraging, and there was small prospect of improvement until the new nation spoke with the firm, united, and effective voice that Hamilton sought to give it.

How Hamilton hoped to strengthen America's international position can be defined by examining his response to the issues of the Nootka Sound crisis of 1790. Great Britain had protested the Spanish seizure of British ships in Nootka Sound on the west coast of Vancouver Island. By the summer of 1790, the British government was actively preparing for war with Spain, and the Washington administration anticipated an attack from Canada on Spanish territory in the Southwest. Apprehensive that the United States might become unnecessarily involved in a war in which it had no real interest, the president asked his cabinet for guidance on an appropriate response in a number of theoretical situations that might arise from an Anglo-Spanish conflict, including a possible British request to move troops across American territory. In the end, settlement of the dispute without war rendered academic both the request and the replies it elicited; but Hamilton's response provides a number of important clues to his general attitude toward America's international position and conduct.

Hamilton divided the question into the theoretical one of the nation's right to refuse consent to the passage of troops and the practical one of the consequences of such an action. He noted the weakness of America and the probable danger of an attempt to stop British troop movements across American territory. While the United States clearly had the right to refuse passage, he maintained, it had neither the financial nor the military resources to prevent the British from doing as they wished. Under the circumstances it seemed to him that cooperation might be wiser than confrontation.

He felt strongly that the government had two primary obligations: to refrain from involvement in the war and to preserve the honor of the United States. It was equally clear that in what might prove to be the first serious test of the new government in international affairs these two obligations might easily conflict. Hamilton concluded that Spain had little reason to expect gratitude or assistance from the United States and that there might be more profit in helping Great Britain, especially if Spain continued to restrict American access to the mouth of the Mississippi. Additionally, refusal to allow passage to the British might mean another war with the former mother country to avoid disgrace, and for a number of compelling reasons that alternative had to be avoided if possible. The British request therefore ought to be honored, for the consequences of refusal—war or disgrace—were worse than the pain of acquiescence. Then, too, cooperation with the British might lead to some advantages. Hamilton finally advised that if the British entered lightly held American territory without permission, a protest should be made to London, though not one strong enough to make war necessary. If, however, British troops in transit forced an American post, then the nation would have to declare war on Britain.

Few pronouncements give a clearer idea of Hamilton's conception of America's role than this one. The Hamiltonian sensitivity to the relationship between means and ends emerges clearly, as does his understanding of the utility of Britain in America's future. The advice reflects also the consonance between his own rise to power and his instincts about the international position of the United States. The country found itself in a weak and friendless position, hemmed in by two more powerful and hostile neighbors, neither of which America could afford to offend. Forced to tread a delicate path between the need for firmness and the prospect of humiliation, any American answer bore the possibility of disaster. Of this Hamilton and Washington were painfully aware.

As has been frequently noted, foreign policy is at best an inexact science, having as its basic ingredient a considerable element of conjecture. Policy makers rarely have full information, and the actions of one nation can seldom be based on exact knowledge of another nation's reaction. Decisions, therefore, must be made according to the government's best estimate of the attitudes and responses of the other parties involved. That assessment must be made in accordance with the answers to a number of questions concerning the nation itself and foreign powers. In calculating a potential foreign response, policy makers ask, "What will happen if we do this?" In formulating policy for the nation, those charged with the responsibility of decision making must ask, "What do we want and how much do we want it?" From such imprecise principles decisions must often be made.

In the situation confronting the United States government in 1790, variants of these questions were asked, but a number of other conditions complicated the search for answers. Apart from Jefferson and Adams, who had served as American representatives abroad during the Confederation period, the cabinet making the decisions had little direct experience in international affairs and no tradition of national policy to guide its actions. In addition, all of Washington's advisers had a somewhat equivocal attitude toward Great Britain; all of them, even Hamilton, had expressed doubts of British trustworthiness during and after the War of Independence. Cabinet members had also become dubious about Spanish intentions. That country, a lukewarm ally in wartime, had given few indications of continuing friendship after the war and had taken some actions that conveyed an opposite impression. Further, Spain's ally, France, a problematical quantity in any case, presented even more uncertainty after the outbreak of its own Revolution.

In such circumstances, the alternatives available to the United States were severely limited, as Hamilton realized perhaps more clearly than any of his cabinet colleagues. At the time and since he has been accused of unseemly haste in acceding to British demands; and in view of some of his subsequent acts, there may be some justice in the charge that Hamilton, the archetypal

Anglophile, used this opportunity, as he did others, to attach his country firmly to the former mother country.

Such an interpretation seems unduly harsh. The Washington cabinet had to estimate the probable consequence of a refusal to allow British troops passage across American territory. Hamilton never doubted the outcome of denial. No good could come from it, and it might well lead to national humiliation, even a threat to independence. While refusal might satisfy national honor or become necessary as a last resort, it would be a futile protest against a powerful neighbor from whose enmity Americans had much to lose and in whose friendship there might be enormous advantage. Rhetorical as he could be on occasion, Hamilton rarely indulged in empty flourishes or refused to accept the consequences of his actions. During the Nootka discussions, he demonstrated both qualities.

It is unfortunate that, since 1938, diplomats and the historians who write about them have been unable to use the word "appeasement" in any but a pejorative sense. Appeasement was often a perfectly reasonable and effective course of action for a weak and vulnerable nation, such as the United States in 1790, in dealing with powerful or predatory neighbors. In his reply to the president, Hamilton was in essence suggesting this course; under the circumstances, it was probably the only realistic one for the United States. Prudence dictated a soft answer to the mistress of the seas, the most powerful country in the world. In his advice during the Nootka crisis, Hamilton seemed moved more by a sense of realism than by any ideological identification with the cause of Britain, though certainly his pragmatic approach to international affairs—and the reliance of his financial system on international trade and capital—did not permit him to forget the possible future utility of a pro-British stance. More importantly, he preferred accommodation to antagonism, and in his discussions of foreign affairs during the Washington years he invariably urged appeasement in the cabinet, perhaps most notably and effectively during the negotiation of Jay's Treaty.

The outbreak of the wars of the French Revolution complicated enormously the search for accommodation with the powers of Europe. Hamilton's response to the problems posed by that cataclysmic event shows another aspect of his approach to international affairs. When general war broke out in Europe in

1793 and France, the nation that had come to America's aid in 1778, once again fought its ancient enemy, a strong party in the United States, both in Congress and outside it, urged on by French agents, loudly proclaimed that gratitude for aid received during the revolutionary war required the nation again to join hands with its erstwhile ally.

In the *Pacificus* papers Hamilton examined the questions raised by these events in Europe and America. Gratitude had no place in international affairs, he said, because it unduly restrained national action and imposed restrictions on it that often worked against the nation's real and enduring interests. In the relations between states, faith and justice were, of course, admirable virtues that could not be "too strongly inculcated nor too highly respected," for they imposed obligations, possessed utility, and were subject to definable rules. The same, however, could not be said of gratitude, and it therefore ought never to be placed on the same level in international relations as in interpersonal ones. Nations should always seek to make their own welfare the primary motive for action. They must never allow gratitude to intrude into the sphere in which the interests of the state, within the limits set by justice and good faith, must predominate. Such sentiments were not intended merely to advance selfish or narrow policies, but to show that a policy regulated by self-interest and bounded by justice and good faith was, and should be, a legitimate objective of the servants of the state. Arguments for a self-denying or self-sacrificing national gratitude for favors received from other nations in the past misconstrued the proper springs of national conduct in the international arena.

Examining the international situation in 1793, Hamilton concluded that the United States had no legal duty to France to enter the war, a conclusion reinforced by a number of other more practical considerations. As in 1790, the dangers of challenging Britain remained: its effective command of the sea, which seemed likely to continue, might ruin American trade; the situation in the Northwest and in the West was still precarious, with British influence there virtually undiminished; and Britain still offered the best prospects for future advantage to America. France, on the other hand, was a more doubtful proposition. Its attitude and policies since the revolutionary change of government were in flux; the activity of its first diplomatic representative in America, Citizen Edmond Genêt, rendered the position of the secretary of state "immensely difficult"; and to many observers like Hamilton its future course, clouded by the horrors and excesses of the Revolution, was impossible to predict.

Under such circumstances, neutrality became the only safe course for the nation while involvement in the war, on either side, was too hazardous; but although there was an administration consensus on the need for neutrality, there was also considerable controversy in the cabinet over the form that neutrality should take. Hamilton wished for a definition that would decrease the aid Americans were obligated to give under the still valid French treaty of 1778, and he sought ways to lessen the impact of neutrality on Britain. Conversely, Jefferson wished a gentler, more indirect expression of neutrality that would allow France to see advantage, or at least the absence of animosity, in America's stance. He hoped to use American policy as a lever for prying concessions from the European powers, in effect forcing them to bid for a beneficent neutrality. "None of the principals involved in the shaping of American foreign policy," Lawrence Kaplan wrote, "wanted involvement in the European war. The sympathies of the president and secretary of state . . . were in full agreement on denying military assistance to the French ally. The secretary of the treasury would not only avoid war but would use the occasion to break the alliance and remove the United States from any obligation to France." The Hamiltonian position was a composite of political, philosophical, and emotional pressures. "France," Professor Kaplan continued, "was an enemy of civilization as long as revolution gripped the nation, while England was the one nation in the world that could protect the world from the French terror as well as the only government that could advance the American political economy."[3] It was perhaps not entirely coincidental that neutrality would enable the United States to reap enormous profits from wartime trade with Europe and the West Indies; not for the last time in American history, profit became the handmaiden of prudence. If the policy of neutrality and the process of strengthening the economy moved America closer to Britain's orbit, Hamilton did not object, for he considered such an arrangement vital to the nation's future.

3. Lawrence S. Kaplan, *Colonies into Nation: American Diplomacy, 1763–1801* (New York, 1972), p. 217. The above paragraph relies heavily on the chapter, "The Hamiltonian Apex, 1793–1796," pp. 216–58.

The negotiations that led to the signing of Jay's Treaty, an agreement that Samuel Flagg Bemis has suggested might more properly be called Hamilton's Treaty, demonstrate the limits of Hamilton's search for accommodation with Britain. In the Anglo-American rapprochement of 1794–95 the secretary of the treasury played a key role. By devising and supporting John Jay's special mission to London, Hamilton defused the ugly clamor for war and in the process thwarted Republican efforts to torpedo his policy by congressional enactment of discriminatory duties on British ships in American ports.

In the months after Washington's decision for neutrality, Britain, instead of appreciating American commercial policy, intensified its sea war against France, seized American goods on the seas, failed to restrain its Indian allies in the West, struck at national sovereignty by impressing American sailors, and by a series of insolent Orders in Council threatened the profitable West Indian provision trade. War might have come from such provocations and the passions they engendered, but, largely because of Hamilton's diplomatic initiative, it did not.

In these negotiations, Hamilton again demonstrated a perhaps too hasty willingness to accommodate the British. In 1794, this haste, if such it was, again went hand in hand with a number of other more pragmatic considerations. First, Hamilton realized that Britain, embroiled in a costly and lengthening war, might be more amenable to American overtures than in the past. It seemed reasonable to suppose that in order to concentrate on the French menace in Europe the British might wish to remove the drain on their resources represented by continuing uncertainty in relations with the United States. This reading of British policy was based in part on a shrewd assessment of the international situation as it might appear to His Majesty's ministers at Whitehall; but it was also based on the requirements of the Hamiltonian financial system for amicable relations with London. The cordial reception that Jay received in London attests to the essential accuracy of these views.

Second, aware as always of the strong interaction between domestic and foreign affairs, Hamilton saw the potential advantages of a settlement with Great Britain. Resolution of some of the touchy problems in the West and the advantages to American commerce and business of an accommodation with the British presented powerful stimulus for opening negotiations. Then, too, the question of war or peace, of ideological commitment to one side or the other—the specters of revolutionary republicanism or reactionary monarchism coming to America—had become emotion-laden issues in domestic politics, splitting both the government and the country into violently opposed factions. Hamilton was not insensitive to the prospects of securing party advantage by concluding a treaty that would confound the pro-French faction and strengthen Federalist influence in the government.

Under no illusions about America's bargaining position vis-à-vis Britain, Hamilton advised Jay to make the best deal he could and to settle as many points at issue as possible. Then, by a series of injudicious conversations with the British minister at Philadelphia, he proceeded to narrow the options open to the American negotiator in London. The inflexibility of the British position, especially on the extremely sensitive question of the interpretation of neutral rights, resulted in large measure from Hamilton's meddling in the negotiations, his overeagerness to indulge the British point of view. Whether he blunted Jay's chief negotiating weapon, an implied threat to join a league of armed European neutrals, by an indiscreet hint to the British minister about America's wish to abstain from European connections remains a matter of historical debate, but there can be little doubt that the British willingness to make concessions lessened as a result of Hamilton's role in the negotiations.

When the treaty came to the United States for ratification and encountered a flood of resentment, Hamilton readily admitted that it was not ideal and in the influential *Camillus* papers defended it on practical grounds: the need for peace, the dependence on revenues generated by trade, the reduction of friction between the two countries. While the treaty left unresolved a number of serious problems between the United States and Great Britain, it did help maintain peace between them; it marked an important milestone on America's road to international respectability; and it marked the apex of Hamilton's diplomatic influence. If the treaty went too far toward appeasement of the British, he regarded the concessions as a necessary part of eighteenth-century diplomacy. "Hamilton's great success," Professor Kaplan noted, "was in understanding the nature of America's link to the Old World and seeking to bend it to the service of the New." He regarded the treaty as an important step in achieving a primary objective of the new federal government:

DEFENCE

OF THE

TREATY

AMITY, COMMERCE, AND NAVIGATION,

ENTERED INTO BETWEEN

THE UNITED STATES OF AMERICA & GREAT BRITAIN,

AS IT HAS APPEARED IN THE PAPERS UNDER THE

SIGNATURE OF

CAMILLUS.

A. Hamilton

NEW-YORK;

PRINTED AND SOLD BY FRANCIS CHILDS AND CO. AND SOLD BY
JAMES RIVINGTON, AT No. 156, Pearl-street; also, at the other Book
Stores of this City.——1795.

establishing a strong, stable nation with the capacity to take an independent stand in the world. Once again, his instincts and his intelligence served the nation well.

In his judgments about the position of the United States and in the policies that he recommended Hamilton was consistent, perceptive, and realistic. The course he charted between 1789 and 1796 admirably suited the condition of the United States at that time, a statement that can seldom be made about the policies advocated by his adversaries. On this basis, Hamilton deserves a place in the first rank as a theoretical exponent of American foreign policy. Instinct and reason persuaded him that existing rules must govern the international game, that nations must eschew unrealistic goals, and that the availability of resources and the nation's reputation and influence must temper its aims. It followed that because the former were limited, the latter should also remain strictly limited, at least temporarily. It may be that on this level Hamilton's attitudes toward the international conduct of the United States formed a model that would be hard to fault for any nation, in the eighteenth century or the twentieth.

Unfortunately, however, government policy operates not only on a theoretical level, but also on the more practical level of implementation, and its effectiveness and that of the men who make it and put it into effect must be judged on that level as well. Here, Hamilton's conduct cannot stand close examination. There is—or perhaps there ought to be—a basic distinction between foreign policy and foreign relations.[4] The former is the area in which the discussion of problems and recommendations is undertaken and decisions made. At such a point, in its embryonic stage, foreign policy is often the proper concern of the cabinet as a whole: it is frequently made as the result of discussions in the cabinet and the representations of Congress and other groups. Like many other major policy questions in their early stages, foreign policy remains an affair of the whole government rather than the preserve of a single department or cabinet member.

4. For a discussion of this question in a modern context, see William L. Turpin, "Foreign Relations, Yes; Foreign Policy, No," *Foreign Policy* 8 (Fall 1972), 50–61.

Washington's habit of circulating questions on important foreign policy issues to all members of his cabinet seems to suggest his acceptance of such a view. There comes a point, however, at which the theoretical discussion of policy must be translated into action, when decisions must be implemented. At that point, foreign policy, the concern with implementation of policy decisions, passes as it did under the first president into the hands of the Department of State or perhaps even a single person.

In molding foreign policy Hamilton possessed considerable, even paramount, influence, which was, of course, legitimate within the operational context of the Washington administrations. The president apparently accepted and even encouraged it. As noted, the course that Hamilton envisaged for the country and attempted with some success to pursue was a reasonable one in the 1790s. A consideration of his role in the international relations of the United States, however, requires some discussion of his impact on the implementation of policy.

Hamilton had extensive influence over foreign policy because of his personal relationship with the president, because of his mastery of detail, and because he continually urged his opinions strongly and eloquently, in writing and orally, in the cabinet and elsewhere. His authority over implementation was rather more limited, for, theoretically at least, this was the province of the secretary of state. How much this administrative detail restricted Hamilton remains debatable. Washington's most recent biographer, James Thomas Flexner, has argued that the president, who believed himself to be fairly experienced in foreign affairs, allowed his secretary of state a free hand only in the administrative details of his department, and that Washington, basically opposed to many of Hamilton's ideas on foreign policy, allowed the secretary of the treasury as little rope. Washington, in other words, was nobody's tool and at least until early in his second term maintained effective control over his able but warring lieutenants. Others, notably Alexander DeConde, have argued that Hamilton had overwhelming influence at almost every level.[5]

While neither view may be entirely satisfactory, there is little

5. James Thomas Flexner, *George Washington and the New Nation, 1783–1793* (Boston, 1970), pp. 400–415; Alexander DeConde, *Entangling Alliance* (Durham, 1958), pp. 501–11.

doubt that Hamilton attempted to influence American relations, particularly with Great Britain, by conversations outside the cabinet and official channels. Indeed, it has been argued that he took such efforts beyond the bounds of diplomatic propriety, carrying them, in the words of one critic, even "beyond the limits of honorable conduct in public office."[6] Deprived of authority over foreign affairs and restricted largely to running his own department, he used other means to assert influence. During the Nootka Sound crisis, for example, he met regularly with Colonel George Beckwith, an agent of the governor-general of Canada, Lord Dorchester, who in turn reported to the British cabinet. At a time when American policy had not been decided, when the government rightly sought to present a united front to the British, Hamilton frequently assured Beckwith that the Washington administration harbored no ill intentions toward the British, that American policy would ultimately reflect this, and that both he and the president felt that way.

Such devious diplomacy was by no means unusual for Hamilton, for he continued to meet Beckwith whenever the latter visited the United States and he later formed a similar relationship with the first British minister, George Hammond, appointed in 1791. The extent of the information that he supplied to Washington about these discussions cannot be accurately established, but the evidence suggests that it was limited and not entirely accurate; on at least one occasion he gave the president an account of a discussion that was somewhat different from the one that appeared in Beckwith's report to his superiors. So accustomed did Hammond become to receiving inside news from the secretary of the treasury that the British minister could only express amazement when Hamilton refused to show him Jay's instructions. In another conversation with Hammond, Hamilton expressed regret for the intemperance of his cabinet colleague, the secretary of state, in his talks with the British minister.

There has been some debate about the intent and significance of these activities. Hamilton's apologists have maintained that they were relatively unimportant, that at most they indicate a little excessive zeal in furthering the ends of government. His critics, on

6. Julian P. Boyd, *Number 7: Alexander Hamilton's Secret Attempts to Control American Foreign Policy* (Princeton, 1964), p. xiv.

the other hand, assert that his actions represent "a sustained effort" to direct American foreign policy in a pro-British direction, that his conduct in the Beckwith business was "not an isolated instance, but [part of] a consistent and characteristic pattern of behavior," and that in following this course Hamilton committed "almost the gravest offense of which a cabinet officer can be guilty in his role of responsible advisor to the head of state."[7]

It is hard to agree with the apologists. There can be little doubt that Hamilton formed his contacts with Beckwith and Hammond consciously and deliberately. Such conduct was inexcusable and may even have bordered on treason, particularly when, as has often been pointed out, it came from a man who emphasized so loudly and continuously the need for a strong and united government. It meant little that Hamilton's motive was above reproach, that he sought to retain strong, united government by helping to secure the accommodation with Britain that he regarded as vital to the nation's well-being. Nor can his actions be condoned by placing them alongside his unquestioned achievements in other areas, for it was inexcusable for a cabinet member to act in a manner that could only decrease the effectiveness of policies upon which his colleagues had agreed. By acting in such a fashion, by interfering in matters clearly outside his departmental province, Hamilton went far toward reducing his stature as a statesman. Ultimately, a government cannot afford to speak with more than one voice on major issues, and it was fortunate that more unpleasant consequences did not follow from Hamilton's conduct. In pursuit of his policy he entered into private discussions with representatives of a foreign power, gave them information they had no business having, and helped undermine the work of more than one American diplomat. His arrogance and his quest for power led him to irresponsible interference in affairs of state. This was not the conduct of a reliable minister and it may be that the president, too, was partly culpable for such a thoroughly undesirable precedent.[8]

7. Boyd, *Number 7*, pp. xii–xiv.
8. According to Hamilton, his 15 July conversation with Beckwith resulted from the president's instructions, given after Hamilton's report of his 8 July talk with the British agent and relayed to Hamilton with Jefferson's knowledge. Beckwith's version of the conversation, however, contained statements made by Hamilton that were not contained in the secretary's report to Washington.

Still, Hamilton's contribution to the making of American diplomatic history must be accounted a great and lasting one. At the end of Washington's presidency, Hamilton helped draft the document that became the Farewell Address.[9] It contained his own and Washington's political testament. In it, he urged on his countrymen the principles that he had sought to implement for the previous eight years. He advised against "passionate attach ment" and permanent alliances with any nation; he advocated as little political connection with other nations as possible. With the French alliance in mind, Hamilton and Washington suggested that foreign entanglements might become impediments rather than aids to securing the national interest. As he had done throughout his years in office, Hamilton again argued that the United States must preserve its freedom of action in the international arena.

Pointing out the weakness of the new nation, he had argued for appeasement of Great Britain in 1790 and for abstention from European wars in 1793, and, recognizing the advantage to be gained from Europe's distress, he had argued for accommodation with the British in 1794–95. To him the important point was always the avoidance of attachments that might become too confining. Thus, he sought to free America from the embrace of the French alliance when his view of the nation's interests dictated that course.

Such ideas formed part of Hamilton's overall conception of national policy. Domestic policy, economic policy in particular, was tied to foreign affairs. The economic health of the nation was essential to the security of the state and to its effective operation in relations with other states. The national policy of Hamilton was designed to achieve strength, stability, and security at home and abroad. In pursuit of that goal the only valid guide to national action was the immediate and long-term interest of the country. Essentially, Hamilton followed a concept of international relations common to eighteenth-century Europe before the French Revolution. It was a view that cast aside considerations of morality, denied the need for international gratitude, and sought short-term alliances that were as unconfining as possible. Hamilton attempted to steer the nation away from firm commitments, toward abstention from European quarrels, and in the direction of

9. Gilbert, *To the Farewell Address*, pp. 123–34.

cooperation with those from whom the greatest advantage could be gained. Always he sought to preserve America's flexibility, its freedom of action in a hostile world, and to avoid burdening the nation with unrealistic and potentially harmful obligations. Flawed though it may be, Hamilton's contribution to the evolution of the nation's stance in international affairs remains a substantial one. A study of his approach remains basic to an understanding of the critical period of the 1790s—and, one may suggest, for the 1970s as well.

BIBLIOGRAPHIC NOTE

The major printed source for future work on Alexander Hamilton must, of course, be the new edition of his papers which has now reached, in time, December 1794, and in volumes, seventeen: Harold C. Syrett and Jacob E. Cooke, eds., *The Papers of Alexander Hamilton* (New York, 1961–). It is a monumental work that, together with the steadily growing number of volumes in the similar editions of the papers of such contemporaries as Jefferson, Madison, and Franklin, provides a solid basis for investigations into Hamilton's life in particular and the revolutionary and early national periods in general. In the category of primary source material, it should also be noted that the best edition of the *Federalist* is now Jacob E. Cooke, ed., *The Federalist* (Middletown, Conn., 1961).

There are two major modern biographies of Hamilton that provide both a comprehensive account of his career and considerable insight into his attitudes and actions. The better is John C. Miller, *Alexander Hamilton: Portrait in Paradox* (New York, 1959). The second is the two-volume work by Broadus Mitchell, *Youth to Maturity, 1755–1788* and *The National Adventure, 1788–1804* (New York, 1957–62). An interesting and important collection of essays on Hamilton is contained in Jacob E. Cooke, ed., *Alexander Hamilton: A Profile* (New York, 1967), which provides discussion of a variety of aspects of Hamilton's life and thought by a group of distinguished scholars. The best treatment of Hamilton's political thought is clearly Gerald Stourzh's brilliant *Alexander Hamilton and the Idea of Republican Government* (Stanford, 1970). Of particular relevance to Hamilton's views on foreign policy is the fourth chapter of this work, "The Foreign Policy of Republican Government," but the whole book is indispensable to future studies of any important aspect of Hamilton's career. Another perceptive and revealing treatment of Hamilton's political thought and career is Adrienne Koch, *Power, Morals and the Founding Fathers* (Ithaca, 1961), in which Professor Koch (who also contributed an important essay on "Hamilton and Power" to Cooke's collection mentioned above) argues persuasively against Broadus Mitchell's view of

Hamilton as "the wise patron of government guidance" with a philosophical and moral basis for his policies.

There are a number of general works on the foreign policy of the
early national period and of Washington's administrations in particular.
Alexander DeConde, *Entangling Alliance: Politics and Diplomacy under
George Washington* (Durham, 1958), the most thorough treatment of
Washington's foreign policy, argues the overwhelming influence of
Hamilton in this area. Felix Gilbert partly supports this view in an
excellent discussion of the intellectual basis of foreign policy under
Washington, *To the Farewell Address: Ideas of Early American Foreign
Policy* (Princeton, 1961). An opposing view is put forward in a more
recent work, James Thomas Flexner, *George Washington and the New
Nation, 1783–1793* (Boston, 1972). Another important work, covering the
period from the beginning of the War of Independence to the War of
1812, is Paul A. Varg, *Foreign Policies of the Founding Fathers* (East
Lansing, Mich., 1963). Perhaps the best survey of American foreign
relations in the Washington years, however, is to be found in the relevant
sections, particularly the chapter on "The Hamiltonian Apex," of Lawrence S. Kaplan, *Colonies into Nation: American Diplomacy, 1763-1801*
(New York, 1972).

On the final and most important achievement in foreign relations of
Washington's presidency, Jay's Treaty, three books are worth noting:
Samuel Flagg Bemis, *Jay's Treaty*, 2nd ed. (New Haven, 1962), the oldest,
most comprehensive and probably still the best discussion of the treaty;
Jerald A. Combs, *The Jay Treaty: Political Battleground of the Founding
Fathers* (Berkeley, 1970); and Charles R. Ritcheson, *Aftermath of Revolu-
tion: British Policy toward the United States, 1783-1795* (Dallas, 1969). The
concluding chapter of Ritcheson's volume, "The Preservation of the
Peace," includes some provocative ideas about the Jay Treaty and the
negotiations surrounding it.

Two recent monographs have dealt specifically with Hamilton's
contribution to American foreign policy. Helene Johnson Looze, *Alexander Hamilton and the British Orientation of American Foreign Policy,
1783-1803* (The Hague, 1969), is useful in providing, for the first time, a
fairly comprehensive treatment of Hamilton's role as a maker of American
foreign policy; but it tends to accept him too uncritically and provides
little or nothing that is new or original. A much better work is Gilbert L.
Lycan, *Alexander Hamilton and American Foreign Policy: A Design for
Greatness* (Norman, Okla., 1970); but this, too, is weakened by too great a
willingness to accept Hamilton at face value. Very much opposed to the
flattering view of Hamilton in these two books is a brief but illuminating
discussion of Hamilton's maneuverings in 1789 and 1790, Julian P. Boyd,
*Number 7: Alexander Hamilton's Secret Attempt to Control American
Foreign Policy* (Princeton, 1964).

THOMAS JEFFERSON

The Idealist as Realist

Lawrence S. Kaplan

No statesman of the revolutionary and early national periods made
a more substantial contribution to the development of American
foreign policy than Thomas Jefferson. From his magnificent
synthesis of eighteenth-century political theory in the Declaration
of Independence to his death fifty years later, Jefferson's idealism,
tempered by pragmatic regard for practical realities, played a key
role in defining a distinctively American position toward the
external world. No one, it might be said, ever blended the
moralistic yearnings of the young Republic for a new international
order with the practical pursuit of national self-interest more
effectively than he.

Examination of Jefferson's amazingly varied career and multi-

The Kent State Research Committee provided financial assistance for the preparation of this essay.

ple talents highlights the renaissance quality of his mind and work.
For another man any one of his accomplishments would have
assured the homage of posterity. Over a span of eighty-three years
Jefferson pursued an astonishing range of activities: he was largely
responsible for founding the University of Virginia; he was an
architectural innovator who helped bring classical forms to the
New World; he was an agronomist experimenting with transplan-
tations of rice and silk to the South; he was a theologian who
attempted to harmonize Christianity with the temper of the
Enlightenment. Above all, he was a scholar in the art of government whose ideas spread through the nation as Jeffersonian
democracy. The prestige conferred by authorship of the Declaration of Independence and the power of the presidency ensured
dissemination of his ideas in a manner rarely available to political
theorists. If his virtuosity did not encompass an appreciation for
the intricacies of finance, that shortcoming stemmed less from a
lack of understanding the techniques of moneymaking than from
a taste that placed spending above getting. Against the bankruptcy
of his Monticello estate must be weighed the credit of a life-style
that warmed guests in the beautiful mansion with their host's
hospitality as much as with fine French wines.

This westerner belonged to an aristocratic family, the Ran-
dolphs of Virginia. His father had improved his status by a wealthy
marriage. As a member of the governing elite of the colony,
Jefferson early experienced British and European influences
flowing across the ocean to Tidewater and Piedmont Virginia.
While there may have been few artists or scientists at the College
of William and Mary in the colonial capital, there were sufficient
men and books to initiate the youthful Jefferson into the life of the
eighteenth-century liberal mind. He enjoyed the best of both the
Old and the New World, sharing the excitement of European ideas
that ranged from Arthur Young's tracts on scientific farming to the
disputed poems of Ossian. Books and papers from European
centers found their way to Jefferson's library and to the drawing
rooms of Williamsburg and Philadelphia. He was very much a
member of the international fraternity of literati that pumped
liberal ideas into the courts of Europe and the coffeehouses of
America—ideas that ultimately pushed both along the road to
revolution. Jefferson's intimacy with such scholarly men as Professor William Small of William and Mary and George Wythe, his
law teacher at Williamsburg, and with such sophisticated men of

the world as Francis Fauquier, lieutenant governor of Virginia during his student days, were experiences he repeated in Philadelphia and Paris in later years. True, the above names almost exhausted the roster of interesting people in colonial Virginia, but the point is that his circle of acquaintances included some of the broadest intellectual interests there; his six years at the village capital provided him with an extraordinary range of ideas.

At the same time, perhaps more than any contemporary, Jefferson captured the best elements in the transatlantic civilization of the colonies. As an American living close to the frontier he appreciated the richness of his environment and recognized the advantages of a land with few people and abundant resources. The agrarian society he so valued bred equality among its members, fostered self-reliance, and opened opportunities for individual growth that the Old World could never provide; his experiences encompassed facets that Europeans could not share unless they came to America. Jefferson understood what the challenge and opportunity of empty land meant in the life of a man; he could see in a practical way government expressing the will of the body politic. He lived in a society free of most of the oppressive traditions of the Old World. His father had surveyed the lands that became the first political units the son encountered. He understood the strengths and weaknesses of Rousseau's natural man; he knew that the theory of Rousseau and Locke was reality for an American.

Membership in the exclusive group that controlled the colony set Jefferson apart from most of his fellows and conferred special advantages on him. Good fortune allowed him to live a life transcending that of the colonial yeoman, whose scarcity of cash and education limited his freedom to roam physically and intellectually; his appreciation of democracy had an aristocratic base in a deferential society. Granted that class distinctions were slighter than in Europe and lacked philosophical and practical support, Jefferson was, nonetheless, a "gentleman," comfortably fixed in his milieu. He could practice the arts of government as proper and entirely natural functions of his place in society: vestryman in his church, magistrate in the local community, delegate to colonial and national legislatures. Of course, opportunity in the abstract beckoned all men—and it was more than just a pious abstraction in America as compared with other societies—but for men of Jefferson's class there simply was a larger share of opportunity.

Others were similarly endowed; his special distinction lay in his genius, in those qualities of mind and spirit that allowed him to range over the whole experience of mankind and distill its essence in lucid prose.

His public career spanned the period from the conclusion of the French and Indian War in 1763 to the end of his second presidential term in 1809, years in which he turned his talents to the creation and maintenance of independence from Great Britain. Jefferson was not concerned with reordering the internal society of America or with indulging private interests. His greatest satisfactions derived from such contributions to political philosophy as were found in the Declaration of Independence or in political practice, from his part in organizing the Northwest Territories, or from the educational theory he bequeathed to the University of Virginia. His primary work, however, was in public affairs, particularly the relations of America with Europe. It could not have been otherwise.

For him, as for all the Founding Fathers, the central event of life was the creation of a nation out of thirteen disparate British colonies. Every step in making the Revolution and in securing it afterwards involved foreign affairs. In such a context, conventional divisions between domestic and foreign affairs lost meaning. In the first generation of the Republic no national leader could escape awareness of the hostile outside world. Europe intruded in every way, inspiring fear of reconquest by the mother country, offering opportunity along sparsely settled borderlands, arousing uncertainties over the alliance with a great power. Unless the new nation settled for a subsistence economy its prosperity rested upon trade with the Old World; the European market held the American economy captive, and no political theory could alter that fact of economic life. There could be no escape from such concerns, any more than from the language Americans spoke, the customs they followed, or the ideas they circulated.

Anglo-American relations dominated American history in the early years of the Republic. Despite a successful military separation, the economic links of tradition proved more enduring than the political, even though many people, Jefferson included, wished it to be otherwise. If an alternative to a British connection existed, it was not to be achieved by retreating into autarchy but by shifting the economy toward France, the wartime ally; it was to

France that those leaders suspicious or fearful of British designs turned during the administrations of George Washington and John Adams.

Anglophiles and Francophiles alike, however, held a different view of Spain, the third major European nation whose interests impinged on those of America. For most Americans, Spain presented an object of aggrandizement and exploitation, a weak state whose territories might be despoiled, or at least kept out of the control of other European powers. As Americans looked southward and westward at insecurely held Spanish territory they envisaged a future continental empire of liberty that would free them from the superpowers of the day.

The record clearly reveals the Jeffersonian involvement in foreign affairs. His service as delegate to both Continental Congresses, as wartime governor of Virginia, and as commissioner to France at the end of the war were all linked to French and British influences in American life. During the Confederation period he represented the United States in Paris, attempting to mobilize support for its continued independence. Upon return to America he became secretary of state, the first in the revitalized union, absorbed in assuring survival of the nation in a hostile world. The French Revolution and its subsequent wars dominated his years as vice-president and president. The magnificent acquisition of Louisiana, though not wholly his doing, deservedly is credited to him; and the disastrous embargo of 1807, though not wholly his mistake, if mistake it was, appropriately is identified with him. Success or failure, Jefferson the public man was of necessity a maker of diplomacy.

Jefferson's enemies of every generation make much of what they consider his deficiencies in character. Most dwell on his inconsistency, pointing out that he shifted from one position to another at critical moments out of fear of consequences, instability of judgment, or passion for power. Thus, his movement from strict to loose construction of the Constitution, from agrarianism to support of manufacturing, from fear of executive power to abuse of it in office, from a love of France to distrust and finally to dependence upon that country under Napoleon have all been used by enemies who would dismiss him as weak, cowardly, opportunistic, or worse. His Francophilism has been interpreted as a personality quirk with dire consequences for the country.

Much of the familiar Federalist criticism of Jefferson withers in the face of close examination. A far better case may be made of excessive consistency, of an allegiance to a conception of society long after it had become obvious that the ideal could not be sustained, or of reliance upon economic weapons against Europe after those weapons were turned against him. Jefferson never questioned what he wanted for America; he envisioned a society of cultivated, independent men on terms of equality with one another, keeping government as close to the local level as possible, living on farms rather than in cities because the agrarian life best propagated the good life. Expansionism became part of the plan because an American empire would remove the corrupt and dangerous model of Europe, as it would if the pattern of international commerce could also be reorganized to incorporate the American alternative to mercantilism, free trade. He identified urban commercial society with class conflict, with oligarchic manipulation of politics, and with European financial control over America, most especially Great Britain's economic interests in its former colonies. To combat such dangers, he believed that right reason applied to the right environment would create a society embodying the best blend of the Enlightenment with the frontier.

He never abandoned his vision of the good society. Apparent deviations were responses to external pressures or were expedients, temporary tactical retreats. He shared with other Founding Fathers a belief that alliances with European powers were unnecessary and potentially dangerous to American independence. His musings about a relationship with Europe "precisely on the footing of China," while fanciful, were genuine; and he knew that in an imperfect world less desirable choices sometimes had to be made to attain more desirable ends. Thus, an alliance with France might be made if Britain threatened the nation's independence; the danger of a connection with Europe had to be balanced against the greater damage that defeat or accommodation with Britain might bring. When France took over the Mississippi outlet at New Orleans, Jefferson contemplated a marriage of convenience to the British fleet and nation. Similarly, he recognized that an embargo on trade would require cultivation of manufactures and urban growth in violation of his preference for an agrarian

America, when he saw the alternative as acceptance of British domination, he took the risk. No one celebrated the virtues of limited government more eloquently than Jefferson, but he realized that they had to be subordinated to the need for a national government strong enough to enforce the embargo, just as in earlier years the state governments of the Confederation, though in his view better custodians of freedom than a more centralized union, had to give way to the Constitution when the Republic's survival was at stake. In 1803, Jefferson's firm commitment to strict construction of the Constitution conveniently expanded to avoid loss of a vast empire in the West.

Jefferson's statecraft invited criticisms. His means occasionally distorted his ends and diminished the stature of the man who tolerated the distortions. Indeed, he paid for his concessions by witnessing before he died some of the unfortunate consequences he had always feared would follow from the promotion of an industrial society, and his reliance on economic coercion exacerbated international tensions while it created new domestic ones. If he did not also pay for France's exploitation of his too ardent sympathy, it was only because he refused to confess to any errors of judgment in a pro-French policy.

Part of the explanation of Jefferson's flexibility lies in his early recognition of the importance of the external world in American affairs and in his firm belief in the permanent hostility of Great Britain. Preservation of the new nation from the baneful effects of those realities required statecraft; if Jefferson sometimes overrated the efficacy of diplomacy, he seldom underestimated the danger of involvement in transatlantic affairs. Ultimately, of course, Americans sought a solution in withdrawal from the European arena into their own empire, into a peculiarly American isolationism wherein obligations to Europe did not exist. In one way or another nearly every American statesman worked to free the nation from dependence upon Europe.

When Jefferson was secretary of state in the 1790s, his countrymen differed violently about the direction of foreign affairs, especially about the American response to the French Revolution and its subsequent wars. The powerful commercial interests of New England and the seaboard towns looked to Great

Britain as a necessary business partner, at least until a viable domestic economy could be created. Many of its leaders equated a pro-British policy with freedom from French ideology and French imperialism. Jefferson and his followers never accepted such views. They believed, at least until after the War of 1812, that Britain intended to reduce America to a position of permanent inferiority in an economic relationship more suffocating than the political connection had been before independence. Like their opponents the Federalists, Jeffersonians responded emotionally to events in France, but they read their import differently. They believed that if the French republic collapsed in its war with monarchical Britain, monarchy if not British rule would return to America.

Jefferson's anti-British animus had deep roots. It grew in part from wartime experiences and received repeated reinforcement during his career. At times his fears approached obsession, but he directed these sentiments more to particular institutions and proponents of policy than to Englishmen per se or to the benign aspects of British culture. However flawed, the British political system surpassed any in Europe; and even when in France desperately seeking help during the Confederation period, Jefferson could in good conscience recommend to French friends that they follow the British political model. If Frenchmen kept in view the example of their cross-Channel neighbor, he told Lafayette, they might advance "step by step towards a good constitution." His feelings for English friends remained as warm as his feelings for Frenchmen. He admired the liberal English reformers whose Anglo-Saxon traditions in law and language he claimed for America—indeed, he who had paraphrased Locke's political philosophy could hardly do otherwise.

In some respects this common heritage exacerbated problems between Britain and America, for the mother country lacked the excuse of ignorance for its abuse of freedom and its threats to liberty. Because Britain had extended its heritage to the New World British behavior became intolerable when it selfishly and abruptly deprived colonists of their right to tax and govern themselves through their own representative bodies. By such actions the ministers of the crown behaved unconstitutionally. In his *Summary View of the Rights of British America*, presented to the First Continental Congress in 1774, Jefferson had observed that emigrants had come to the colonies as free men, voluntarily

adopting the mother country's system of law; they wished to
continue their union by submitting to a common sovereign, "the
central link connecting the several parts of the Empire thus newly
multiplied." All that Americans wished from Britain, he argued,
was a restoration of lost liberties, a recognition of their rights as
Englishmen. In failing to respond to this understanding of Anglo-
American relations, the British invited application of the principles
of natural right philosophy, which permitted, even demanded,
separation from a ruler who had broken the social contract; for as
Carl Becker has said, by 1774 such an interpretation had become
"familiar doctrine to all men."

Jefferson and his colleagues thought that if the right of
revolution was accepted as natural, circumstances justified it and
they made their case in the Declaration of Independence.
Whether they read history and law accurately, the nature of the
charges they brought against their sovereign continued to absorb
Jefferson's attention for more than a generation. Throughout his
public career he saw British policy as part of a plot to subvert
American liberties. That plot ranged from the imposition of taxes
and the incitement of Indian massacres to destruction of American
trade and suspension of the rights of self-government—all for the
"establishment of an absolute tyranny over these states." British
policy did not change after independence. As Jefferson left office
in 1809, he saw the Orders in Council of 1807 as merely another
version of the crown's long-standing attack on "trade with all parts
of the world"; impressment was a means of forcing captive
Americans "to bear arms against their country"; intrigues among
Federalists and Indians were continued royal attempts to excite
"domestic insurrections" and to incite "the merciless Indian
savages." The hostility that had provoked the Declaration of
Independence in 1776 also provided the rationalization for the
embargo in 1807.

Of course, experiences in the critical decade after the Treaty
of Paris, when he served as minister to France and as secretary of
state, had reinforced the Jeffersonian image of Britain as a
malevolent force in American affairs. The Orders in Council of
1783, directed against American trade and removing it from
imperial preference, corroborated his worst fears. By following the
advice of Sheffield rather than the more liberal inclinations of
Shelburne the British intended to maintain control over American
commerce with minimal reciprocity under their navigation system.

British mercantilists abolished subsidies for critical American exports, denied American ships entry into the West Indies, and accepted American goods in Britain on terms no more favorable than those granted European nations. Such was the price of independence, for British ministers correctly anticipated that the impotent government of the Confederation could not implement retaliation by higher duties on British goods or exclusion of British ships from American ports. To many it seemed that Britain had determined to exploit those structural weaknesses and take advantage of the inability of the states to act in concert.

The first minister in London, John Adams, recognized to his despair that Whitehall's policy would enrich Britons at the expense of Americans, and might destroy the new nation in the process. In a brief visit to London in 1786, Jefferson experienced firsthand the contempt for America that the arrogant British had been demonstrating to Adams. His impressions were even darker than those of his Massachusetts friend, for while the king had at times been civil to Adams, he snubbed Jefferson, moving the latter to rage, "That nation hates us, their ministers hate us, and their king more than all other men."

The French connection, so frequently and so pejoratively identified with Jefferson, derived largely from the foregoing emotion and from the problems that evoked it. To escape the web of British mercantilism and to foil expectations of a collapse of the republican experiment, France became a counterweight to British influence and an instrument of American survival; Jefferson saw opportunity, he thought, to use that country's friendship and alliance as a balance to British power and to build more satisfactory commercial arrangements in international trade. He had not forgotten the enormous service that French arms, supplies, and money had rendered in the revolutionary war; nor had he forgotten the self-interest that had inspired that aid. He hoped to exploit such impulses for further service.

Like Franklin before him, he found the task of winning French friendship a highly congenial one. From his first contacts with Frenchmen during the war he had prized the manners and customs they had brought with them; lengthy and spirited talks with Lafayette and Chastellux in Virginia foreshadowed the pleasure he found in French culture and cuisine. While he may not have been quite the traitor who "abjured his native vittels" for foreign food, as Patrick Henry claimed, he did become a lifelong enthusiast for French food and wine. More importantly, he found in Paris a lively appreciation of the American model of the good society which French reformers wished to use in reshaping their own country. When Jefferson became minister he assumed rightly that he would receive the homage his predecessor had won, and he basked in the veneration of the new American society as he followed a scenario limned by that great diplomatic impresario, Benjamin Franklin. Jefferson, like Franklin, sought to exploit the sympathy of the French intelligentsia for America to bend French political and economic policies to the service of the United States.

These objectives monopolized Jefferson's time in France between 1784 and 1789. Initially, the minister concentrated on securing treaty relations with European powers modeled on the 1778 commercial treaty with France. To the new Republic political recognition was an important mark of international respectability; the psychic value apparently outweighed the practical. Such treaties seemed to confer legitimacy, almost as if the more agreements one made, no matter how little trade resulted from them, the more certain the permanence of the United States became. Sweden and Prussia signed liberal treaties with America, without affording any substantial material advantages. Those contracts reflected the optimism of 1776 when Americans expected, as Thomas Paine's *Common Sense* suggested, that the world would applaud the new nation's challenge to British leadership in international trade and its arbitrary control of the seas. The next step, expansion of the Congressional Treaty Plan of 1776, would be European acceptance of free trade and freedom of the seas, in which the advantage of a small maritime country would be united with the larger conception of a foreign policy following moral law. Philosophes and Physiocrats and their American disciples, among whom were Benjamin Franklin and Thomas Jefferson, tended to imbue free trade with nearly mystical qualities; to them it was a panacea for the world's ills, a cure for wars and international rivalries. It followed, as Felix Gilbert has said, "that in a reformed world, based on reason, foreign policy and diplomacy would be unnecessary, that the new world would be a world without diplomats." It also followed that in such a world Americans would reap enormous economic advantage.

Experiences with the French alliance toned down some of Jefferson's expectations for the implementation of such a new order, but despite his awareness of the limitations of treaties and

THE PROVIDENTIAL DETECTION

of the shortcomings of European altruism, he continued to believe that the words of the philosophes and the sentiments of French liberal circles could be shaped to American advantage. He spoke the language of the Physiocrats when he argued for the removal of trade barriers, pointing out that such barriers on the Continent pushed American commerce into British ports. By appealing to the reformers for support he hoped to serve his country's interests and those of the new international order, the postrevolutionary world that would be governed by the laws of nature. At the same time, while waiting for that new order, he urged upon the ministers in power a full reciprocity of economic policy on the practical ground that all the sacrifices France had made to achieve independence for its ally would be wasted if America returned to the British connection by the back door of economic dependence.

On paper, Jefferson's initial negotiations had some small success. The combined efforts of the Physiocrats and the Anglophobes, particularly those in the foreign ministry, overcame many of the obstacles to direct trade. The French lifted import duties on American whale oil as a result of his pleas, and he made spectacular if insubstantial gains in breaking down exclusive arrangements that Philadelphia entrepreneur Robert Morris had made with the powerful syndicate of financiers, the Farmers-General, who controlled the French tobacco market. New trade opportunities opened to Americans.

Few of them lasted, however. The antiquated economic structure of *l'ancien régime* could not tolerate the innovations Jefferson advocated. Suspicious from the beginning of the freer access to their domestic market, the Farmers-General found their prejudices confirmed when they observed that American merchants used their French profits to buy more goods from British manufacturers rather than to reinvest in France. Such a turn of events might have been predicted, for the French lacked both goods and credit to replace the British, even if the tug of habit could have been resisted sufficiently to nudge American importers from familiar connections across the Channel.

Appreciating these obstacles, Jefferson hoped to surmount them by having the French compete with the British in products needed in the American market and by having them develop more sophisticated and flexible marketing techniques. That effort failed. For one thing, even his allies in the foreign ministry, Vergennes and his successors, did not support it vigorously; but perhaps more importantly, it soon became apparent that the allies were working at cross-purposes, with the Americans seeking strength and independence through the French, while the latter looked with equanimity on continued American dependence upon France. Vergennes hoped to exploit the uncertainties of America's future, for as long as the United States could not meet its international obligations, France's role as its protector would remain paramount. In the Quai d'Orsay expectations of continued influence over American policy counterbalanced American dependence upon the British economy and inability to pay the French debts. Moreover, the ministers would be making a virtue of necessity, for no diplomat could make permanent constructive change in the rigid economic structure of prerevolutionary France.

The frustrations engendered by American impotence in foreign affairs and a recognition of the limits on its power of persuasion in the international arena heightened Jefferson's sensitivity to the key events of the last years of his mission to France: the Constitutional Convention in America and the Revolution in France. In his own mind these events were related. Reports from home of dissatisfaction with the Confederation produced conflicting emotions. Suppression of Shays's Rebellion in 1786 and the reputed dominance of Robert Morris's faction in Philadelphia made him despair over the future of the Republic; the avarice of financiers and the anarchy of farmers disturbed him equally, for he saw in both dangerous threats to the safety and security of the nation. Although concerned over the damage demagogues might do to the Republic, he nevertheless retained his sympathy for the complaints of farmers and frontiersmen that stimulated protests against the government.

Rebellion became embarrassing at a time when French reformers looked to the United States as a model. News of transatlantic repression invoked the irony of despotism coming to the New World just as the Old sought to emulate the principles of 1776. In this frame of mind Jefferson reacted to news from Philadelphia. Patrick Henry and James Monroe described the work of the convention as illiberal and aristocratic and fed his initial suspicion of the new Constitution.

Suspicion did not remain the final Jeffersonian position on the federal union contrived at Philadelphia, and he did not return to America in 1790 pessimistic about its future. The views of James Madison and his own recent experiences led him to the conclusion that a stronger government was necessary to assure the nation's survival. Safety in a hostile world required a centralization of power and a unified voice in foreign affairs. He accepted a post as secretary of state in Washington's cabinet on the assumption that the new government would strengthen the nation's hand in international affairs, that it would resolve the problems of diplomacy that the impotence of the Confederation had exposed. Long before the convention assembled at Philadelphia, he had observed that a primary object of his treaty negotiations was to take commerce out of the hands of state governments and to place it under the control of Congress until the states removed the imperfections of the Confederation by a new compact; while the convention deliberated he asserted that the states ought to be "made one as to all foreign, and several as to all domestic matters."

Indeed, one of the unifying forces in Washington's cabinet during much of his first administration was the broad agreement of its members about the need for a strong government and a powerful executive to manage it. Factional antagonisms that later divided the nation—problems of strict vs. loose interpretation, of Anglophilism vs. Francophilism—existed in embryo at the outset of the Washington era, but in 1790 pressures over the immediate course of the nation's foreign policies overwhelmed them.

Although Jefferson returned home with distrust of Britain and admiration for France, he brought with him no illusions about Franco-American relations. His experiences had revealed important qualifications about the nature of French benevolence. Such optimism as he displayed rested not on any agreements between the two governments or decrees that France had made in America's favor, but on expectations about the more liberal regime that appeared in the making after destruction of the Bastille. As he took up his duties France had not yet revealed the full dimensions of change; in 1790, as in 1787, it still closed the West Indies to American ships and retained its monopoly of American products entering France. Jefferson felt that France had not yet seen its self-interest, had not yet recognized the mutual advantages that would flow from the new politico-economic system proposed by America.

To effect a new relationship with France and to break the old one with Britain required a centralized government strong enough to command the respect of its peers in the international arena. In this view Jefferson was at one with John Jay and Alexander Hamilton. Like the former (who had been secretary for foreign affairs under the Confederation) he believed that if Europeans saw an efficient and well-administered national government, with its trade and finances prudently regulated, they would be disposed to cultivate American friendship rather than risk its resentment. This theme, which Jay stressed in the third *Federalist*, found a harmonious response in Jefferson, and he could even join with Hamilton when the New Yorker asserted in the eleventh *Federalist* that "a steady adherence to the Union" might allow the new nation to tip the scales of European competition in the New World for the benefit of Americans. Thus, a commonly recognized impotence in foreign affairs provided a powerful stimulus for strengthening the powers of the central government. The Founding Fathers, even when they could agree on little else, all sought to exploit European disadvantage for America's advantage.

Historians have not always recognized that Hamilton and Jefferson shared belief in a strong executive able to resist congressional encroachments upon its power in foreign affairs. Jefferson earlier had expressed approval of the constitutional device that freed the central government from the interference of state assemblies on matters of taxation; now with the new government in operation, he thought that the federal legislature's natural tendency to interfere with presidential responsibilities must be resisted. In a memorandum to Washington, presented shortly after taking office, the new secretary of state questioned the propriety of presidential consultation with the Senate about diplomatic exchanges. Arguing that there was no constitutional requirement for such solicitation and that the practice would create an unfortunate precedent, Jefferson interpreted senatorial powers as extending no further than approval or disapproval of nominees. Even then, he envisioned the decision as basically presidential—almost exclusively so, "except as to such portions of it as are specially submitted to the Senate. Exceptions are to be construed strictly." Jefferson's rigid construction of the Constitution in 1790 was hardly distinguishable from that of the Hamiltonians around him, including the secretary of the treasury himself.

If the Jeffersonian vision of American foreign policy began

with an executive free of congressional constraints and the shortcomings of the Confederation, it included other elements customarily identified with his great rival, Hamilton: repayment of obligations to foreign creditors through assumption of the debts of previous governments and the promotion of American shipping through an effective navigation system. New England merchants and Philadelphia creditors welcomed these facets of the Hamiltonian program, and, to a point, so did Madison and Jefferson. While it is true that from the outset Jefferson had many reservations about his cabinet colleagues, especially when he suspected them of monarchical tendencies, he could work with them during the early years of Washington's administration. He could tolerate Treasury intrusion into his department by Hamilton's involvement in consular affairs, as long as he believed that Jeffersonian views received a fair hearing. His rivals in the cabinet in those early years were "good men and bold men, and sensible men."

Not even the Nootka Sound affair in the summer of 1790 fully revised that judgment. Although Jefferson strongly opposed Hamilton's wish to grant a British request for the passage of troops through American territory in the event of war between Spain and Britain over the Pacific Northwest, he had no knowledge of Hamilton's intimate connections with British agents. Nor did he adamantly oppose concessions to the British per se. His point simply was that concessions ought to be reciprocal; the United States ought not surrender a bargaining weapon in advance. In their first cabinet debate on foreign affairs Hamilton and Jefferson differed more on tactics than on ideology.

Of course, Hamilton's early hostility to discriminatory legislation against British shipping did evoke criticism from Madison and Jefferson, but not the deep emotional response it was to arouse in 1793–94. Hamilton, after all, had a navigation system, and that was a step in the right direction. It took time before Jefferson's mind converted Hamilton's behavior into a dangerous passion for monarchy and a fatal dependence on Britain.

In part, at least, Jefferson's tolerance for failure of punitive measures against the British may have flowed from the concurrent insensitivity toward America displayed by the liberal regime in France. While the revolutionists had reformed their government under the National Assembly, nothing in those reforms served the interests of the United States. To his chagrin, Jefferson realized that the new bourgeois rulers of France had no more intent than the mercantilists of the old regime to permit liberal terms for American goods in French markets. That realization caught him between anger and embarrassment, for it coincided with a contretemps in relations between the two nations. Madison's navigation law (which failed to discriminate between ships of countries with commercial treaties and those without them) had given rise to a French protest, to which Jefferson normally would have been sympathetic. He recognized that in spirit, if not in letter, it was unfair that British and French ships would receive equal treatment in American ports, and he wished Congress to make special concessions to the French in return for the concessions they had made during his ministry; but French intransigence threatened to undermine support for such an arrangement.

Still, Jefferson sought to exploit the situation. The behavior of the National Assembly freed him from some inhibitions over past French favors and permitted him a degree of flexibility. That France did not see its own advantage in at least removing prerevolutionary restrictions from the West Indian trade seemed incredible to him. His impatience flared into anger when the French consul in New York insisted upon the recall of two consuls whom Congress had sent to the French islands. Jefferson resisted that demand, ultimately winning a minor victory when the American consuls were permitted to remain as "commercial agents." That success signified little and the secretary knew it; he harbored no illusions that an entente had been established between the two countries.

Much of his distress in office, then, stemmed less from the Francophobic character of the Hamiltonians than from the fact that the French refused friendly gestures when they were offered. Neither Madison's persistent attempts in Congress to fashion a navigation system that would benefit French commerce nor Jefferson's illuminating reports on the whale oil and codfish industries (with their clear invitation to France to replace those who had built "their navigation on the ruin of ours") struck responsive chords in Paris. Assuming the impossibility of weaning Americans from British ties, the French middle-class leaders of the Revolution wrote off American commerce. They even revoked the minor concessions that Jefferson had so painfully extracted during his ministry in France. The arrival in 1791 of a new French minister, Jean Baptiste Ternant, did not help matters. Ternant found Hamilton more congenial than Jefferson, so when the latter presented a plan for exchanging with the French full privileges of natives in each other's ports, the negative response did not surprise him. To the minister, free trade seemed to reward Britain at the expense of France.

War in Europe, particularly between France and Britain in 1793, changed the immediate course of Franco-American relations. It revived Jefferson's hopes for a new identity of interests between the two countries, although he recognized the danger of American involvement in the European conflict through obligations incurred in the alliance of 1778. For all his rising anger against Federalists and Britons, Jefferson did not envisage American troops or ships fighting alongside the French in the West Indies or anywhere else any more than did Hamilton. Yet the opportunity for exploiting a new French mood to strike out at British suzerainty over trade and arrogance over maritime claims proved too glittering to resist. The republican government of France opened West Indian ports to American ships and dispatched a more amiable minister to negotiate a liberal commercial treaty based precisely on Jefferson's scheme of mutual naturalization. Small wonder that the secretary's expectations outweighed fears as Europe plunged into the wars of the French Revolution.

There was a link between the worsening of Jefferson's relations with Hamiltonians at home and improvement of his relations with France. From 1793 to the end of the decade, first as secretary of state and then later as vice-president, he saw the Republic in peril in America and the Republic in peril in Europe. France's part as warrior against British monarchy and imperialism sharpened his antagonism toward British agents in America; increasingly, he saw the Federalist faction as a tool of British interests seeking to restore monarchy to America. Such a goal explained the uses to which Hamiltonian power would be put; it explained the failure of his own efforts to reduce British influence and enhance the interests of American democrats. The whole Hamiltonian program—from funding the national debt and establishing a national bank to Anglo-American reconciliation and a pro-British trade policy—became in his mind part of an enormous invisible conspiracy against the national welfare. The European war unmasked Hamilton's real purpose. Such was the Jeffersonian image of Federalism; of course there was a mirror image of Jeffersonians in the minds of their opponents.

Naturally, this Jeffersonian angle of vision enhanced the importance of France as a counterweight to domestic and foreign enemies. While hardly a new position, its urgency intensified after 1793, and introduced a new and ugly dimension into American debates on foreign affairs and domestic politics. The French republic took on symbolic overtones. According to Jeffersonians, France struggled for more than its own survival—the survival of liberty everywhere was at stake. A British victory would reimpose its rule in America, either directly or through Britain's faithful American servants. Many of Jefferson's friends perished in the struggle for republicanism in France; although he deplored the losses, he endured them stoically, even philosophically, regarding his friends as soldiers fallen in the battle for universal liberty. "My own affections have been deeply wounded by some of the martyrs to this cause," he told William Short on 3 January 1793, "but rather than it should have failed I would have seen half the earth desolated; were there but an Adam to an Eve left in every country. Left free, it would be better than it now is." Written a month before France declared war on Britain, this letter expressed Jefferson's deep commitment to the cause of revolutionary republicanism. Given that predisposition, his fear of counterrevolutionary Britain and its supposed American agents intensified. The mild challenge raised by Britain in the Nootka Sound affair of 1790 had become three years later a matter of the life and death of a society.

The immediate problem for Washington's advisers, however, was the position of the United States toward the belligerents. To resolve that difficulty, Jefferson laid down a precedent for recognition of foreign governments: de facto control by the government in power. Possession of domestic power and ability to fulfill international obligations were the tests of legitimacy. Even before Washington raised the question of recognition in the cabinet, Jefferson had spelled out his position in a letter to the American minister in France. "I am sensible," he told Gouverneur Morris on 12 March 1793, "that your situation must have been difficult during the transition from the late form of government to the reestablishment of some other legitimate authority, that you may have been at a loss to determine with whom business might be done. Nevertheless when principles are well understood, their application is less embarrassing. We surely cannot deny to any nation that right whereon our own government is founded, that every one may govern itself according to whatever form it pleases, change these forms at its own will; that it may transact its business with foreign nations through whatever organ it thinks proper, whether King, Convention, Assembly, Committee, President, or anything else it may use. The will of the nation is the only thing essential to be regarded." Jefferson never questioned that the republican government of France should have its minister received, its financial claims honored, and its role as an ally affirmed; when Washington raised these questions after the execution of the French king and the extension of the European war, the secretary of state immediately perceived the mind of Hamilton guiding the president. It outraged him that America seemed more cautious in its support of a republic than it had been in its allegiance to a monarchy. With feeling he asked, "Who is the American who can say with truth that he would not have allied himself to France if she had been a republic?" [1]

In defending the alliance Jefferson marshaled evidence from many authorities on international law of the seventeenth and eighteenth centuries, from Grotius to Vattel. He won his case, at least over recognition and legitimacy of treaties, if not over neutrality. If his position was based on the moral worth of republicans expressing the will of the people rather than on *de facto* control of France by the Girondists, realism needs redefinition. The scholars of international law help little in understanding

---

1. The immediate problem for the Washington administration was the precise posture the United States should strike toward the belligerents when one of them was an ally. It was at this juncture that Jefferson laid down a policy that has been accepted as a precedent for American recognition of foreign powers: a doctrine based on *de facto* control of the society by the government in power. Possession of power and the ability to fulfill obligations to other nations were the appropriate tests of legitimacy. The traditional criteria for recognition deserve scrutiny in light of the periodic practice in the twentieth century of deviating from this approach, of refusing recognition to governments in Mexico, Russia, Manchuria, and China on the grounds that these governments assumed power by force, held it by repression, and displayed hostility to American interests and values. If such were truly deviations from tradition, the contemporary response has been to justify the position by circumventing the Jeffersonian stance and pointing to American concern with government by consent of the governed and the right of rebellion to remove tyranny. In other words, the American outlook on world affairs had always entailed a moral judgment to be rendered against a regime imposed on an unwilling people and disruptive of the proprieties of international conduct.

the Jeffersonian position, for they can be cited either way, as Jefferson himself did when he dismissed that "ill understood scrap in Vattel" that Hamilton had used to deny recognition and then a few months later cited that same Vattel to refute the French minister's demand for a more friendly neutrality. For both Hamiltonians and Jeffersonians the nub of the matter seems to have been the legitimacy of a revolutionary transfer of power. For the former destruction of a hereditary monarchy by revolution stripped from the usurpers all international obligations owed to their predecessors; for the latter, revolutionists merely made legitimate what had been doubtful before by exercising a natural right to alter the form of government.

Neither Hamilton nor Jefferson appeared willing to accept the full implications of *de facto* government as these had been spelled out in Pufendorf's assertion that the actual possessor of sovereignty, however acquired, was entitled to the allegiance of his subjects so long as no claimant appeared with a better, "more legitimate" right. In the absence of such a claimant, Pufendorf asserted, reason dictated that the possessor should continue to hold power. Although this argument fitted nicely into Jefferson's interpretation in 1793, one wonders whether he would have been so solicitous for recognition of a monarchical government if it had come to power by counterrevolution against a republican regime, whether he would have been so insistent upon receiving ministers and authenticating an alliance if the government in question had been British sponsored or Anglophile. It is reasonable to conclude that for reasons of morality and national interest Jefferson would have taken Hamilton's stance in opposition to a *de facto* government if the question turned on the situation of 1814 when a monarchy dependent for survival upon Great Britain replaced Napoleon. Perhaps it was merely fortuitous that the first secretary of state found morality on the side of *de facto* legitimacy in 1793.

Belief in Federalist subversion of America's republican experiment dominated Jefferson's mind for the remainder of the decade. Obsession with Hamiltonian maleficence led him at times to startling judgments couched in picturesque language. Washington appeared elliptically as one of the "Samsons in the field & Solomons in the council . . . who have had their heads shorn by the harlot England." On another occasion he prepared to leave Monticello for a visit to London (which he expected to find under

French occupation) to "hail the dawn of liberty and republicanism in that island." His conviction that the Federalists had accepted a British definition of neutral rights and an inferior position in the British Empire merged with the conviction that they also planned a monarchical government for America. Washington was their captive, and while John Adams resisted Hamiltonian pretensions, the second president was also an adherent of a form of society inimical to Jeffersonian values. So the world seemed to Jefferson, retired in Virginia from 1794 to 1796 and then isolated in the vice-presidency during Adams's administration. A quasi-war with France coupled with assaults upon the liberties of Republicans lent credence to a nearly paranoid view of America that Jefferson did not alter until he became president.

Yet even in his moments of deepest despair over the direction of American policy under the Federalists, Jefferson resisted his natural impulses to expand the relationship with France, for he knew the limits of counterbalance. Even as he tangled with his rival over neutrality in 1793, Jefferson had no wish to bring the United States into the European war. His opponents were far less fastidious on isolation when Britain was involved. What Jefferson wanted was a benevolent neutrality that would assist France rather than Britain; with it he wished to pressure the British for commercial concessions in return for abstention from the conflict. He failed. Once a proclamation of neutrality had been issued, the possibilities for manipulating it to the advantage of Britain passed to Hamilton, and he made the most of them. There is, however, no evidence that for all his unhappiness Jefferson would have risked a war with Britain. He, rather than Adams, might have reaped the unhappy consequences of Jay's Treaty—and he might have handled them less well.

Jefferson's disavowal of Minister Edmond Genêt during his last year in office and subsequent willingness to let the French alliance lapse at the beginning of his presidency provide an appropriate frame for the comment of France's minister in 1796, Pierre Adet, that Jefferson was an "American and, as such, he cannot be sincerely our friend. An American is the born enemy of all the European peoples." Adet recognized a basic Jeffersonian premise, that in the midst of war and revolution he had given his fervent blessings to the French cause—but France essentially was an instrument of policy rather than an object of it. Its society, its people, its culture all evoked a genuine Francophilism. In Jefferson's statecraft with France, however, there were always *arrières pensées*.

In picking up the pieces of the Revolution and making them part of an empire, Napoleon Bonaparte recognized Jefferson's unreliability, though he missed no opportunity to manipulate him. The first consul wisely concealed information about the return of Louisiana to France, anticipating Jeffersonian distress at the prospect of a French neighbor replacing Spain on the Mississippi. More than pressure from westerners or taunts from Federalists moved the president in 1803. France, more than Spain, posed an obstacle to American expansion and had to be removed. With Louisiana safely secured, Jefferson could resume his policy of seeking to balance British power with French. The charges of Francophilism reached their climax in 1807 with the embargo, when the president seemingly fitted his scheme of economic coercion into Napoleon's Continental system. Such an attempted accommodation, however, was hardly a mark of servitude; it was rather a gamble based on the assumption that France posed a lesser threat than Britain. However tyrannical the French emperor might be, his rule would pass away, while the threat of parliamentary tyranny in Britain would remain. Moreover, the British danger hit closer to home by virtue of that nation's control of the sea. "I cannot," as Jefferson phrased it, "with the Anglomen, prefer a certain present evil to a future hypothetical one." The nation's survival required playing one power off against another, while keeping free of entanglements with either. The dismal end of the embargo, and war in 1812, revealed the dangerous defects in that gambit.

Jefferson's handling of foreign affairs appeared to move from one position to another—from alliance with France in the 1790s, to threat of alliance with Britain in 1803, to collaboration with Napoleonic schemes in 1807; from restrictions upon congressional authority over diplomatic appointments in 1790, to assertions of congressional prerogative over neutrality in 1793, to enlargement of presidential power in the enforcement of the embargo in 1808; from an appeal for a Chinese isolation from the world within an agrarian society, to a concurrent encouragement of trade with

France in the 1780s, to an advocacy of domestic manufactures
during his presidency. The exigencies of politics accounted for
some of the shifts, but most were more apparent than real.

The primacy of American independence from the Old World
remained a constant in Jefferson's thinking. He preferred an
agrarian society to an industrial one; but if he had to accept the
latter, he wished for an industrial America cut loose from British
controls, performing the role France had failed to provide. To
ensure insulation from Europe's troubles he pressed for westward
and southern expansion to free American borders from the
anxieties of war and to make room for the growth of the Republic.
Jefferson's early encounters with division and disunity in the
Revolution and Confederation had qualified his dedication to
states' rights; his major involvement with them was when he felt
impotent to control the central government. While he never
denied the virtues he had celebrated in limited government, his
early advice to Washington and his own behavior during his
presidency suggest that when opportunities for vital action by the
executive offered themselves the president ought not to be
inhibited by excessive deference to congressional or state authority.

The pragmatic strain in Jefferson's management of foreign
affairs, which permitted him to accept conditions inhibiting his
freedom of action, also permitted him to shape those conditions
to his ideas of the needs of the nation. If commercial ties with
Europe were indispensable—and they were—he wished them to
be conducted with minimal political entanglements as he
preached in his first inaugural. He shed no tears for the demise of
the French alliance. If developments abroad served the interests of
a small maritime power, he could exploit them without surrendering either American interests or principles. Philosophers of the
Old World might be enlisted in the American cause, just as the
conflicts among European states might serve American trade or
territorial advances. Such sentiments marked Jefferson's view of
France and his policy toward it.

Whether Europe or America derived more gain from his
dalliances remains debatable. What is certain is Jefferson's consistent belief in the justice of his policies; they were moral by virtue
of their American character. For all his expediency he never
separated national self-interest from morality in the management
of foreign affairs. His determination to recognize the French

republic in 1793 rested on justice as well as on utility. Recognition appeased his moral sense while it appealed to his practical streak, much as did his ideas on neutral rights and free trade. A characteristic American approach to international relations has been the casting of national interests on a moral base; Jefferson's contribution was to shape this conceit and to seek a relationship with the external world that followed from it.

BIBLIOGRAPHIC NOTE

Any treatment of Jefferson as a diplomatist should begin with Henry Adams, *History of the United States during the Administrations of Jefferson and Madison*, 9 vols. (New York, 1889–91). Adams's biases, particularly his inability to take Jefferson's statesmanship seriously, have affected twentieth-century scholarship. Contemporary studies of diplomacy in the Jeffersonian era either reinforce Adams's charges of Francophilism and insensitivity to the realities of power or react against them. Bradford Perkins, *The First Rapprochement: England and the United States, 1795–1805* (Philadelphia, 1955) and *Prologue to War: England and the United States, 1795–1805* (Berkeley and Los Angeles, 1961), distributes blame for the breakdown of Anglo-American relations on both sides, but allocates a slightly larger share to Jeffersonian statecraft. Alexander DeConde, on the other hand, dealing with the 1790s in *Entangling Alliance: Politics and Diplomacy under George Washington* (Durham, 1958) and *The Quasi-War: The Politics and Diplomacy of the Undeclared War with France, 1797–1801* (New York, 1966), emphasizes Federalist partisanship for Great Britain as a major source of America's difficulties.

Dumas Malone's magisterial but still incomplete biography, *Jefferson and His Time*, particularly volume 2, *Jefferson and the Rights of Man* (New York, 1951), volume 3, *Jefferson and the Ordeal of Liberty* (New York, 1962), and volume 4, *Jefferson the President: First Term, 1801–1805* (New York, 1970), offers a sympathetic and reasonably objective picture of his diplomatic career from his ministry in France to the end of his first administration. Gilbert Chinard, *Thomas Jefferson: The Apostle of Americanism* (Boston, 1929), with its special emphasis on France, and Merrill Peterson, *Thomas Jefferson and the New Nation* (New York, 1970), are the most useful one-volume biographies. Lawrence S. Kaplan, *Jefferson and France: An Essay on Politics and Political Ideas* (New Haven, 1967), shares Chinard's claim that Jefferson's French policy was not under the influence of French ideology but operated consistently under the assumption that Great Britain was the greater threat to American interests. Beckles Willson, *American Ambassadors to France, 1777–1927: A Narrative of Franco-American Diplomatic Relations* (London, 1928), contains a sketch of Jefferson's contributions as minister to France from 1784 to 1789. W. K. Woolery, "The Relations of Thomas Jefferson to American Foreign Policy, 1783–1793," *Johns Hopkins University Studies in Historical and Political Science* 45 (Baltimore, 1927), develops particularly Jefferson's position toward France. Merrill Peterson, "Thomas Jefferson and Commercial Policy, 1783–1793," *William and Mary Quarterly* 12 (3rd series, 1965), 584–611, emphasizes Jefferson's hopes of using France as a counterbalance to Great Britain's economic power over America. Gilbert Chinard, "Jefferson and the Physiocrats," *University of California Chronicle* 33 (1931), 18–31, observes that the differences in the economic ideas of Jefferson and the Physiocrats were greater than the similarities. Robert R. Palmer, "The Dubious Democrat: Thomas Jefferson and Bourbon France," *Political Science Quarterly* 82 (1947), 400–504, notes Jefferson's doubts of French abilities to assimilate a major revolution.

Samuel Flagg Bemis, "Thomas Jefferson," in Bemis, ed., *The American Secretaries and Their Diplomacy*, 10 vols. (New York, 1927–29), has a good capsule account of Jefferson's role as the first secretary of state. Charles M. Thomas, *American Neutrality in 1793: A Study in Cabinet Government* (New York, 1931), presents the dilemma facing the Washington administration as a result of the Anglo-French war. Albert H. Bowman, "Jefferson, Hamilton, and American Foreign Policy, *Political Science Quarterly* 71 (1956), blames Hamilton for most of Jefferson's problems in 1793. Meade Minnegerode, *Jefferson, Friend of France, 1793: The Career of Edmond Charles Genêt* (New York, 1928), is a bitter attack on the secretary by a descendant of the French minister. A more balanced view is offered in Harry Ammon, *The Genêt Mission* (New York, 1973). Philip M. Marsh, "Jefferson's Retirement as Secretary of State," *Pennsylvania Magazine of History* 69 (1945), 220–24, is sympathetic to Jefferson's isolation in a Hamiltonian cabinet.

Adrienne Koch, *Jefferson and Madison: The Great Collaboration* (New York, 1964), deals with the close relationship between the president and his secretary of state. Mary P. Adams, "Jefferson's Reactions to the Treaty of San Ildefonso," *Journal of Southern History* 22 (1955), 173–88, comments on his militant reaction to the Spanish cession of Louisiana to France. Louis M. Sears, *Jefferson and the Embargo* (Durham, 1927), remains the standard treatment on the subject despite the pacifism that he dubiously attributes to Jefferson.

FROM INDEPENDENCE TO WAR:

JAMES MADISON

and American Foreign Policy

Patrick C. T. White

George Washington's main purpose, he wrote in 1793 as the wars
of the French Revolution engulfed Europe, was "to keep our
people in peace." That task proved a delicate and challenging one,
and if the first president of the United States achieved that goal his
successors found it increasingly difficult and finally impossible.
The early decades of independence for countries that have thrown
off the imperial mantle are seldom easy, as the twentieth century
has so clearly demonstrated; what is true today was also true for
the thirteen colonies after recognition of their independence in
1783. For more than two decades after that extraordinary event,
presidents struggled with the problems of defending American
interests overseas, creating a viable economy at home, and

Extensive documentation for the views expressed in this essay may be found in
Professor White's *Nation on Trial: America and the War of 1812.*

shaping institutions to govern the new nation. Few men played a more central role in these critical years than James Madison, for he molded the Constitution of 1787, made foreign policy as secretary of state between 1801 and 1809, and as president led the United States into its first foreign war. Wars are the cruelest test for nations, and it was Madison's misfortune to take a divided country into a conflict in 1812. While a majority of his party supported what Calhoun called the second war for liberty, a substantial and purposeful minority passionately believed otherwise.

This deep party division tragically complicated the making of foreign policy, and finally pitched the United States into a war it was ill prepared to fight and not ready to sustain. No president can escape unscathed from the ruinous divisions an unpopular war inflicts upon the nation. When Daniel Webster could cry out in 1814 that the war was being fought to conquer Canada rather than to defend America's national interests, it is obvious how deep the divisions in the country had become. More than a century and a half later Lyndon Johnson suffered the same torments and damage when he involved the United States in a venture in Vietnam that too many of his countrymen believed ill judged, immoral, and harmful to the nation.

Madison was born on 18 March 1751 in King George County, Virginia. As the son of a well-known planter whose forefathers had settled in that region late in the seventeenth century, he entered a secure and established world. He was related to Edward Pendleton, a distinguished lawyer and revolutionary leader, and to John Taylor, a leading states' rights lawyer. By inheritance and upbringing, then, he naturally viewed property rights as vital to the nation. He did not hold this view narrowly, for his subsequent reading of Locke led him to the same conclusion; the right to acquire property, Madison believed, formed the basis of a just and stable society. Because of his frail health, Madison received his early education at the hands of tutors. For university training he went not to William and Mary College where so many of his contemporaries received their education, but rather to the College of New Jersey at Princeton where the climate better suited his health and where the academic standards were more exacting.

At Princeton Madison read Greek and Roman history and

steeped himself in the writings of Locke, Hume, Addison, and Montesquieu. He absorbed the great English dissenting tradition that was such a vital part of the eighteenth century. His teachers were clerics and so he wedded a deep and lasting Christian ethic to his dissenting thought. The education he received helped shape his political beliefs; from his reading of Livy he discovered the virtues of republican government, from Cicero he learned of the dangers of the military dictatorship of a Caesar. Thucydides warned him of the disasters that fratricidal war might inflict upon a country, and Plutarch stressed the virtues of citizenship. If classical civilization gave Madison an understanding of the state, his reading of Addison, Pope, and Swift gave him a sense of style, manner, and grace. Overriding this, his Protestant ethic instilled in him a conception of man's relation to God. He believed that there were limits to the state's power over the individual, and he accepted Locke's doctrine that men could not be governed without their consent.

When Madison graduated from Princeton in 1771 he was unsure of the profession he wished to pursue. He thought of law, but found politics more fascinating. The principles and forms of government, he once wrote, were too important to be ignored by inquisitive minds. In April 1776, at the age of twenty-six, he was elected a delegate from Orange County to a convention in Williamsburg, Virginia. After a vigorous debate this assembly instructed its delegates to the Continental Congress to call for independence from Great Britain. Madison, who was both young and inexperienced, took no part in the debate but supported the resolution on independence and celebrated its passage. In 1780, he became a delegate to the Continental Congress where he served four years. The experience he gained there shaped his views both of the nature of politics and the extent to which power should be delegated to the individual states. The year Madison entered Congress was a somber one, marked by American defeats at Charleston and Camden and the announced treason of Benedict Arnold. Through these distressing times Congress debated and bickered, showing neither a unity of purpose nor a determination to wage war effectively. Madison shared Washington's fear that one head might gradually turn into thirteen disparate ones, with fearful consequences. The answer to that problem, Madison asserted, lay in greater "authority and vigour in our councils."

At the same time, defining America's future interests con-

cerned him. It was imperative that the government assert its claims
to the Mississippi River. Spain and Britain had jointly controlled
that river by the 1763 treaty. When Spain entered the war against
Britain in 1779 it ignored the United States claim to the area once
held by the mother country. Madison composed a state paper
laying effective claim to the disputed territory, arguing that the
Mississippi was a natural boundary, insisting that America could
make more effective use of the territory than Spain, and asserting
that to surrender the claims of the individual states to the area
would dangerously weaken the war effort. Madison also rejected
the Spanish closing of the mouth of the Mississippi to navigation
(a right exercised because Spain controlled both banks of the river
there) as both harmful to America and its allies and a defiance of
natural law. A great tide of American settlers, he suggested, would
inevitably settle the West, and it was only right that the future be
recognized now. If this was neither Manifest Destiny nor a sense
of mission—and it was not—it was nonetheless a clear recognition
of the vital importance of the West to the new nation.

By 1782 the defeats that had haunted the United States had
turned to victories and Great Britain accepted peace. The negotiations by John Jay, Benjamin Franklin, and John Adams, which
culminated in the triumphant Treaty of Paris in 1783, proved the
prescience of Madison's view. The agreed terms reflected the skill
of the American negotiators and the feelings increasingly voiced
in Britain that the attempt to crush colonial aspirations was an
unworthy task. The treaty itself recognized the independence of
the United States, gave it fishing rights in specified regions of
British North American waters, drew a boundary that gave the
United States the Mississippi River down to the thirty-first parallel,
provided for the evacuation of American territory by British
troops, and pledged the United States to work for the restoration
of sequestered Loyalist property as well as to create no impediments to the collection of legitimate British debts.

It is an all-too-familiar occurrence that internal disorder
follows colonial independence. The United States was no exception to this rule, although its troubles were less turbulent and
destructive than most. Nevertheless, the difficulties were real
enough to convince Madison that neither internal tranquillity nor
foreign relations could be secure until a new and stronger federal
authority was created. He observed in 1783 that if the men who
had made the Revolution regarded peace with Britain as the end

of their labors, if they remained indifferent while anarchy and domestic turmoil dissolved the bonds of government, they would reap the contempt of their fellows and the condemnation of posterity. Peace alone would be insufficient; he demanded that the true purpose of the Revolution be realized: "Let them, by a government adequate to the ends of society, secure those blessings to which the virtues, sacrifices and sufferings of America have undeniable claims."

The years after 1783 demonstrated the truth of Madison's prophecy. State quarreled with state, economic instability threatened the union, and domestic insurrection challenged the central authority. Foreign danger matched this internal tribulation. Great Britain excluded the new nation from the imperial trading system and closed the West Indies to the United States. Even worse, the failure of America to protect both the loyalists and their property and the inability of the federal authority to prevent individual states from placing impediments in the way of collecting British debts gave London an excuse to keep the Northwest posts. Beyond that, Spain closed the Mississippi River to navigation through Louisiana in 1784. Only the determined opposition of Madison and the stubborn resistance of the southern states prevented the United States from ratifying a proposal that would have accepted that closure for twenty-five years in return for American access to Spanish markets.

With all its risks and consequences this continued instability could not be tolerated. While the nation had violated its treaties with Britain, France, and Holland, those foreign powers had not yet been rigorous in retaliation; but that moderation, Madison warned, should not be taken for "permanent partiality" to American faults. The solution lay at hand: a new framework of constitutional government to replace the discredited Articles of Confederation. For some years Madison had devoted his thoughts and energies to an examination of the means to achieve this. He called for a constitutional convention; when it met in 1787 he was ready to take up the challenge. A shining constellation of talent gathered at Philadelphia—"an assembly of demi-gods," as Jefferson put it. Washington, Jefferson, Franklin, Randolph, and Hamilton were only some of the nation's leaders who attended and lent their gifts to its deliberations. As important as their talent was the commitment of the majority to a nationalist vision of a strong central authority. Madison had observed that the "great desideratum" in government was a modification of the concept of sovereignty to make a centralized government a neutral party between interest groups and factions, to keep one part of society from violating the rights of another, and to prevent the agents of government from becoming interests adverse to society. To reconcile the conflict between those who wished to retain the strength of the individual states and those who wanted a centralized national authority Madison proposed a compromise that would preserve the "due supremacy of the national authority" without excluding local authority where it was "subordinately useful." The result was a "mixed government" that embodied the federal principle, preserved local government, and secured liberty and freedom.

Ratification of the Constitution had to follow its making, and here Madison with Hamilton and Jay excelled. In the *Federalist* papers they produced a defense of the new Constitution that stands as one of the most eloquent tracts on political theory in the English language. It was, as Jefferson observed, "the most authentic exposition" of the federal Constitution, and its clarity of style and force of argument helped convince the nation of its utility.

One of the chief purposes of the new Constitution, wrote Madison, was to act as a bulwark against foreign dangers and serve as the guardian of American commerce. Between 1787 and 1793 he pressed for a foreign policy that would realize these twin goals. Madison's efforts were first directed at the imbalance of American trade with Britain. Since the United States imported from the United Kingdom twice as much as it exported there, America had become dangerously dependent upon British credit and goods. To assure the reality as well as the form of independence it was imperative, Madison argued, to diversify American trade by directing a greater proportion to France. To this end, he introduced a variety of measures in the House of Representatives including preferential duties for the ships of nations that signed trade treaties with the United States. Since Britain had not, and indeed, since it had abruptly rejected a reciprocal trade agreement with the United States in 1784, its ships would suffer discriminatory tonnage duties in American ports. The pro-French nature of this measure, which would additionally have raised the price of goods in the United States, proved too much for Hamilton and Washington, and they rejected it; but an act giving American ships preferences in home ports was enacted. It should be observed that

Hamilton's opposition to these measures did not make him less a nationalist than Madison. The former believed that continuing and developing closer ties with Britain would better serve America's interests. Their increasing divisions on foreign policy when combined with their deepening differences over domestic matters led to the formation of the Federalist and Republican parties, a development that had been neither envisaged in the Constitution nor favored by Washington.

The outbreak of war in Europe placed new pressures upon the United States. In 1793 Britain and France became locked in a savage struggle that did not finally end until the defeat of Napoleon at Waterloo. The distinguished naval historian, G. J. Marcus, turned to Livy's description of the Second Punic War to find a parallel for that exacting struggle. The latter had written in *Historia*, "Never did any other states and peoples of greater strength and resources engage in war against each other; nor were there states of any other times possessed of such resources and power." The war in Europe posed a particular dilemma for the United States, for it enlarged and deepened the divisions between those who argued for the maintenance of closer ties with Britain and those who wanted to encourage a more intimate friendship with France. Some Republicans believed that the treaty of 1778 with France both morally and legally obligated the United States to come to its aid in the likely event that its possessions in the West Indies were attacked. Others, like Jefferson and Madison, felt that American neutrality should be used to extract concessions from the warring powers. Both of these alternatives seemed far too dangerous to Hamilton, for if either led to war with Britain the future of the Republic would be imperiled. The Neutrality Proclamation issued by Washington bore the imprint of Hamilton's views and called only for "conduct friendly and impartial towards the belligerent powers." The cabinet division over policy spilled into public print. In a series of eight newspaper articles, Hamilton defended not only the Neutrality Proclamation but also the general direction of American foreign policy. Madison, who was convinced that Washington's policy wounded national honor and disregarded "stipulated duties to France," answered Hamilton's defense of the proclamation in five tightly reasoned commentaries. Yet he did not criticize the idea of neutrality, for like Jefferson he wanted only to lean toward France. Rather, he challenged the manner in which the policy was decided and announced. He took a legalistic and constitutional view of Washington's actions and drew upon the intentions of the framers of the Constitution in 1787 to shape his criticism. The president's need to act swiftly to protect the nation's interests was, to Madison, a secondary consideration. This was the first debate in the long history of argumentation over executive privilege and the making of foreign policy.

The events that swiftly followed the Neutrality Proclamation further illustrated Madison's determination to pursue a policy sympathetic to France. The first occurred when Secretary of State Jefferson issued a report on the state of American commerce in which he asked that economic coercion be used to compel Britain to lift its restrictive economic policies. In January 1794, Madison introduced a series of resolutions in the House to this end. He proposed that high barriers be placed against British ships and goods until London accepted the principle of reciprocal trade. He admitted that such a mercantilist system would benefit France, but he saw merit rather than disadvantage in that result. To Federalists, however, the Madison plan was a "wild system" that would strike at the foundations of American business and commerce; despite Madison's passionate advocacy of his proposals the House rejected them and instead implemented a temporary trade embargo with Britain.

Following this measure Washington sent John Jay to London to negotiate the differences with Britain. This mission presented Madison with the second opportunity within a year to outline his foreign policy. Jay was instructed to secure the withdrawal of British troops from the Northwest posts, to deal with the vexatious questions of Loyalist debts and boundary disputes, and to soften the blows being struck at neutral rights. It was a mission designed to stop the drift toward war with Britain. When Jay returned to the United States with the treaty, however, he had only secured the first issue, provided for commissions to settle the second, and failed almost completely to reach agreement on the last. That most prized of objects, the complete opening of trade with the West Indies, eluded his grasp, for the concessions on that critical issue were so trifling as to seem an affront rather than an olive branch. The ratification of the treaty proved to be as stormy as the events that had led to its negotiation. Jay was cursed for failing to defend American rights at sea, and for not wringing concessions from Britain over the West Indies trade. He ruefully observed that he could find his way across the country by the light of his burning effigies

It is not enough to beat the servants of the state; the real question was whether Jay could have secured better terms in the face of British unwillingness to make concessions to a small neutral power—concessions that would, in Britain's judgment, fatally weaken its ability to wage war against France. The alternatives to Jay's Treaty would have been not more favorable terms for America, but war with Britain, and neither Washington nor Hamilton were prepared to take that risk. Madison viewed this posture as self-serving. The treaty was, he insisted, "a ruinous bargain" and could only be explained away by Jay's "blind partiality" for Great Britain. Even worse, he charged, it showed that the Federalists were now a "British party" whose purpose was to secure "an exclusive connection with the British government," sacrificing in the bargain America's commerce and national honor. Beyond that Madison called for the president to submit to the House the papers relative to the treaty, and he boldly asserted the right of the House to pass the legislation necessary to execute its terms. A majority of that body's members felt that such an action would strike at the heart of the treaty-making powers of the president, and rejected Madison's claims.

The election of 1796 followed the ratification of Jay's Treaty. Madison supported Jefferson for the presidency, but he himself decided to retire from public life. He adamantly insisted that he would serve in neither state nor federal offices. His desire on this point, he wrote, was "sincere and inflexible." Certainly his contribution to the nation had been sufficient to justify a withdrawal from the political scene. He, more than any other, had shaped the federal Constitution under which the country lived; he, more than any other, had developed the Republican party, for he, not Jefferson, had organized its structure and led it in the House; and he, more than any other, had formulated a Republican foreign policy as an alternative to the one conceived and practiced by the Federalists.

If Madison was resolute in his determination to retire from political life, both events and his deep commitment to politics pulled him inexorably back into the mainstream of American life.

The presidency of John Adams with its Alien and Sedition Acts was the immediate occasion for his return to national affairs. The quasi-war with France that had erupted in 1797 distressed him, but the Alien and Sedition Acts, which struck at the heart of American liberty, moved him to profound anger. The Virginia and Kentucky Resolutions were the answers he and Jefferson formulated to this harsh exercise of federal authority. Madison did not claim the right of the state to nullify national legislation; rather he formulated the more intricate doctrine of interposition, the right of the individual state to judge when the federal compact had been broken and its further right to interpose its power between the national authority and the people.

The election of Jefferson to the presidency in 1800 opened a new career for Madison. The president called him to serve as secretary of state; although his health still troubled him, he readily accepted the offer, for he was bound to Jefferson by ties of party, principle, experience, and friendship. Madison brought to his new office both strengths and weaknesses. His powers of advocacy had been admirably illustrated during the debates on the Constitution, but advocacy is not enough in the making of foreign policy. Here the accidents of chance, the interests of other nations, and the recognition of the possible as well as the desirable are critical qualities in decision making. Madison's dispatches had a legalistic, even wooden quality, and too often they read like lawyers' briefs. State documents are not necessarily designed to fire the imagination, but they should reveal a sure and complete grasp of the complexity of world affairs. Madison may have disliked Hamilton's *Realpolitik*, but the latter's grasp of reality frequently served America's interests better than a theoretical defense of abstract principles. Further, the nationalism that had moved Madison to call for the Constitutional Convention and that had shaped his view of America's destiny sometimes blinded him to Britain's dilemma; to survive the dreadful wars of the French Revolution and Napoleonic era England had to utilize every weapon at its command, to exploit its control of the seas, and in so doing had perforce to conflict with American interests in neutral trade. Madison's deeply held conviction that logic and reason shaped men's views fell before the fury of Napoleon's ambitions and the British determination to thwart them.

Men act, Madison had written in his "Vices of the Political System of the United States," from a "prudent regard to their own good, as involved in the general and permanent good of the community." He thought that nations should also act that way. "The wars which afflict mankind are not produced by the intrigues or cupidity of the weaker nations, who wish to retain peace whilst their neighbours are at war." They are rather, he wrote, the "offspring of ambition" or commercial competition. It was in the interest of great powers to act with wisdom and generosity toward lesser powers, for no country remained omnipotent for long, and those that once held the world stage would later become supplicants to the very nations they once mistreated and reviled. Consequently, he concluded, all nations would be best served by supporting a system of international law that dispensed justice evenly to all mankind.

These principles were soon tested. Fortunately, the first year of Madison's tenure as secretary of state was quiet, for the great war in Europe had come to a temporary halt. The Peace of Amiens was signed in 1801 and the issues that had so bedeviled America at sea disappeared. Yet peace was an illusion and the actions of Spain and France soon forced Madison to confront a threat to the security of the United States. The blow fell when Spain transferred Louisiana to France and then shortly thereafter closed the mouth of the Mississippi River to American commerce. Madison reacted swiftly and positively. The Mississippi River, he wrote, was everything to the commerce of the West: "It is the Hudson, the Delaware, the Potomac and all the navigable rivers of the Atlantic States formed into one stream." Furthermore, western states considered navigation on it a "natural and indefeasible right" and would fight to preserve it. An even greater danger loomed, however. Napoleon had sent a powerful army to Santo Domingo with orders to crush a slave revolt there and then establish a great French empire in the Mississippi region. To forestall this danger-ous enterprise Madison wanted to secure New Orleans and West Florida. He agreed with Jefferson that if France took possession of New Orleans the security of the United States would depend on the British. The cession of Louisiana to France would change the relationship between that country and America; indeed, he said, "the worst events are to be apprehended." Secretary Madison therefore instructed American representatives in Paris to purchase New Orleans from France and West Florida from Spain. The transfer of territory, he argued, should be made on the supposition that France did not want war with the United States. The claim to

West Florida was less firm. The communication through the rivers of Florida, he observed, was "so natural, so reasonable and so essential" that annexation must eventually take place. For such a diplomatic triumph the United States needed good fortune as well as good management. Fortune smiled upon America, for Napoleon's army at Santo Domingo was decimated, and when the French emperor's grandiose dreams of empire collapsed he hastily sold all of Louisiana to the United States rather than see it fall to Britain. Spain proved more difficult, for the United States had no lever of power to exert upon it. Not until 1810 when Spain was totally occupied with the peninsular war did American forces march in and take that area. Even without Florida, the Louisiana Purchase was victory enough, the one unqualified diplomatic success of Jefferson's presidency. It marked the creation of an American empire that Madison could call an empire of liberty, for its settlers would be Americans cherishing the rights, liberties, and aspirations of the men who had made the Revolution in 1776.

Unhappily, the disaster of war in Europe followed the triumph of the Louisiana Purchase. When Napoleon renewed hostilities with Britain, the United States found itself and its commerce once again cruelly squeezed between the two great powers. Napoleon's swift military victories against the allies in Europe forced Britain to depend upon sea power to fashion a final victory, and in the process neutral rights were summarily ignored. The British reapplied the Rule of 1756 which forbade a nation to trade with European colonies during war if that trade had been prohibited in peacetime; they extended blockades from single ports (the traditional practice) to include entire coastlines; they expanded the definition of contraband from arms and accouterments of war to foodstuffs; and they ended coastal trade in Europe by neutrals. When Napoleon's Berlin and Milan decrees declared the United Kingdom in a state of blockade, Britain retaliated by commanding all ships destined for the Continent to call first at a British port for clearance. Then, when Napoleon decreed that any ship following such instructions would be seized when it reached France, the nature of the American dilemma was clear. Under such circumstances seizure of American ships by either Britain or France was a certainty.

If this were not enough, Britain again began to impress American sailors. The Orders in Council restricted commerce, but impressment affected men. The necessity for maintaining the

JAMES MADISON   93

strength of the Royal Navy lay at the bottom of this British practice. The combination of savage discipline, appalling living conditions, and low wages drove its sailors to desert. Many of them signed onto American ships and Britain was determined to halt the atrophy of the force that was critical to prosecution of the war. Britain therefore stopped and searched neutral vessels on the seas for sailors who had escaped His Majesty's service. More importantly, it seized as its own those who had been born in the United Kingdom but who had become naturalized American citizens. At the time, international law did not recognize the right of people to transfer national allegiance. Once born in a country, one remained a citizen of it always. The practice of naturalization, ruled the law officers of the crown, was "novel" and could not be used to avoid answering the call to service issued by His Majesty's government.

Madison responded to this attack upon American commerce with a scathing denunciation of British practices. In a lengthy pamphlet entitled "Examination of the British Doctrine Which Subjects to Capture a Neutral Trade Not Open in Time of Peace," he scourged Britain for limiting the trade of neutrals during wartime. From Grotius to Vattel, from the practices of the Hansa towns to the treaties with Spain, Madison showed how Britain distorted international law, overthrew accustomed practices, and subverted American interests. "The innovation," he wrote, "which she endeavors to enforce as a right of war, is under that name a mere proposal for extending the field of maritime capture, and multiplying the sources of commercial aggrandizement; a warfare, in fact, against the commerce of her friends, a monopolizing grasp at that of her enemies." He responded with the same anger over impressment. In a series of closely reasoned dispatches to Monroe and Pinckney in London in 1806 Madison denounced the practice as intolerable and demanded that it cease. "Taking reason and justice for the tests of this practice, it is peculiarly indefensible, for it deprives the dearest rights of persons of a regular trial, to which the most inconsiderable article of property captured on the high seas is entitled, and leaves their destiny to the will of an officer, sometimes cruel and generally interested, by his want of mariners, in his own decision." He instructed his representative to bring the British government "more and more to understand their own interests as well as our own"; but it was an error to think that British and American interests coincided. Enlightened self-interest might be much praised, but it was in precious short supply during the Napoleonic Wars. Britain would neither surrender the right to impress nor moderate the conditions that made it necessary.

Matters worsened when a new and more determined government came into office in London. It included Lords Canning and Castlereagh, two of the greatest diplomats in Britain's history; they had resolved to destroy Napoleon. The news of the formation of this new cabinet arrived hard on the heels of fresh intelligence about new restrictive Orders in Council. Then came the *Chesapeake* affair. A British frigate attacked this American vessel on its first cruise in June 1807; four of its crew were killed, eighteen of them wounded, and four alleged deserters seized. This flagrant and unwarranted breach of international law could have led to a complete rupture with Britain. Even Canning, described by John Quincy Adams as that "implacable and rancorous enemy" of the United States, was ready to admit error though less ready to apologize for the incident. The British minister in Washington, David Erskine, saw war as imminent. It might be difficult, he said, to "induce the Nation to determine upon a war with England upon Commercial disputes," but an appeal to national honor could arouse the passions of the people. Jefferson chose to save the nation's honor by other means. The French minister in Washington observed that the president did not want war with Britain and "that Madison dreads it still more."

Jefferson selected an embargo. Madison, who throughout his career had favored the use of economic coercion in diplomacy, supported it. Indeed, the secretary of state drafted the message, which the president sent to Congress with slight alterations. Madison believed that the measure would force Britain and even France to modify their policies. He believed that a secondary benefit would accrue to the United States, for the loss of Europe's markets would stimulate the development of American manufacturing. Unfortunately, Madison overestimated the effect of the embargo abroad and the willingness of Americans to submit to its strictures at home. Britain found alternative markets for its goods in South America; Napoleon refused to lift his decrees; and the United States saw its commerce ruinously damaged. Boston, Savannah, and New Orleans had an air of desolation, and depression gripped the West as agricultural prices plummeted. A great experiment in diplomacy had failed. Conceived as a means to defend America's interests and coerce its enemies, it had

impoverished the country, divided the nation's councils, and was
held in contempt by Britain and France. John Quincy Adams wrote
in 1811 that its only redeeming feature was that it had postponed
war. It had; but the problems it had been designed to resolve
remained, and it was Madison's ill luck to inherit them.

Jefferson retired from the presidency exhausted by his efforts
but comforted by the belief that history would judge him
generously for his unselfish efforts to preserve peace. Madison,
whose service and experience made him the natural candidate of
the Republican party, succeeded him. He faced formidable problems: the *Chesapeake* affair hung fire, the Orders in Council
remained in force, and the embargo lay in ruins. Perhaps a new
president could find fresh solutions to old problems; but could
Madison rise to the occasion? Certainly Senator Adair of Kentucky
thought him "too fearful and too timid to direct the affairs of the
nation," although Albert Gallatin found him "firm when the storm
arises." The first test came with the formation of the cabinet and
here Madison displayed a dangerous weakness. Except for Albert
Gallatin as secretary of the treasury he appointed a cabinet bereft
of talent and devoid of energy and drive.

Unhappily for America, Congress showed no more unity of
purpose or determination of spirit. Some Republicans were ready
to arm the nation; others demanded further negotiations; still
more Federalists wanted close ties with Britain. Congressional
sniping at Gallatin and the incompetent secretary of state's failure
to inform the Senate of the president's policy—a procedure,
Madison wrote, that was "indispensable to the advantageous
conduct of the public business"—did not help matters. The
embargo was gone and the remaining nonimportation act was due
to expire. Few wished to renew a measure that harmed American
commerce more than it hurt Britain or France. As an alternative
Nathaniel Macon introduced a bill that permitted American ships
to trade overseas, but closed the ports of the United States to the
contesting powers in Europe. This was designed to punish those
who injured the United States, but when it emerged from a
quarrelsome Congress it had been emasculated beyond recognition. Macon's Bill No. 2 simply provided that trade with Britain and
France would be renewed—with the proviso that if either of the

offending powers rescinded its oppressive decrees the United States would, if the other did not follow suit in ninety days, apply an embargo against the recalcitrant belligerent. This was a mean and dishonorable measure, for it rewarded one guilty party and provided an opportunity for the unscrupulous to blackmail the United States.

That is what happened, for France announced in the duc de Cadore's letter of August 1810 that the Berlin and Milan decrees were repealed, provided that Britain rescind its Orders in Council. It is not difficult to understand Napoleon's motives for this action; he desperately needed American supplies and hoped that by gulling Madison into accepting the Cadore letter he would secure the repeal of the British blockade. He succeeded on the first count but failed on the second. The president grasped at the French move with unseemly haste, but Britain refused to believe that Napoleon had acted in good faith. Even Pinckney, the American minister in London, said that the continued French seizure of American vessels made his efforts to secure Britain's repeal of the blockade impossible. Instructed to argue that the Cadore letter was valid, he privately admitted that he was defending a lie.

If Macon's Bill failed there was little the United States could do. It could continue to negotiate in the hope, however vain, that Britain and France would listen to reason; it could again try economic coercion, although that, too, offered faint promise; it could submit to conditions as they were, although that would be craven; or it could prepare for war. Madison and the Congress opted for the first alternatives. Despite the many grounds of discontent and discouragement, Madison wrote, America was ready to participate in any new experiment for "a cordial and comprehensive adjustment of matters between the two countries." Beyond that a new nonintercourse act was applied to Britain. The embargo as conceived in Macon's Bill was not imposed. Because too many knew that France was still violating American commerce, it was decided simply to prohibit the importation of British goods while allowing American exports to flow anywhere overseas.

Though such halfhearted measures had little merit, the president knew that the nation was not ready for more aggressive moves; but if American action raised the risk of war with Britain, such a course at least had the advantage, as Madison himself observed, of confronting the country with one adversary at a time.

At this juncture two considerations severely restricted presidential maneuverability. In the first place, lack of congressional support justified presidential caution, for the Congress abandoned a pending measure to raise fifty thousand troops and it abolished the Bank of the United States. The lack of men and money dictated prudence, as did presidential involvement in the Florida annexation movement. Madison had long recognized the strategic and commercial importance of that Spanish territory, and he ardently desired to make it a part of the United States. In an exercise of presidential power that would have delighted a Theodore Roosevelt, Madison occupied West Florida, an act that might even have brought war with Spain, Britain's ally. Defensive considerations, the declining stability in the region that might provide a pretext for British occupation to prop up Spanish authority, in part prompted the annexation. The president provided the rationale for the act. the crisis justified unilateral and decisive action, and the act was "understood to be within the authority of the Executive." Such vigorous extensions of presidential power are not usually associated with the author of the Virginia and Kentucky Resolutions.

Great Britain's response to these events in America gave little cause for optimism. The new British minister in Washington, Augustus John Foster, told the president that London would not lift the Orders in Council until it had clear proof that Napoleon's decrees had been absolutely and unconditionally withdrawn. Because that proof could not be provided, England and America moved closer to a final break; but hope was to be found in the Twelfth Congress which met late in 1811, for its members soon showed that they were of a different mettle from their predecessors. Congress was not united in its views, nor did it consistently pursue a clear and coherent policy; but it did show a firmer grasp of reality and a more determined sense of direction. Its nucleus consisted of a group of young activists, the War Hawks: Henry Clay of Kentucky and Felix Grundy of Tennessee were thirty-four years old, John Calhoun of South Carolina was twenty-nine, John Harper of New Hampshire, thirty-two, and Peter Porter of New York, thirty-eight. Defeat of the old members was, said Robert Wright of Maryland, "the sentence of the nation against the doctrine of submission." These new nationalists were determined to see things through to the end. They did not remember the Revolution for most were born just before or during it. War held no terror for them; Jefferson might say that "one war in a lifetime is enough," but they had no patience with such reasoning. They were supremely confident that war with Britain would be short and swift, victory sweet and certain. Clay would take Canada with the Kentucky militia; even Jefferson thought that, at worst, taking Canada would be merely a "matter of marching."

The Hawks dominated Congress and its committees. In addition to making one of their number, Clay, Speaker of the House, they chaired all the major committees: Foreign Affairs, Naval Affairs, Military Affairs, and Ways and Means. Each of these committees contained a substantial number of the young activists. The views of this group were soon expressed in the report of the Foreign Affairs Committee stating that the country could no longer remain indifferent to the wrongs inflicted by Great Britain. Justice and humanity had restrained America from taking up arms, but "forbearance was no longer a virtue." The time had come to put the nation into the "armor and attitude" demanded by events. One of their number later reported that they had "crossed the Rubicon."

The debate that followed the report showed clearly the mood of Congress; one after another, members rose to call for war. The issue, as Senator Robert Wright of Maryland put it, had narrowed down to war or submission—and with the antitemporizers in the ascendancy, sentiment for the latter was fast dissipating. From the last days of 1811 to the middle of 1812, the country drifted toward war.

A number of serious frictions between the two countries prevented reconciliation. Impressment remained a threat to safety and an affront to sovereignty, and it appeared to Americans that British officials were inciting the Indians on the frontier to war. In March 1812, the Henry letters that Madison sent to Congress seemed positive proof of British perfidy: a British agent, John Henry, had been snooping around New England to determine whether, in the event of war, the Federalists there would look to England rather than to Washington for guidance. There was not much in the letters, but they gave rise to outraged cries against British interference in American affairs.

In the early months of 1812, despite the clamor in Congress, Madison, with the assistance of his new secretary of state, James Monroe, continued negotiating for resolution of the points at issue between the United States and Great Britain. It was a hopeless task. The increasing influence of a group in England calling for repeal of the Orders in Council and reconciliation offered some hope, but when the Perceval government rejected a softer line toward America, it pushed the president toward the conclusion that Britain preferred war to repeal of the orders. Ironically, as American patience wore thin, the British government was moving toward a conditional repeal of the hated measures; but the assassination of the prime minister slowed that move until it was too late. Whether repeal alone would have satisfied American demands remains a matter of conjecture. As long as impressment continued, no American was safe at sea, and if the flag could not protect the citizens who sailed under it, America could not be a truly sovereign state.

When combined with western grievances and fears, the cumulative effect of a decade of British actions finally moved the president to call for war, although continued French attacks upon American commerce made his final decision more difficult. A case for war with both Britain and France could be made, as Madison told Jefferson, but such a war would alienate the Federalists, divide the Republicans, and be impossible to fight. So he chose to face Great Britain as the power that had committed the greatest and most unforgivable transgressions. The president waited until the *Hornet* arrived from England in late May with the latest intelligence, and then, after a fruitless last round of talks with the British minister had shown that Britain was still inflexible, he acted. On 1 June 1812 he sent his war message to Congress, citing the just causes for war in order of their importance: impressment, blockades, and the Orders in Council. His choice of priorities was fair and substantial. Impressment struck at the sovereignty of the Republic by challenging its ability to protect its own citizens, while the Orders in Council damaged its economy in a way that became increasingly unbearable with the passage of time.

The president's message set off fierce and protracted congressional debate, but finally, on 18 June, by a vote of nineteen to thirteen in the Senate and seventy-nine to forty-nine in the House, the United States declared war. The nature of this vote revealed a deeply divided nation rather than a united one. Many Federalists felt that by striking at Britain the United States was attacking the last hope of ordered good government in a world gone mad with revolution. Some Republicans thought that the United States was not yet armed for war and that hostilities should be postponed

until the needed forces could be recruited. Others believed that
republican institutions were still too fragile and untested to stand
the shock of war.

Madison was largely responsible for this confusion, for as
president he should have carried the nation with him in a spirit of
unity and determination. Majority votes are sufficient to pass tax
legislation, but not enough for war; for that, near unanimity is
required, and Madison's failure was a failure of presidential
leadership. On the great issues of war and peace it is the
president's duty to unite a quarrelsome and divided Congress and
to so address the nation that it places its full support behind his
policies. Undoubtedly, presidential eloquence alone would not
have persuaded all who doubted the wisdom of Madison's
actions, but the lack of it made opposition easier to embrace. The
president would have been wise to follow the advice given by
Winston Churchill to the British foreign secretary Sir Edward Grey
in 1915: "I beseech you at this crisis, not to make the mistake in

falling below the level of events. Half-hearted measures will ruin all. . . . You must be bold and violent. You have a right to be."

Circumstances, of course, were against Madison; he was not a man of boldness or of violence. His belief in economic coercion and his hope that reason could overcome ignorance were insufficient to change the policies of great powers involved in a great war. A small, neutral United States had little chance of escaping untouched from the implacable violence of the Napoleonic world war. Chance and fortune had served as Madison's companions in the Louisiana Purchase, but they were unhappy associates in the years of his presidency. There can be little doubt that if it had not been for the Napoleonic Wars there would have been no War of 1812. The issues that led to the latter sprang from the former. The question that bedeviled the United States was how best to protect the national interest in the face of affronts to sovereignty and injury to trade. Madison believed in a system of "perfect freedom" of trade. He had argued for such a system in the formation of the new nation and he called for it as president, but neither Britain nor France shared that view and neither would pursue policies that would lead to it. The tools of economic coercion the United States used to loose Europe from its system were insufficient for the task. The efforts to protect American citizens on the seas proved equally inadequate. Impressment forcibly removed over six thousand American sailors from their ships for service in the Royal Navy. Neither Washington nor Adams, Jefferson nor Madison could design policies to prevent that. When the United States took its place among the nations of the world, Madison asserted, "they assumed and established a common Sovereignty on the high seas, as well as exclusive sovereignty within their territorial water." The declaration of this principle, however, did not establish its practice.

Madison went to war to resolve these dilemmas. His success must be judged, in part, by how he waged war and the terms he secured in peace. In the beginning America suffered disastrous reverses; commanders were weak, troops ill disciplined, and objectives badly chosen. The opposition forces, though small in number, were tightly disciplined regulars brilliantly led by General Isaac Brock. As the war progressed, however, the quality of America's leadership improved and its soldiers acquitted themselves well in battle. By 1814 it was clear to Britain that it could not effectively continue the war except at exorbitant costs. The duke of Wellington, that greatest of soldiers, advised the prime minister, Lord Liverpool, that troops in Canada had held that colony better than he could have hoped and that since a stalemate had been reached the time had come to negotiate a peace. Madison had reached the same conclusion. The United States might, indeed, launch a major invasion of Canada, but the campaign would be bloody and protracted. Furthermore, the Royal Navy, now that Napoleon had been defeated, would devastate the Atlantic seaboard. Finally, the country needed relief, for the swelling tide of domestic opposition to the war threatened national unity.

The peace negotiated at Ghent settled upon a restoration of the situation at the outbreak of war. No mention was made of the maritime issues that had caused the war. This has led some to argue that this was proof the war had been needlessly fought; but by 1814 all the maritime disputes had disappeared with the defeat of France. More importantly, Britain would never again impress American citizens. Daniel Webster warned that to do so would lead to immediate war with the United States, and Britain took this solemn declaration to heart. Beyond that, as Gallatin observed, the war had renewed the spirit of American nationalism and rededicated the nation to its early purpose. While Britain and the United States were to have many dangerous differences later in the nineteenth century they never fell into war again. The lessons of the War of 1812 had not been lost upon them.

Certainly Madison's foreign policy had a distinguishing stamp to it. He believed in domestic freedom based upon personal liberty. He recognized the importance of controlling the Floridas and the Mississippi and he sought to expand American trade overseas. In a violent world he attempted to uphold the nation's rights through economic coercion, but he failed to recognize that it was a frail weapon when used against France and Britain in the era of the Napoleonic Wars. He failed to recognize, too, that a nation without effective armed forces was hardly in a position to extract meaningful concessions from great powers in conflict. Once he had decided upon war he failed to inspire the nation to meet the challenge that lay before it. Yet he did not enter the war for mean or narrow reasons, but rather to preserve the nation whose creation was so much a product of his talent and genius. If he made mistakes in policy and erred in judgment, his work still stands as a monument to his principles.

BIBLIOGRAPHIC NOTE

The War of 1812, one of the most contentious in American history, has captured the attention of historians, partly because it was the first fought by the new Republic and partly because it aroused such domestic opposition. In assessing the war and its causes few historians have been charitable to Madison. Henry Adams, the first and still one of the greatest students of the period, in his multivolume history of the administrations of Jefferson and Madison, damned the president for indecisiveness, weakness, and inability to control events. More recently, both Bradford Perkins, in *Prologue to War* (Berkeley, 1961), and Reginald Horsman, in *The Causes of the War of 1812* (Philadelphia, 1961), have stressed the complicated origins of the war and the importance of European affairs in bringing on the final rupture in Anglo-American relations. Perkins has also drawn attention to the importance of economic matters in relation to the Orders in Council, and he has pointed out Madison's inability to act with determination. Roger Brown, in *The Republic in Peril: 1812* (New York, 1964), has carefully analyzed the part of party division in the coming of the war and has also questioned Madison's qualities of leadership. In *Foreign Policies of the Founding Fathers* (East Lansing, Mich., 1963), Paul Varg suggests that Madison's policies were idealistic but argues that he could use power politics when it suited his interest and that the president inclined toward France as a counterweight to the pro-British proclivities of Hamilton.

A careful study of the period that emphasizes maritime factors in bringing on the war is A. L. Burt, *The United States, Great Britain, and British North America from the Revolution to the Establishment of Peace after the War of 1812* (New Haven, 1940). An interpretation of the war that stresses the role of the West is the old but still provocative work by Julius Pratt, *The Expansionists of 1812* (New York, 1925). This should perhaps be read in conjunction with Warren H. Goodman's introduction to the historiography of the causes of the war, "The Origins of the War of 1812. A Survey of Changing Interpretations," *Mississippi Valley Historical Review* 28 (1941–42), 171–86. An excellent account of the war, its causes, and the diplomacy that ended it appears in Harry L. Coles, *The War of 1812* (Chicago, 1965), a volume in the Chicago History of American Civilization series.

The diplomacy of Ghent is discussed in the following: Fred L. Engelman, *The Peace of Christmas Eve* (New York, 1962), F. A. Updyke, *The Diplomacy of the War of 1812* (Baltimore, 1915), Raymond Walters, Jr., *Albert Gallatin: Jeffersonian Financier and Diplomat* (New York, 1957), and Bradford Perkins, *Castlereagh and Adams: England and the United States, 1812–1823* (Berkeley, 1964).

A nicely written and provocative view of the president's approach to the problem of war or peace appears in Abbot Smith, "Mr. Madison's War," *Political Science Quarterly* 57 (1942), 229–46. In an illuminating essay, Walter LaFeber has argued that Madison worked for the territorial expansion needed by the rapidly growing American population, pressed for mercantile laws to develop manufacturing and agriculture, and saw that domestic faction could be absorbed in an expanding empire on land and sea. LaFeber's views appear in "Foreign Policies of a New Nation," in William Appleman Williams, ed., *From Colony to Empire* (New York, 1972). Irving Brant's multivolume biography of the president, *James Madison*, 6 vols. (Indianapolis, 1941–61), strives—not always successfully—to restore his stature as a statesman. Brant argues that in order for Madison to be effective in diplomacy he needed to deal with men whose understanding matched his own. The absence of such qualities in the president's opponents added to the partisan opposition at home that soon bordered on disloyalty. One of the most recent and distinguished studies of Madison, Marvin Meyers, *The Mind of the Founder: Sources of the Political Thought of James Madison* (Indianapolis, 1973), suggests that Madison's contribution to the founding of America should not be underestimated and that throughout his career he remained the finest and foremost voice of eighteenth-century liberalism. It has been common practice to rank Madison as an "average" president, in the class of Hayes or Hoover, but as Leonard Levy has suggested, the time has come for a reassessment of Madison's extraordinary talents and accomplishments.

JOHN QUINCY ADAMS

Empiricism and Empire

Norman A. Graebner

John Quincy Adams was born to opportunity. He was scarcely twenty-two years of age when his father took the oath of office as the country's first vice-president. John Adams's earlier diplomatic tours had permitted his son to study in England and Holland and to serve as secretary to the American legation in St. Petersburg. The Adams family heritage, moreover, had prepared him well for the heady intellectual environment of sharp minds and sharper pens that emerged with the new government. Never again would national debate reach those early standards. Thomas Jefferson and James Madison were much in the vanguard, but the younger Adams, by nature and upbringing, preferred the style and thought of the high Federalists, led by Alexander Hamilton. This became especially true after 1793 when national controversy moved into the realm of external policy. Adams learned his lessons well. More than any other American he carried the Federalist tradition in foreign affairs into the subsequent age of the Virginia dynasty.

Historians have judged John Quincy Adams the most accomplished diplomatist in this country's history. Such distinguished
performance required above all solid intellectual formulations of
policy. That Adams possessed remarkable qualities of mind was
evident long before 1817. His unique perceptions of international
affairs first emerged when he defended President George Washington's Neutrality Proclamation in April and May 1793. The
Marcellus papers, which preceded by two months the appearance
of Hamilton's noted *Pacificus*, revealed at the outset the funda-
mentals that would guide Adams's thought and action throughout
his diplomatic career. His rejection of the plea that the United
States support France dwelt on the importance of interest and
power, not good intentions, in the conduct of foreign relations.
Having treaties of peace with France, England, Holland, and
Prussia, the nation had no corresponding obligation to judge the
merits of their respective causes. While men might privately
lament the impending bloodshed and misery of the world, a
nation far removed from Europe, a nation whose happiness
depended upon freedom from all European interests and politics,
had a duty to remain "the peaceable and silent, though sorrowful
spectators of the sanguinary scene." Neutrality, believed Adams,
would serve the interests of American commerce; partisanship
would serve no countervailing purpose. Had the king of France
remained on his throne and inaugurated the existing war against
Europe, the French treaty of alliance—the legal and moral foundation of the pro-French arguments leveled at the Washington
administration—could impose no obligation on the United States.
No treaty, Adams argued, "can ever oblige one nation to adopt or
support the folly or injustice of another." How could the United
States aid the French cause when France had declared war on all
the naval powers of Europe? To rush to their aid would risk
destruction and ruin.

Adams's able defense of Washington's controversial policies
propelled him into long periods of service abroad. The president
assigned him to the Netherlands in 1794; his father, when he
became president, kept him in Berlin from 1797 to 1801. Shortly
after his return to the United States, Adams entered the Senate
and there defended the troubled foreign policies of Thomas
Jefferson and James Madison against the assaults of the New
England Federalists, his erstwhile allies. In 1809, Adams again went
abroad, this time as Madison's appointed minister to St. Peters-

burg. Whatever the contribution of Adams's diplomatic experience in Europe to his ability as secretary of state, he himself was
not greatly impressed by his early achievements.

In external characteristics Adams scarcely resembled the
suave, even-tempered, reassuring diplomatist of the classic mold.
He was short and bald, with a belligerent demeanor and a rheumy
affliction that caused his eyes to run incessantly. If he at times
antagonized his associates, he was scarcely more charitable
toward himself. On one occasion he confided in his diary: "I am
not satisfied with myself this day, having talked too much at
dinner. . . . Yet, in the estimation of others, I pass off on the
whole better when I talk freely than when silent and reserved. This
sometimes stimulates me to talk more than is wise or proper. . . .
Nor can I always (I did not this day) altogether avoid a dogmatical
and peremptory tone and manner, always disgusting, and especially offensive in persons to whose age or situation others
consider some deference due." On occasion Adams's diary notes
were even more pitiless; he saw himself as "a man of reserved,
cold, austere, and forbidding manners; my political adversaries
say, a gloomy misanthropist, and my personal enemies, an unsocial
savage. With a knowledge of the actual defect in my character, I
have not the pliability to reform it."

Beyond his dogged convictions that neither time nor circumstance would alter, Adams possessed every other quality essential
for diplomatic distinction. His understanding of Europe and its
relationship to the New World was profound. He understood with
equal precision the limits of effective American diplomacy. For
Adams no less than for Washington and Hamilton, United States
foreign policy had one major purpose: to serve the interests of this
country, defined in commercial and geographical terms. He
recognized, as had Hamilton in the *Federalist*, the natural separation of the New World from the Old and the essential advantages
the United States enjoyed in its world relationships. Throughout
his career Adams denied that a genuine foreign policy could
pursue abstract objectives. If he favored liberty, he refused to
anchor the nation's foreign policies to its achievement. The means
of enforcement, he knew, were not within his control; nor could
such an objective be the subject of fruitful negotiations.

European diplomats always found Adams direct, reliable, and
realistic. Even when he insisted on the diplomatic equivalent of
any concession and refused to surrender any advantage, diplomats

found him simple mannered and courteous. On occasion they noted his reserve; but one foreign diplomat in St. Petersburg described him as a bulldog among spaniels.

Adams's residence in St. Petersburg during the closing years of the Napoleonic Wars made him a natural choice to represent the United States in the negotiations with Britain at Ghent after the War of 1812. With the establishment of peace in 1815, Madison transferred him to London where, like his father in 1785, he assumed the task of negotiating issues left unresolved by war.

In 1817 the third member of the Virginia dynasty, James Monroe, invited Adams to join his cabinet as secretary of state; John Adams advised his son to accept. Jefferson lauded Monroe's choice, noting their complementary characters: "Adams has a pointed pen; Monroe has judgment enough for both and firmness enough to have *his* judgment control." Jefferson's was a Republican view, recognizing differences in personality, not philosophy. Monroe and Adams had occupied opposite poles during the great debates of the Washington years, and Adams's earlier convictions were as firm as ever. "The President, I am sure," he wrote to his mother, "will neither require nor expect from me any sacrifice of principles inconsistent with my sense of right." That the two men functioned as an effective team measured not only the overwhelming conversion of the Republicans in power to the older Federalist notions of proper diplomatic behavior, but also Adams's acceptance of his subordinate role in policy making.

Adams managed the technical aspects of diplomacy with remarkable skill. His diligence compelled him to read all dispatches sent and received by the State Department. Monroe, equally experienced in foreign affairs, maintained a close surveillance over Adams's correspondence. When, on occasion, Adams objected to Monroe's presidential statements or accepted them only after futile argument, it was because the president had again reacted to events abroad from the standard of simple Republican virtue rather than from a clear recognition of the interests and genuine intentions of the United States. Ultimately it was Adams and not Monroe who gave leadership and direction to American foreign relations during the eight years of their close association.

Adams worked independently, often as a minority of one. He

alone among the nation's leaders knew Europe's leading statesmen personally, especially Czar Alexander, Talleyrand, and Castlereagh. Although Adams believed that his perceptions were keener than those of his less experienced cabinet colleagues, members of Monroe's powerful cabinet opposed him on numerous occasions. Recognizing both the secretary's independence of mind and his refusal to accept views regarded as rash by the diplomatic corps, the French minister, Hyde de Neuville, wrote of Adams, "I know that he has dared to declare himself very strongly on many occasions against indiscreet and purely speculative ideas."

For Adams partisanship was as dangerous as it was inexcusable. Earlier he had lamented the Jeffersonian attacks on Washington's foreign policies as well as the opposition of the New England Federalists to Jefferson and Madison. Of all the wartime deformities in need of elimination, the most disgusting was the "rancorous spirit of faction." To Adams, unrestrained partisanship was rooted in politics and personal ambition; to his critics, therefore, he would seldom attribute sincerity.

Adams believed that his judgments should be measured by recognized standards of propriety, their accuracy in reflecting world conditions, and their possible contribution to the country's welfare. He rebuked the members of the press who criticized him far more savagely than he did those diplomats who sometimes appeared unnecessarily obdurate: "There is not one [editor] whose friendship is worth buying, nor one whose enmity is not formidable. They are a sort of assassins who sit with loaded blunderbusses at the corner of streets and fire them off for hire or for sport at any passenger whom they select." More pointedly Adams passed judgment in his diary on the editors of the *Aurora* and the *Democratic Press*, both of Philadelphia: "They are both men of considerable talents and profligate principles, always for sale to the highest bidder, and always insupportable burdens, by their insatiable rapacity, to the parties they support."

If, as secretary, Adams faced opposition in the cabinet, the Congress, and the press, he towered over the Washington diplomatic corps. Those compelled to negotiate with him never ceased to admire his intelligence and learning, his industry and self-discipline, his unwavering pursuit of his country's interests, which he grasped more surely than any other man of his age. Adversaries questioned only his doggedness and disposition. British Minister Stratford Canning described Adams in his memoirs as "much above par in general ability, but having the air of a scholar rather than statesman, a very uneven temper, a disposition at times well-meaning, a manner somewhat too often domineering. . . ."

The professional respect Adams enjoyed rested in large measure on the essential honesty of his policies. For him the path of virtue was not always clear, nor would it always be crowned with success; but he believed that an otherwise sound policy would be wiser and more enduring if it were essentially virtuous. Perhaps there were occasions, especially in time of war, when deception was justifiable; but fraud was never acceptable when force would not be equally justified. Fraud must be practiced sparingly, he warned, for it "tends when discovered to impair the confidence of mankind in the sincerity and integrity of him who uses it." Stephen Decatur had offered his famous toast, "Our country! . . . may she always be in the right; but our country, right or wrong." Adams would disagree: "I cannot ask of heaven success, even for my country, in a cause where she should be in the wrong. . . . I disclaim as unsound all patriotism incompatible with the principles of eternal justice. But the truth is that the American union, while united, *may* be certain of success in every rightful cause, and may if it pleases never have any but a rightful cause to maintain."

From the beginning Adams recognized the limits of American power and influence in Europe. Toward the Continent, emerging from a quarter-century of war, he urged a posture of strict neutrality. Europe, he wrote in 1815, "consists only of victors and vanquished, between whom no permanent state of social repose can exist. May we persevere in the system of keeping aloof from all their broils, and in that of consolidating and perpetuating our own union." In his noted oration of 4 July 1821, Adams insisted that the United States had conducted its foreign relations in a spirit of friendliness and reciprocity; it had recognized the independence of other countries and maintained its own. America sympathized with the cause of liberty. "Wherever the standard of freedom and Independence has been or shall be unfurled," Adams said, "there will her heart, her benedictions and her prayers be. But she goes not abroad, in search of monsters to destroy. She is the well-wisher to the freedom and independence of all. She is the champion and vindicator only of her own. She will commend the general cause by . . . the benignant sympathy of her example." Any shift from liberty to force, he warned, might make the United

States dictatress of the world and no longer the ruler of its own spirit. To his principle of neutrality Adams added that of nonintervention.

Toward the North American continent Adams was an expansionist, but one who looked to geography, not to war. He believed that the continent was destined to be one nation in language, religion, society, and politics. During November 1819, Secretary of the Treasury William H. Crawford informed him that many British and French citizens regarded the United States as ambitious and encroaching. Adams replied that to argue otherwise would be useless: "Nothing that we could say or do would remove this impression until the world shall be familiarized with the idea of considering our proper dominion to be the continent of North America. From the time when we became an independent people it was as much a law of nature that this should become our pretension as that the Mississippi should flow to the sea." A year later, in conversation with Stratford Canning over the future of Oregon, Adams declared that the London government had certainly concluded that "there would be neither policy nor profit in cavilling with us about territory on this North American continent." When Canning asked if the secretary included Canada in his claims, Adams responded: "No, there the boundary is marked, and we have no disposition to encroach upon it. Keep what is yours, but leave the rest of the continent to us."

To underwrite his hopes for peace and security in a still challenging world, Adams looked to a stronger union, based on centralized government, and to a reasonable level of military preparedness. "No nation can enjoy freedom and independence," he wrote, "without being always prepared to defend them by force of arms." He once reminded Monroe, "We shall have no valuable friends in Europe until we have proved that we can defend ourselves without them." Adequate power—which Adams doubted the country would ever create except in time of war— dared not encourage a mood of belligerency, however. He advised the country to employ every means available to settle disputes amicably and never to enter a war "without a fair prospect of attaining its objects," nor should it remain in a war unless the gains were clearly commensurate with the costs. Such principles and purposes guided him in every diplomatic confrontation of his secretarial years.

◇◇◇

European statesmen recognized the importance of France to the restoration of the European balance of power after the Napoleonic Wars. The allies desired a great and powerful France because French power was "one of the essential foundations of the social structure" of the Continent. The restoration of the Bourbons, as even the British agreed, would serve the interests of all nations in a stable Europe. Despite the later condemnation of the Congress of Vienna for its free assignment of territory, the decisions of that notable international conference underwrote the principle of balance. The Quadruple Alliance that followed in November 1815 represented the efforts of Europe's leading statesmen to carry into peacetime the equilibrium created by the coalition against Napoleon. The later conferences at Troppau (1820), Laibach (1821), and Verona (1822), which adopted interventionist policies toward Italy, Spain, and Portugal, split the great powers. British leaders could detect no threat in liberal uprisings to the allied purpose of maintaining Europe's essential equilibrium. Castlereagh, Britain's greatest foreign minister, broke down in 1822 over his failure to nullify Europe's reactionary policies and took his own life. His brilliant successor, George Canning, withdrew British participation from the affairs of the Quadruple Alliance.

Americans could scarcely approve the principles that guided the Congress of Vienna. Much of the press ridiculed the Vienna settlements because of their apparent disregard for national sovereignty in their high-handed redistribution of territory. American writers were equally distrustful of the principle of legitimacy that restored the monarchs to their thrones. Europe, it seemed, had returned to an age of despotism. Even Czar Alexander's Holy Alliance (formed at Paris in September 1815 by Austria, Russia, and Prussia), with its large standing armies, seemed devoted less to peace and justice than to repression and war. To American observers Europe appeared unstable, harboring ideals far different from those of the United States and filled with combustible materials that any spark could reignite into war. *Niles' Register* in August 1817 warned its readers that the United States could hardly trust the friendship of monarchies. Adams had expressed similar fears: "The Royalists everywhere detest and despise us as Republicans." He later repeated his doubts: "There is already in all

governments of Europe a strong prejudice against us as Republicans, and as the primary causes of the propagation of those
political principles, which still make the throne of every European
monarch rock under him as with the throes of an earth-
quake. . . ."

Adams recognized the fundamental purpose of Europe's
postwar state system: to prevent the resurrection of preponderant
power and to restrain threats to the region's stability; but with
time he also became critical of the czar's Holy Alliance, complaining that Europe had cast off Napoleon only to return to divine
right. Still, through subsequent years the league appeared successful, at least in Europe; in Latin America the challenge to the status
quo seemed too distant for the European powers to control.
Adams saw clearly that threats to Europe's stability were internal,
that tensions endangering the peace centered on relations between peoples and their rulers. He saw clearly why Russia's
Alexander patronized the European system: "His territories are the
most extensive, his military establishment the most stupendous,
his country the most improvable and thriving of them all. . . . his
circumstances point his policy to a faithful adherence to the
general system, with a strong reprobation of those who would
resort to special and partial alliances, from which any one member
of the league should be excluded."

Eventually the czar suggested that America concur in the
principles of the European league and become a formal member.
The compact bound members only to the preservation of peace,
and should the United States find itself at odds with one or more
members of the Holy Alliance, it could count on the interposition
of the czar in its behalf. In precise diplomatic language, Adams
instructed Henry Middleton, United States minister in Russia, to
reject any such proposal: "As a general declaration of principles,
. . . the United States, not only give their hearty assent to the
articles of the Holy Alliance, but will be among the most earnest
and conscientious in observing them. But . . . for the repose of
Europe as well as of America, the European and American political
systems should be kept as separate and distinct from each other as
possible."

If Europe's great powers desisted, because of predictable
costs, from imposing on one another, they scarcely seemed
capable of imposing on the New World. Europe's balance served
the American interest in achieving a stable and independent

hemisphere, but it did not necessarily equalize the capacity of the European powers to influence American affairs or even their intention of doing so. Toward France both the administration and the press expressed indifference. They regarded that power as neither f iend nor enemy. The French government, fearful of British influence in the United States, anticipated considerable benefit from maintaining close and friendly ties with Washington. Shortly after the Congress of Vienna Adams reminded Monroe that Continental powers such as France would attempt to separate the United States from England, but France by itself posed no threat.

Russia, like France, seemed to lack the power or the intention to challenge American interest in the New World. Observant Americans recognized the contrast between the government and society of Russia and of the United States, but they harbored no feelings of fear or distrust. Adams admitted that he trusted Czar Alexander more than any other monarch in Europe. As a Continental power with a large army, Russia wielded major influence in Europe and the Middle East; elsewhere Britain exerted a moderating influence on Russian ambition. Indeed, many Americans, Adams among them, hoped that Anglo-Russian rivalry would restrict the power of both countries outside the Eastern Hemisphere.

The complacency that determined American attitudes toward the Continent did not exist with regard to England, which had the power, and seemingly the interest, to interfere in American affairs. Adams had hoped that Napoleon's retention of power in France might serve as a counterweight to British power. There was little conviction in the United States after 1814, however, that England, having shaken off the restraints of France, would convert the Treaty of Ghent into an instrument of peace. The press freely predicted renewed war, although not necessarily in the immediate future. Adams shared this postwar distrust of England. He wrote to his mother, Abigail, that although British ascendancy in Europe would decline, that country would continue to seek the ruin of the United States. British animosity toward France had been satiated by victory, but, warned Adams, "their feelings against America are keener, more jealous, more envious, more angry than ever."

Believing the United States to be in danger because of Britain, Adams was bitterly critical of the peace societies that not only opposed armaments but also placed enormous faith in the czar's ability to maintain peace. Old John Adams expressed his son's view when he addressed the Masssachusetts Peace Society in July 1816: "Our beloved country, sir, is surrounded by enemies of the most dangerous, because the most powerful and most unprincipled character. Collisions of national interest, of commercial and manufacturing rivalries, are multiplying around us. Instead of discouraging a martial spirit, in my opinion it ought to be excited. We have not enough of it to defend us by sea or land." Similarly, John Quincy later complained that the peace societies, by corresponding with the czar, were endangering the security of the United States. Instead of championing the position of America, these groups were openly endorsing the ideas and leadership of a foreign ruler who had his share of faults and ambitions. Adams believed that it was time for Americans to concentrate on matters at home and devote their energies to more productive enterprises.

For Adams peace with England was essential for American security and well-being. Britain alone of Europe's leading states had the power to injure the United States. "My special duty at present," Adams wrote from London in May 1816, "is to preach peace. . . . I am deeply convinced that peace is the state best adapted to the interest and happiness of both nations." As secretary a year later he resumed negotiations which he had begun in London on issues still unsettled since Ghent. During the peace negotiations of 1782 his father had sought the dismantling of all fortifications along the Canadian-American frontier. After the War of 1812 the younger Adams had pressed the British for such an agreement, but again without success. Still undaunted, Adams repeated the offer in London during March 1816. The British government, hoping to avoid a naval race with the United States on the Great Lakes, finally accepted Adams's overture. The result was the Rush-Bagot Agreement, signed in Washington during April 1817, which limited British and American naval armaments on the lakes to those required for the enforcement of customs regulations. This treaty, the first reciprocal naval disarmament agreement in modern history, removed a potential source of friction and expense and admirably served the interests of both Britain and the United States.

During the following year Adams achieved the long-standing

American quest for fishing rights off the Labrador and Newfoundland coasts. While in London he insisted that in the original
division of the empire in 1783, Britain had granted the inshore
fisheries on the northern coasts to the United States. The British
agreed to American fishing on the high seas and suspended
trespass proceedings against New England fishermen. Adams later
resumed his conversations on the fisheries question, determined
to eliminate the English use of the word "liberty" when referring
to American access to both the Grand Banks and the open seas.
Privately Adams was opposed to compromise, preferring that the
administration demand full American fishing rights along the
northern coasts and establish them by force if necessary. Over-
ruled by Monroe, Adams proposed that the United States forfeit
the right of drying and curing on the shore and reserve full rights
to fishing. Ultimately Albert Gallatin, who managed the final
negotiations in 1818, achieved more extensive inshore fishing
rights than Adams's instructions had demanded. The new treaty
granted American fishermen permission not only to catch fish
along extensive sections of the northern coasts but also to dry and
cure fish on any of the unsettled coasts of Labrador. The British
resisted the American effort to guarantee these fishing rights even
in time of war, but, as a compromise, they granted Americans
liberty "for ever" to take fish along the northern coasts.

As late as 1815 the United States and Britain had conducted a
flourishing trade without benefit of any formal commercial treaty.
On 3 July of that year Adams signed a commercial convention in
London that, except for the prohibition of discriminatory duties,
merely reaffirmed existing practice. The convention provided for
reciprocal consulates, freedom of commerce between the United
States and British territories in Europe, as well as equality of
treatment of the products, ships, citizens, and subjects of each
country in the ports of the other. The convention permitted
American ships to trade in the British ports of Calcutta, Madras,
Bombay, and Penang in South Asia.

Unfortunately the Anglo-American convention of July 1815
failed to gain full reciprocal arrangements, for Britain refused to
permit American ships in the saltwater ports of British North
America and the British West Indies. These restrictions, by
permitting English traders to engage in a triangle traffic denied to
Americans, canceled the advantages of full reciprocity in direct
United States–British commerce. For Adams this policy was totally

objectionable. The regulation of commerce, he wrote, "should be by arrangements to which both parties consent and in which due regard is paid to the interests of both."

Adams confronted the uncompromising London government with a series of congressional acts in 1817, 1818, and 1820 that imposed special tonnage duties on British ships entering the United States from ports closed to American vessels, and Congress eventually eliminated the importation of all British West Indian goods except those brought directly from the colony where they were grown. These restrictions injured the West Indian economy and prompted Parliament to open some colonial ports to American ships in 1822. At the same time it enumerated American products that might compete with those of Canada. In March 1823, Congress, under Adams's direction, opened United States ports to British ships coming from colonial ports, but only from those ports to which American ships were admitted. At the same time Congress authorized the president to impose a 10 percent discriminatory tariff on colonial goods imported in British vessels until London eliminated all colonial preferences. By 1826 the British had again cut off American trade with their West Indian islands. Adams failed to negotiate conditions of greater reciprocity than those that had existed in 1822.

Adams's success in defining the boundaries of the Louisiana Purchase demonstrated the breadth of his vision and the virtuosity of his performance. In the Convention of 1818 with England he negotiated the boundary line from the Lake of the Woods westward along the forty-ninth parallel to the Rocky Mountains. West of the Rockies, however, British fur-trading interests were centered south of that parallel, largely along the valley of the Columbia River. London, therefore, demanded the Columbia as the boundary between the mountains and the Pacific. Adams, who would settle for no less than a usable port along the Oregon shore, had been convinced by New England seamen that the Columbia River would never meet that need, largely because of the dangers of the bar that blocked its entrance. He understood also that the Juan de Fuca Strait and Puget Sound (both north of the Columbia but south of 49°) constituted one of the world's best inland waterways. For these reasons Adams demanded no less than the extension of the forty-ninth parallel to the Pacific. When British negotiators proved intractable on this point, Adams agreed to a policy of joint occupancy with Britain in the Oregon country west of the Rockies for a period of ten years, an arrangement that either country could terminate on one year's notice. Thus Adams delayed the final Oregon settlement until a time when the diplomatic advantage would pass to the United States.

Adams's subsequent diplomatic achievement, perhaps his greatest, came in 1819 when in the Adams-Onís Treaty he not only acquired Florida for the United States but also defined the southern boundary of the Louisiana Purchase from the Gulf of Mexico to the Pacific Ocean. Florida in 1817 was still under Spanish rule, but that region had become a problem for the United States government—and for the citizens of Georgia—simply because the Madrid regime was too plagued with political and military disorders elsewhere to maintain order in its colony. British adventurers in Florida periodically armed and incited the Indians to raid north of the boundary. Monroe dispatched General Andrew Jackson to punish the Indians for their destruction of American lives and property. Carrying out his instructions with considerable vigor, Jackson in 1818 pursued a band of marauding Indians into Florida where he captured and executed two British agents as well as two Indian chiefs. Spain protested the action, and Jackson's enemies in Congress demanded his dismissal.

President Monroe and all members of the cabinet, except Adams, agreed. They argued that Jackson had exceeded his instructions and committed an act of war against Spain, which required an official disavowal. Adams reminded the cabinet that Jackson's actions were defensive, that he had entered Florida not to make war on Spain, but to terminate the Indian depredations. Jackson had discretionary powers; to disavow them, believed Adams, was unthinkable. He admitted in his diary that he had pushed his case to the limit; but he added, "If the question was dubious, it was better to err on the side of vigor than of weakness—on the side of our own officer . . . than on the side of our bitterest enemies. . . ." Adams's argument carried. On 23 July 1818 the secretary charged to the complaining Spanish minister, Don Luis de Onís, that Spain had an obligation under treaty to keep order in Florida. The fort at St. Mark would be restored only to a Spanish force strong enough to hold it against an Indian attack. Peace between the United States and Spain, he warned, required that "henceforth the stipulations by Spain to restrain by force her Indians from all hostilities against the United States should be faithfully and effectually fulfilled." If Spain could not control the Indians, then it had no choice but to cede Florida to the United States.

Meanwhile on 10 July 1818 the French minister in Washington, Hyde de Neuville, informed Adams that Spain, recognizing its weakness, would cede Florida to the United States, provided that Washington would assume the claims of American citizens against Spain, estimated at some five million dollars. Onís immediately took up the negotiations, raising the issue of the still undefined southern boundary of the Louisiana Purchase. Spain hoped to push the line eastward and northward as far as possible; Adams sought a boundary that would bring as much of Texas and the Southwest as possible into the United States. Onís, on 11 July, proposed a western boundary that would separate the United States from Spanish Mexico at a line moving northward between Adeas and Natchitoches to the Red River and thence to the Missouri. Adams rejected this outright. So uncompromising was Madrid that in October Adams threatened to break off the negotiations. Then on 31 October the secretary presented a note to Onís outlining what he termed the final United States offer. The boundary was to be a line running from the mouth of the Sabine River to its source, from there north to the Red River and its source in the southern Rockies, up into the mountains to the forty-first parallel, and from there west to the ocean. This was altered slightly by Adams in the course of the negotiations.

By 15 February Onís had agreed to Adams's revised boundary, including the forty-second parallel, but he insisted that the river lines follow the middle rather than the south bank of the streams. Adams countered that Spain would have no settlements near those rivers and that the middle of streams never lent themselves to precise lines of demarcation. He insisted before the cabinet that the United States adhere to the principle of owning the rivers and islands in them. On 20 February Onís capitulated, observing that Adams had given him more trouble than the president. The Spanish minister recalled the words a suitor once addressed to Philip IV: "Sire, your Majesty has no influence with the Minister of Grace and Justice, for he refuses me what you have granted."

On 22 February 1819, Onís and Adams signed the Transcontinental Treaty. "It was, perhaps," he wrote in his diary, "the most

important day of my life. . . . May no disappointment embitter the
hope which this event warrants us in cherishing, and may its
future influence on the destinies of my country be as extensive
and as favorable as our warmest anticipations can paint!" Later,
members of Congress urged Adams to put the treaty aside and
claim the Rio Grande. The secretary reminded one congressman
who came to criticize that he and Henry Clay were excellent
negotiators in theory. Then he leveled a strong rebuke: "In the
negotiations with Spain we had a just claim to the Mississippi and
its waters, and our citizens had a fair though very precarious claim
to indemnities. We had a mere color of claim to the Rio del Norte,
no claim to a line beyond the Rocky Mountains, and none to
Florida, which we very much wanted. The treaty . . . barely gives
up to Spain the colorable claim from the Sabine to the Rio del
Norte. Now, negotiation implies some concession upon both
sides. If after obtaining every object of your pursuit but one, and
that one weak in principle and of no present value, what would
you have offered to Spain to yield that also?" The congressman
had no answer.

Spain's challenge to the United States lay not only in that
nation's weakness in Florida but also in its precarious position
throughout the Western Hemisphere. Napoleon's invasion of
Spain in 1808 had terminated Madrid's effective control of Spanish
America. Provisional *juntas* maintained by Spain's ruling classes
continued to claim jurisdiction over the empire, but by 1812 their
New World influence was purely nominal. Freed of Spain's
commercial restrictions, the various regions of Latin America
opened their commerce to the world. British and Yankee ships
entered South American ports in large numbers. When war broke
out between the restored Spanish monarchy and the now rebellious colonies, the struggling South Americans looked to the
United States for economic, military, and moral support.

Within the United States, editors, congressmen, and administration officials favored Latin American independence with almost
total unanimity; but on the proper national response to Latin
America's plight there was no agreement at all. Abbé de Pradt, the
prolific European writer, emphasized not only the importance of
Latin America to Europe but also the possibility that, inasmuch as

Spanish control was doomed, the great European powers might establish the region's independence on terms that would keep the new nations attached to Europe. Determined to sever Europe's ties with the New World, editors led by William Duane of the *Aurora* demanded United States guardianship of Latin American independence. In Latin America, he argued, this nation would find "the corrective of European jealousy, and the resources with which to defeat and counterplace the intolerant and malignant selfishness of European nations." In Congress the powerful Clay denounced the administration for neglecting American interests and the cause of liberty.

Monroe and Adams would not be stampeded. They recognized the overwhelming preference of their countrymen for Latin American independence, but they refused to commit the United States before the European powers had revealed their intentions or the patriots of South America had demonstrated their capacity to establish their independence and maintain a semblance of order. The open congressional support for Latin America appalled Adams. "There seemed to me," he complained in June 1816, "too much of the warlike humor in the debates of Congress—propositions even to take up the cause of the South Americans; predictions of wars with this country to the end of time, as cool and as causeless, as if they were talking of the expense of building a light house. . . ."

As the public pressure for involvement continued, Adams reminded his father that Latin America had replaced the French Revolution as the great source of discord in the United States: "The republican spirit of our country not only sympathizes with people struggling in a cause, . . . but it is working into indignation against the relapse of Europe into the opposite principle of monkery and despotism. And now, as at the early stage of the French Revolution, we have ardent spirits who are for rushing into the conflict, without looking to the consequences." Because he doubted that the people of South America were capable of self-government, Adams viewed the revolutions with little sympathy. Monroe, who was somewhat more sympathetic, argued that the United States could render Latin Americans no service more useful than to refrain from any action that might provoke direct European intervention. He explained his views in a letter to Jackson in December 1818, although later he omitted the key passage: "By this policy we have lost nothing, as *by keeping the*

Allies out of the quarrel, Florida must soon be ours, and *the Colonies must be independent, for if they cannot beat Spain, they do not deserve to be free."*

During 1818 the ultimate course of United States policy toward Latin America began to emerge. In March, Monroe requested a congressional appropriation for a commission of inquiry to South America. Hoping to compel the administration to recognize the independence of the Argentine, Clay attached an amendment appropriating eighteen thousand dollars for a United States legation in Buenos Aires, and he even stepped down from the Speaker's rostrum to enter a strong plea for his measure; but the House remained unconvinced and voted down the amendment, 115 to 45. Shortly thereafter Adams expressed his contempt for Congress in his diary: "The present session will stand remarkable in the annals of the Union for showing how a legislature can keep itself employed when having nothing to do. . . ." The proposed appropriation "for a minister to Buenos Ayres has gone the way of other things lost upon earth, like the purchase of oil for light houses in the western country." In July the president's fact-finding commission returned to Washington, hopelessly divided. Still the administration continued to respond to changing conditions both in Europe and in Latin America. By the summer of 1818 Monroe and Adams concluded that the great European states would never agree on measures to restore Spanish sovereignty in South America, especially since Britain clearly favored Independence. At the Conference of Aix-la-Chapelle, which opened in September 1818, England opposed the use of force against the Latin Americans; but Castlereagh's rejection of Adams's suggestion for a concerted British-American policy encouraged further caution in Washington.

Throughout 1819 and 1820 Adams moved slowly and deliberately, proclaiming official American neutrality toward the struggles of Latin America though reminding Monroe that any successful revolution eventually reaches a stage when those fighting for independence merit recognition when that recognition no longer constitutes a departure from the obligations of neutrality. He warned the president, however, that the justice of a cause was not in itself "sufficient to justify third parties in siding with it." Finally in February 1821, ratified copies of the Transcontinental Treaty were exchanged in Washington This eliminated the one remaining international argument against recognition of Latin Amer-

ican independence. That year the striking victories of the revolutionary forces all but destroyed Spain's remaining authority in
South America. Clay secured passage of two resolutions in the
House, one expressing interest in South American independence,
the other encouraging the president to recognize the independence of the new nations whenever he believed it expedient.
Shortly thereafter, in March 1821, Clay and Adams discussed Latin
America at length, each regretting their years of deep disagreement, though Adams still argued the administration's case for
delay. "That the final issue of their present struggle would be their
entire independence of Spain I have never doubted. That it was
our true policy and duty to take no part in the contest I was
equally clear. . . . So far as they were contending for independence, I wished well to their cause; but I had seen and yet see no
prospect that they would establish free or liberal institutions of
government. . . . Arbitrary power, military and ecclesiastical, was
stamped upon their education, upon their habits, and upon all
their institutions. Civil dissension was infused into all their seminal
principles. War and mutual destruction was in every member of
their organization, moral, political, and physical. I had little
expectation of any beneficial result to this country from any future
connection with them, political or commercial."

Monroe recognized the changing conditions in a special
message to Congress on 8 March 1822. He declared that Chile, the
United Provinces of the Plata (Argentina), Peru, Colombia, and
Mexico were fully independent and thus could rightfully claim
recognition by other nations. Congress responded by appropriating funds to meet the expense of "such missions to the independent nations on the American continent as the President might
deem proper." After formal recognition of the five new states,
Latin American representatives added both numbers and variety to
the Washington diplomatic corps.

Further delay, Monroe explained to Madison, would have
produced deep resentment in Latin America and opened the way
for renewed European encroachments. Even as Monroe sought the
exclusion of European influence from the Western Hemisphere he
reassured the European powers that the United States had no
intention of controlling the new governments or of creating a
separate American system. Neither Monroe nor Adams revealed
much concern for the nature of the Latin American regimes; nor
did they favor the immediate assignment of ministers to the new

capitals. No commercial treaties, based on reciprocity, could possibly affect Britain's dominance of Latin America's foreign trade. A race with England for markets or monopolies in the new nations was in Adams's view "neither a wise nor an honest policy."

Britain made clear its commercial and political preference for Latin American independence at the Conference of Aix-la-Chapelle in 1818. Britain's new foreign minister in 1822, George Canning, refused to follow the American lead out of deference to Spain and the Holy Alliance. So guarded had been Monroe's recognition policy that it produced no break with Spain. British policy, unlike that in Washington, focused on Europe, especially when the Holy Alliance, over London's objection, voted to send a French army into Spain to put down a liberal revolt. In 1822 when the invading French successfully restored Ferdinand VII to his full royal prerogatives in Spain, Canning suspected that France might attempt to restore the Spanish empire as well. Even more threatening was the possibility that France might use its influence in Spain to lay the foundation for another French empire in America. In 1823 Canning warned the Paris government against any move to acquire portions of Spanish America by conquest or cession. When French policy in Spain continued to cause unease in London, Canning in August turned to Richard Rush, the American minister, suggesting that Britain and the United States issue a joint declaration disavowing territorial ambitions in Latin America but warning Europe, except Spain, against intervention.

Rush was highly flattered by Canning's recognition of America's growing importance in the Atlantic world, but insisted on referring the matter to Washington unless Britain recognized the independence of the Latin American nations immediately. This Canning refused to do. Instead, he delivered a secret warning to Paris. The French government responded with the famed "Polignac Memorandum," which assured the British that it had no intention of dispatching an expedition to the New World. Thus Canning, through unilateral action, had resolved the immediate challenge to British policy.

In a long communication of 19 August 1823, Rush relayed Canning's proposal to Washington. Monroe received the dispatch on 9 October. He did not regard Europe as a threat; still he favored Canning's proposition and sought reassurance from his old friend Jefferson, in quiet retirement at Monticello, who in a classic response reiterated his concept of the two spheres which advocated the noninterference of the United States in European affairs and the noninvolvement of Europe in the affairs of the New World. For him it was imperative that this country, if it desired to maintain the status quo in the Western Hemisphere, not take a stand against the existing order in Europe. Only one nation, Britain, could challenge American interests in the New World; it was the part of wisdom, therefore, to enlist that great power in the cause of emancipating the American continents from European influence. Madison likewise endorsed Canning's proposal.

Meanwhile Adams had responded to the French invasion of Spain by reasserting the doctrine of no transfer. France's policy in Spain was not Adams's major concern; what troubled him was the possibility that Spain might cede Cuba to Britain as the price of an Anglo-Spanish alliance. In April 1823, Adams sent a long note to the American minister in Madrid, Hugh Nelson, warning the Spanish government that the United States would oppose the transfer of Cuba to any European power. Such a transfer, wrote Adams, not only would affect Spanish-American relations but would also subvert the rights of the Cuban people and justify the United States in supporting any resulting independence movement. When Canning assured Washington that Britain had no intention of acquiring the island, Monroe suggested to the cabinet that the United States issue a statement of self-denial also. Adams objected; he saw no reason for the United States to bind itself permanently against the possibility that Cuba might one day solicit union with the United States. Monroe assured London informally that the United States had no designs on Cuba.

Russia had also posed a threat to United States interests in the Western Hemisphere and provoked another historic response from Adams. Before the 1820s rumors of Russian encroachment along the Pacific coast of North America as far south as California had produced only indifference in Washington. In Adams's view, Russia lacked both the navy and the merchant marine to establish distant colonies; but in 1821 the Russian emperor issued a ukase that excluded foreigners from trading, fishing, or navigating within one hundred Italian miles of the northwest coast from the Bering Strait to the fifty-first parallel of north latitude. Both Britain and the

United States objected. At a cabinet meeting on 28 June 1823, Adams introduced the question of Russian claims. He believed the United States should contest them, especially since that country had no settlements in the disputed region. On 17 July, Adams informed the Russian minister, Baron Tuyl, that the United States would contest Russia's right to any territorial establishment on this continent and that this nation assumed the principle that "the American continents are no longer subjects for *any* new European colonial establishments." On 22 July he penned a note to Middleton in St. Petersburg: "There can, perhaps, be no better time for saying, frankly and explicitly, to the Russian Government that the future peace of the world, and the interest of Russia herself, can not be promoted by Russian settlements upon any part of the American continent. With the exception of the British establishments north of the United States, the remainder of both the American continents must henceforth be left to the management of American hands." Thus Adams asserted the principle of noncolonization.

When Monroe returned to Washington with the opinions of Jefferson and Madison corroborating his own, Russia had created another crisis. Baron Tuyl warned Adams that the czar would not recognize the new governments of Latin America and that, unless the United States remained neutral, Russia might support a European invasion of the former Spanish empire. This Russian threat merely confirmed convictions in Washington that Canning's proposal should be accepted; but Adams refused to be frightened. He doubted that France intended armed intervention in Latin America; moreover, the British navy was powerful enough to prevent it. The secretary suspected that Canning's overture was aimed less at obtaining unnecessary United States support than in preventing, through a self-denying agreement, future American expansion into Texas and the Caribbean. When the cabinet met on 7 November, Adams proposed that the United States decline the British overture and take its stand against the Holy Alliance unilaterally. "It would be more candid, as well as more dignified," he said, "to avow our principles explicitly to Russia and France, than to come in as a cock-boat in the wake of the British man-of-war."

Adams favored an overall American policy that would combine a letter to Russia with one to France in a single statement of national intent. To this Monroe agreed; but the president still hesitated to reject the British proposal. The news that France had captured Cadiz caused him to despair for the future of South America. Calhoun, equally fearful of Europe, proposed that Rush be given discretionary power to accept Canning's overture, if necessary. Adams argued that Spain had no more power to restore its control in the Western Hemisphere than had Chimborazo to sink to the bottom of the sea. "But if the South Americans were really in a state to be so easily subdued, it would be but a more forcible motive for us to beware of involving ourselves in their fate."

A week later Adams delivered his note to the Russian minister. In moderate language he explained that the United States was a republic and thus was attracted to the Latin American states by the very principles that repelled the czar. He hoped that Russia would nonetheless maintain its policy of neutrality; but Russia quickly created further alarm when another note reminded the United States of the Holy Alliance's success in putting down revolutions in Europe and its obligation to guarantee tranquillity everywhere, including Latin America. As gloom settled over the Potomac, Adams told the cabinet, "My purpose would be in a moderate and conciliatory manner, but with a firm and determined spirit, to declare our dissent from the principles avowed in those communications; to assert those upon which our own Government is founded, and while disclaiming all . . . interference with the political affairs of Europe, to declare our expectation and hope that the European powers will equally abstain from the attempt to spread their principles in the American hemisphere, or to subjugate by force any part of these continents to their will." He thus formulated the principle of "hands off"; Monroe accepted it and decided to proclaim this new American purpose toward the Western Hemisphere in his December message to Congress.

On 21 November, Monroe read a preliminary draft of his forthcoming message to the cabinet. Adams was shocked. "Its introduction," he recorded, "was in a tone of deep solemnity and of high alarm, intimating that his country is menaced by imminent and formidable dangers, such as would probably soon call for their most vigorous energies and the closest union." What distressed Adams especially was Monroe's reversion to his old Republican innocence in taking up the cause of revolution in Spain and Greece, two areas in which he had no intention of acting. He urged the president to reconsider the entire subject: "This message would be a summons to arms—to arms against all Europe, and for objects of policy exclusively European— Greece and Spain. It would be as new, too, in our policy as it would be surprising. For more than thirty years Europe had been in convulsions, . . . and we had looked on safe in our distance beyond an intervening ocean, and avowing a total forbearance to interfere in any of the combinations of European politics. This message would at once buckle on the harness and throw down the gauntlet. It would have the air of open defiance to all Europe. . . . I did not expect that the quiet which we had enjoyed for six or seven years would last much longer. The aspect of things was portentous; but if we must come to an issue with Europe, let us keep it off as long as possible."

Adams was especially disturbed at Monroe's open endorsement of the Greek independence movement, for he had long argued against United States involvement in that cause. The Greek revolutionary movement had slowly gathered strength until by 1821 it posed an immediate threat to Ottoman rule. Sultan Mahmud II retaliated with such violence and destruction that he aroused anti-Turkish sentiment throughout western Europe and the United States. In 1822 *Niles' Register*, dwelling on Turkish barbarities, chided the country for not taking up the cause of Greek liberty and independence. In his annual message of December 1822, Monroe expressed regret that a country that had contributed so much to civilization should live under a gloomy despotism, but concern for the Greek cause still languished. Then in 1823 Edward Everett, professor of Greek literature at Harvard and editor of *The North American Review*, championed Greek independence and enlisted the support of Daniel Webster. Adams remained unimpressed, and he argued strongly against any American meddling in the affairs of Greece and Turkey, especially since the country was not prepared financially or militarily to intervene. When Crawford and Calhoun in the cabinet expressed great enthusiasm for the Greeks, Adams recorded his disgust; he maintained his opposition in the critical cabinet debates on the president's message during late November.

For Adams it was essential that Monroe not antagonize the Holy Alliance needlessly. If the European powers chose to challenge the United States, Washington should meet the issue but not create it. If the Holy Alliance really intended to restore the colonies to Spain, which Adams doubted, the United States had perhaps been too hasty in acknowledging South American independence. "If they intend now to interpose by force," Adams warned, "we shall have as much as we can do to prevent them, without going to bid them defiance in the heart of Europe." Arguing steadily against any American involvement in European affairs, Adams summarized his views before the cabinet: "The ground that I wish to take is that of earnest remonstrance against the interference of the European powers by force with South America, but to disclaim all interference on our part with Europe; to make an American cause, and adhere inflexibly to that." Adams had added to "hands off" his principle of abstention.

This concept of two worlds Monroe embodied in his celebrated message to Congress on 2 December 1823. The so-called Monroe Doctrine declared specifically that the American continents were no longer open to European colonization and that the United States would regard any effort of the European powers to extend their government to any portion of the Western Hemisphere as a threat to its peace and safety. On the other hand, Monroe assured the nations of the Old World that the United States would not interfere with their dependencies in the New World or involve itself in purely European matters. Meanwhile Adams prepared documents to Britain and Russia. He assured Canning that the United States intended to pursue separate but parallel policies in Latin America. Together Adams and Monroe had wedded American policies to the status quo in the Atlantic, a status quo that, if threatened, would have the defense of the British navy itself. Adams's communication to Russia concluded with a strong warning against European interference in the affairs of the Western Hemisphere. The secretary regarded this dispatch, dated 27 November 1823, as the most important state paper of his career.

Early in 1824 Adams resolved the conflict with Russia in the Northwest. New England traders demanded access to the fur seals and sea otters in the Aleutians far north of 51°. Adams reminded Stratford Canning in Washington that the United States had no territorial claims as far north as the fifty-first parallel, and assumed that British interests would be sufficient to counter Russian demands. To Russia Adams suggested a boundary at 55° north latitude. In St. Petersburg the Russian government accepted Adams's noncolonization principle as well as the American right of access to unsettled regions north of the line of division. To keep all of Prince of Wales Island under Russian control, the Russians proposed the boundary of 54°40'. In the Convention of April 1824, Russia gained its preferred boundary but gave up all pretensions to a *mare clausum* in the north Pacific.

Even as the April convention disposed of the Russian threat in the far Northwest Adams's allies laid the Greek issue to rest in Congress. These triumphs for the concept of two worlds as embodied in the Monroe Doctrine were the last of Adams's secretarial years. Through eight years it was his recognition of geographic factors as the foundation of national interests and diplomatic advantage that underlay his varied goals and successes. Adams detected more assuredly than his contemporaries that European influence in the Western Hemisphere was declining. This assumption encouraged his anticipation of Latin American independence, his vision of an expanding republic on the North American continent, and his disinclination to compromise on issues purely American. Recognizing the limits of United States power outside the Western Hemisphere, he argued against all verbal commitments that transcended easily demonstrable national interests or any intention of the government to act. Adams understood that such involvements served no national requirements and ultimately disappointed everyone who took the rhetoric seriously. Rejecting the need of threats of war, he settled for what diplomacy could accomplish. Where he possessed the diplomatic advantage, as in the Rush-Bagot and Adams-Onís treaties, he pursued the American interest as he defined it. Where the nation's advantage was doubtful, as on the questions of Oregon and commercial reciprocity, he either postponed the settlement until the superior interests and advantages of the United States became apparent or simply accepted less than he desired. Where the issue was revolution in Latin America, Greece, or Spain, he abstained from involvement totally. The essence of Adams's statesmanship was his ability to define a clear hierarchy of national interests to be pursued. Adams never permitted his objectives to outrun the means available to him.

Adams's diplomatic achievements were remarkable. What he had contributed to the nation's thought was less tangible but no less impressive; but Adams's ultimate purpose transcended even such triumphs and looked rather to some lasting contribution to the good of the world. Referring to a projected convention for establishing neutral and belligerent rights in wartime, he confided in his diary: "When I think, if it possibly could succeed, what a real and solid blessing it would be to the human race, I can scarcely guard myself from a spirit of enthusiasm, which it becomes me to distrust. I feel that I could die for it with joy, and that if my last moments could be cheered with the consciousness of having contributed to it, I could go before the throne of Omnipotence with a plea for mercy, and with a consciousness of not having lived in vain for the world of mankind."

BIBLIOGRAPHIC NOTE

The mind and the work of America's greatest secretary of state are best approached in his own writings, public and private; nowhere does the new national feeling of the post-Ghent era appear more prominently than in his diary, a classic that reveals the chilling candor and sharp intelligence of an extraordinary mind: Charles Francis Adams, ed., *Memoirs of John Quincy Adams, Comprising Portions of His Diary from 1795 to 1848*, 12 vols. (Philadelphia, 1874–77). The Worthington C. Ford edition of *The Writings of John Quincy Adams*, 7 vols. (New York, 1913–17), remains useful though it stops short of the presidential years. Most of Adams's important public papers are in the series American State Papers, *Foreign Relations*, especially volumes 4 and 5.

In smaller compass, Allan Nevins has compiled a convenient one-volume edition of the *Memoirs* (New York, 1951), and Walter LaFeber collected in paperback a short, sensible selection of excerpts from the letters, speeches, and papers of Adams under the title *John Quincy Adams and American Continental Empire* (Chicago, 1965).

The best biography—definitive and indispensable—remains the two-volume study by Samuel Flagg Bemis, *John Quincy Adams and the Foundations of American Foreign Policy* (New York, 1949) and *John Quincy Adams and the Union* (New York, 1956). The early sketch by Dexter Perkins in volume 4 of the American Secretaries of State and Their Diplomacy series, edited by Samuel Flagg Bemis (New York, 1928), provides a solid appraisal based on multiarchival research. George A. Lipsky's topical approach in *John Quincy Adams: His Theory and Ideas* (New York, 1950) is useful to students. For a contemporary assessment by a self-confessed disciple see William H. Seward, *Life and Public Services of John Quincy Adams* (Auburn, N.Y., 1850).

For the context of Adams's diplomacy, the best introduction is George Dangerfield, *The Era of Good Feelings* (New York, 1952), a masterful, gracefully written account of post-1815 America. The same author's *Awakening of American Nationalism, 1815–1828* (New York, 1965), contains excellent chapters on the Transcontinental Treaty and the

Monroe Doctrine. On the former subject, Philip C. Brooks, *Diplomacy and the Borderlands: The Adams-Onís Treaty of 1819* (Berkeley, 1939), remains definitive; for the latter, Dexter Perkins's monumental three-volume work *The Monroe Doctrine* (Gloucester, Mass., 1927) retains its preeminence. For U.S.–Latin American relations in the Adams era see Arthur P. Whitaker, *The United States and the Independence of Latin America, 1800–1830* (Baltimore, 1941); J. Fred Rippy, *Rivalry of the United States and Great Britain over Latin America, 1808–1830* (Baltimore, 1929); William W. Kaufmann, *British Policy and the Independence of Latin America, 1804–28* (New Haven, 1951); John A. Logan, Jr., *No Transfer: An American Security Principle* (New Haven, 1961); and Charles C. Griffin, *The United States and the Disruption of the Spanish Empire, 1810–1822* (New York, 1937). The president's famous message of December 1823 can be found in many collections, perhaps most conveniently in volume 2 of the widely available Richardson edition of the *Messages and Papers of the Presidents*.

A sophisticated analysis of Adams's diplomacy from the end of the War of 1812 to the enunciation of the Monroe Doctrine in 1823 is the concluding volume of Bradford Perkins's trilogy on Anglo-American relations, *Castlereagh and Adams* (Berkeley, 1964). For the Ghent negotiations see the titles mentioned in the essay on Madison in this volume. For an evaluation of a key theme in Adams's economic diplomacy consult F. Lee Benns, *The American Struggle for the West India Carrying-Trade, 1815–1830* (Bloomington, 1923), a work that George Dangerfield regards as seminal and "quite essential" for an understanding of a complex subject.

Adams's secretarial relations with important American contemporaries are discussed in Harry Ammon, *James Monroe: The Quest for National Identity* (New York, 1971); Raymond Walters, Jr., *Albert Gallatin: Jeffersonian Financier and Diplomat* (New York, 1957); and J. H. Powell, *Richard Rush: Republican Diplomat, 1780–1859* (Philadelphia, 1942). For the views of European diplomats toward Adams see Stanley Lane-Poole, *Life of Stratford Canning*, 2 vols. (London, 1888), and "Correspondence of the Russian Ministers in Washington, 1815–1825," *American Historical Review* 18 (January, April 1913): 309–45, 537–62. Vernon G. Stetser traces Adams's relationship to United States commercial policy in his *The Commercial Reciprocity Policy of the United States, 1774–1829* (Philadelphia, 1937).

CHARLES
WILKES

and the Growth of
American Naval Diplomacy

Geoffrey S. Smith

If mentioned at all by diplomatic historians, Charles Wilkes appears as a cocksure and irresponsible naval officer whose role in the *Trent* affair of 1861 brought the United States and Great Britain to the brink of war. To emphasize that dramatic act to the exclusion of all else, however, obscures two important aspects of diplomacy. Wilkes's prior career suggests that scientific exploration was both a prelude to and a handmaiden of antebellum expansionism; in addition, as Peter Karsten demonstrated in his provocative study of the naval aristocracy, an examination of the careers of American naval officers may clarify neglected dimensions of the nineteenth-century American response to the external world.

This essay is based on the author's forthcoming biography of Wilkes. Professor Smith received financial assistance from the Canada Council.

135

To appreciate that response and enhance understanding of America's quest for power and prestige in the nineteenth century, one must turn occasionally from such avowed leaders of the period as John Quincy Adams, James K. Polk, and William H. Seward. Then, as now, diplomacy was more than presidential decision, ministerial exchanges, or "what one clerk said to another clerk." Then, if not now, the naval officer often became a diplomat, an initiator and resolver of crises. Even in the era preceding the golden age of Annapolis, it is not surprising that the naval outlook in antebellum America included respect for a proper balance among scientific advancement, commercial expansion, and the advantages of republican government. For much of the nineteenth century Americans did not properly appreciate the increasing need for a strong navy. General sentiment against a peacetime military establishment combined with frugality in government resulted in jeers at Yankee cockboats following in the wake of British men-o'-war. The Atlantic Ocean and the English fleet were thought adequate for coastal defense; but so narrow a view minimized the nonmilitary and diplomatic functions executed by the navy, for during much of the century, and especially in peacetime, it emerged as a sharp cutting edge of American diplomacy. Its explorers were prominent in the diplomatic maneuvers for control of the West, especially the Pacific Northwest.

The manner in which one naval officer—a scientist, explorer, publicist, wartime commander, and self-avowed definer and defender of the national interest—thought about the role of the United States Navy in world affairs suggests that Charles Wilkes deserves a more prominent place among the makers of American diplomatic history than he has been accorded. As one of the first and most important explorer-diplomats, as a representative of mid-century naval interests and outlooks, and as an "embodiment of the wide-ranging energies and aspirations of the American people," Wilkes adds a useful (if usually neglected) dimension to the relationship between navalism and diplomacy in his day. Understanding his part in the acquisition of Oregon heightens awareness of the dynamics of American expansion. His career also coincided with an important period of technological innovation, highlighted by the transition of the navy from wood and sail to iron, steel, and steam. He reached maturity during the reform movement that resulted in the establishment in 1845 of the U.S. Naval Academy at Annapolis. A transitional figure whose sternness and discipline epitomized the "old navy," Wilkes nonetheless exhibited feelings for technological efficiency, scientific exploration, naval strategy during war, and the political and commercial destiny of the United States. In these and other ways, Wilkes foreshadowed the work of post–Civil War navalists Robert W. Shufeldt, Stephen B. Luce, and David D. Porter, those influential but still underestimated precursors of Alfred Thayer Mahan.[1]

Charles Wilkes, a grandnephew of the famous English dissenter John Wilkes, was born 3 April 1798; his early years coincided with America's naval war with France and with the successful demonstration of national sea power during the War of 1812. His death, on 8 February 1877, occurred as American diplomacy entered what historian David Pletcher called "the awkward years," when naval strength touched nadir. Wilkes's father, the son of a Loyalist who returned to America after the revolutionary war, became a New York merchant with commercial connections that directed his family's attention toward the Atlantic. As Charles grew up his interest centered increasingly upon science and the sea. He was an able student with several private tutors, and he concentrated on mathematics, navigation, and draftsmanship. His older brother, a major influence upon him during adolescence, served with the navy in the War of 1812; in his "Autobiography" Wilkes fondly recalled the celebrations held in New York City to honor American naval victories in that war. At the age of seventeen, against his father's wishes, he entered the merchant marine and got his first whiff of salt air on a voyage to Europe. A second voyage placed him under the command of a former officer in the French navy, a contact that led to Wilkes's appointment as a midshipman in the United States Navy on 1 January 1818.

Early in his naval career Wilkes recognized the need for greater national attention to the scientific aspects of navigation and naval technology. From 1824 to 1826, while preparing for his lieutenant's examination, he studied with a Swiss immigrant, Dr. Ferdinand Hassler, who in 1802 had founded what became the United States Coast and Geodetic Survey. From that experience, and from subsequent surveys of Narragansett Bay and St. George's Shoal, Wilkes developed a clear view of the practical importance

1. See the essay in this volume on Mahan.

of hydrography, geodesy, magnetism, and astronomy to navigation. In addition, Hassler's lack of discipline and his primitive surveying instruments provided constant irritation, which strengthened Wilkes's desire for the day when the nation would no longer depend upon European equipment or experts.

The versatile Wilkes put his ideas to work in 1833 when he assumed direction of the Naval Depot of Charts and Instruments. He soon transferred the depot from the western part of Washington, D.C., to Capitol Hill, both to bring his scientific work to the attention of Congress and to facilitate his astronomical experiments; he was the first American to construct an observatory and employ fixed astronomical instruments. He grew stronger in his belief that by expediting the charting of Atlantic ports and coastal waterways, naval surveys and exploration would strengthen developing commercial interests and lead to America's nautical independence.

The idea of a global exploring expedition assumed priority in Wilkes's assessment of the needs of the navy. Such an expedition, initially proposed by John Quincy Adams in 1825 and championed thereafter by Jeremiah N. Reynolds of Ohio, might strengthen the interdependence of science and the navy and augment the reputation of both. Moreover, such an expedition would require a skilled commander, and Wilkes, already a surveyor of ability and an embryonic naval scientist, felt himself uniquely qualified for the post.

Before the navy could become an instrument to further national scientific prestige, shipboard attitudes of both captains and crew had to change fundamentally. Wilkes's introduction to sea life left him disenchanted with naval mores. Although as a navy regular he valued discipline and order as preconditions of nautical efficiency, he recognized that life in the old navy left much to be desired: "No school could have been worse for the morals and none so viciously constituted." Younger men who conceived of the navy as an institution of national prestige were frustrated that older officers, in the absence of a merit system, stood above law and made others "subservient to their pleasures, caprices, and gratifications." "Debauching and drunken blackguards," masquerading as captains, men who often did not acknowledge the existence of scientific aids to navigation, served neither the nation's nor the navy's interests. Hamstrung by the lack of an educated officer corps, troubled by petty bickerings among officers, and debilitated by a lack of pride, the navy needed reform. To redress these shortcomings Wilkes favored creation of a naval academy, but he also stressed the necessity of officers first securing training through a sea cruise; while naval midshipmen were reasonably well educated, their knowledge of shipboard procedures was often abysmal.

Wilkes's attitude toward naval reform affected his feelings about politics in general. A social aristocrat in Jacksonian America, he found the system of political patronage demoralizing and believed that "good men should be above it." He believed that the dictates of party harmony necessitated sacrificing personal integrity; freedom of choice could scarcely exist in the political realm. This antipolitical animus was understandable. Institutional politics had blocked naval reform in the early nineteenth century; sectional and personal politics sabotaged the proposed exploration of the Pacific Ocean and northwest coast in 1825; and soon after Congress created a navy-directed scientific expedition in May 1836, personal jealousies, interdepartmental bickering, and the mismanagement of the navy secretary threatened that project.

Influenced by Wilkes's scientific reputation, Secretary of the Navy Mahlon Dickerson had proposed that he command one of the expedition's smaller vessels; but the commander-designate, Thomas ap Catesby Jones, balked at this suggestion, contending— in unmistakable old navy rhetoric—that Wilkes's attainments were of a "peculiar nature." Seeking a senior officer who would command respect on the quarterdeck, Jones further explained that Wilkes might take charge of instruments and surveying, but that under no circumstances might he be considered "as a commander, or for any other performance of regular navy duty."

Characteristically, Wilkes angrily refused to accept what amounted to a civilian's role in the expedition. Anticipating later navalists who zealously guarded their prerogative over scientific fields related to navigation, he berated Jones's lack of interest in science and ridiculed plans for twenty one civilian scientists to accompany the expedition. Their presence would make navy regulars (many of whom possessed scientific skills) inconsequential "hewers of wood and drawers of water." To protect his reputation, Wilkes detached himself from the expedition and returned to New York, where he continued his scientific work during the next few months.

While he was away, preparations for the expedition bogged

down. What Congress had planned as a voyage of exploration to aid American whaling interests in the Pacific, to facilitate trade with Latin America, and to augment the status of national science had instead become an acute embarrassment to President Martin Van Buren. Even John Quincy Adams, a staunch advocate of the voyage, remarked that all he wanted to hear about the expedition was that it had sailed. Most of the blame for the delay can be attributed to Dickerson who, after securing from several scientific groups the names of men competent to accompany the voyage, hesitated to convene them, failed to pay them, and proved unable to provide necessary equipment. It seemed to many that the delay might allow rival British and French expeditions, then preparing to put to sea, to steal the thunder of the American navy.

When Captain Jones resigned his command because of poor health in November 1837, and when Secretary Dickerson failed to find a suitable replacement, Van Buren took matters into his own hands by transferring supervision of the project to his capable secretary of war, Joel R. Poinsett. Unwilling to let the prestige of discovery go by default to England and France, the president urged Poinsett to expedite preparations for the voyage. Poinsett, who was an able administrator and an advocate of science, soon settled upon Lieutenant Charles Wilkes to lead the expedition. In Poinsett's view the latter's lack of seniority did not prejudice his qualities as seaman and navigator. In fact, Wilkes's scientific competence made him one of the few officers qualified to command the voyage and to bring it to a successful conclusion.

Wilkes's appointment in April 1838 threatened to disrupt preparations for the expedition. Far from being the first choice, he had served primarily as a shoreside scholar. This fact, plus the two-year delay in mounting the expedition, raised criticism in many quarters. Wilkes's earlier resignation, together with his well-known quick temper and impulsiveness, exacerbated the feelings of colleagues and politicians. Lieutenant C. K. Stribling, who equaled Wilkes in rank, termed the appointment "highly injurious" to the morale of senior officers; a congressman wondered how a junior officer could command respect on so arduous a voyage; another lawmaker proposed that vessels assigned to the expedition be transferred to the coast squadrons for routine duty. Although failing to remove Wilkes from his command, Captain Beverly Kennon, a highly respected officer, succeeded in forcing the administration to divest the expedition of "all military charac-

ter." By so doing, Kennon hoped to prevent the Wilkes appointment from setting a potentially dangerous precedent; his plan
precluded a departure from the usual custom of selecting commanding officers from the senior ranks of the navy. The most bitter
criticism of Wilkes, however, came from Lieutenant Matthew
Fontaine Maury, whose personal interest in the voyage stemmed
from hydrographic abilities equaling his adversary's. Maury
scorned Wilkes as "a cunning little Jacob" who had campaigned
long and hard for the post. Claiming that his rival had barely
enough sea service to familiarize himself with ordinary ship
routine, Maury decried the promotion of a shore-bound sinecur-
ist—an armchair admiral—over the heads of many meritorious
officers.

Such attacks did not bother Wilkes. With Poinsett's full
support he moved swiftly to take charge of the project. He
personally supervised the equipping, repairing, and final selection
of vessels assigned to the cruise; he reassigned sailors and soothed
their dissatisfactions with the move; he named an old Brooklyn
friend, William L. Hudson, to be second in command; he reduced
the number of civilian scientists assigned to the voyage, arguing
that naval personnel were fully qualified for the scientific tasks
related to navigation. Finally, he tested and calibrated his instruments at the Naval Observatory in Washington to assure their
accuracy. The expedition received a sort of public official blessing
in late July when Van Buren, Poinsett, and the new navy secretary,
James Kirke Paulding, visited the squadron at Hampton Roads,
Virginia.

Despite initial progress and evidence of executive approval, a
serious and potentially dangerous problem remained. That problem stemmed from Wilkes's fiery personality, and from his
dissatisfaction that promotion had not accompanied his new
command. Named to a post of high responsibility, entrusted with
a mission of international scientific importance, and representing
the nation and the navy before the world, he felt sharply the lack
of power and prestige that accompanied professional advancement. Nor did the carping of the crew and their underhand
references to the "lieutenant-commodore" mitigate his injured
pride. He brought these facts to the president's attention. Speaking for himself and Hudson, he reminded Van Buren that a failure
to rectify the existing state of affairs would do "great injustice" to
the expedition and its commanding officers. Only patriotism

prevented his resignation, he wrote, adding that the failure to promote him might even threaten the success of the mission.

Unwilling or unable to recognize that the administration's failure to raise his rank stemmed at least in part from a desire to avoid further controversy, Wilkes considered it a blow to his *amour propre,* and successful execution of the mission became his obsession. The presumed "slight" (or, more precisely, Wilkes's own sensitivity to it) no doubt contributed to his subsequent transformation into a shipboard martinet. Pique also led to his hiding a commodore's uniform and pennant aboard the flagship *Vincennes* for later use. Characteristically, he planned to resolve the difficulty himself.

The exploring expedition represented in microcosm the variety of functions executed by naval officers in the 1840s and 1850s. Instructed to "extend the empires of commerce and science; to diminish the hazards of the ocean; and [to] point out to future navigators a course by which they might avoid dangers and find safety," Wilkes took command of a flotilla consisting of 6 ships, 83 officers, and 342 enlisted men. The last global voyage wholly dependent upon sail, the expedition left Hampton Roads on 8 August 1838, only three months after Matthew C. Perry crossed the Atlantic in the *Fulton*—the initial transoceanic voyage by a steam-powered vessel. As one of a number of contemporary episodes matching civilized man against primitive nature, the Wilkes expedition featured human elements of courage, tragedy, and humor as it endured an arduous journey of nearly four years. Ranging from the waters of the Antarctic and South Pacific to the Juan de Fuca Strait, Wilkes and his colleagues surveyed approximately two hundred eighty islands, about eight hundred miles of coastline and contiguous territory in Oregon and Alta California, and some fifteen hundred miles along the Antarctic continent. Although the expedition did not make many new discoveries in the Pacific, the maps and charts resulting from the voyage anticipated Matthew Fontaine Maury's *Physical Geography of the Sea* (1855), providing American merchantmen with new certitude as they plied maritime routes.

Like other expeditions of the 1840s and 1850s, the one led by

Wilkes helped clarify and expand the navy's role in the development of the nation's diplomacy. In the middle years of the century the navy's primary tasks, aside from showing the flag and protecting national interests, centered on commercial, scientific, and political reconnaissance. As gatherers and interpreters of useful information, Wilkes and his colleagues helped construct the foundations upon which the post–Civil War navalists would build a new navy that would become a powerful ally of America's burgeoning network of global trade and commerce.

An important part of Wilkes's work was a series of warnings to the Navy Department about the need to strengthen the American presence in Polynesia and the Pacific Northwest. In addition to surveying oceanic channels, recommending and publicizing points of potential commercial and strategic interest, and informing Washington of the need to augment American power throughout the Pacific region, Wilkes and his colleagues became unofficial diplomats, representing a growing world power in such remote places as Brazil, New South Wales, Manila, and Singapore. The expedition also proved that during the 1840s Manifest Destiny denoted as much a maritime as a territorial force. Indeed, the personnel of the expedition became "maritime frontiersmen," mirror images of the thousands of mountain men, traders, pioneers, adventurers, and army surveyors who trekked westward to the Pacific. Harbingers of an increasingly complex, globally oriented society just beginning to crowd commercial, religious, and technological frontiers, the explorers gathered reams of scientific, economic, and political information at such points of future American interest as the Philippines, Samoa, Hawaii, California, and the Oregon Territory.

The expedition played an important though underrated part in the diplomacy of continental expansion. It enabled Wilkes to emphasize the danger of traversing the bar at the mouth of the Columbia River, and the destruction of one of his ships, the *Peacock*, publicized the inadequacies of Columbia Bay as an ocean harbor. More importantly, he pointed out the strategic importance of the area adjacent to Forts Tacoma and Walla Walla, the commercial potential of the Juan de Fuca Strait and Puget Sound, and the magnificence of the harbor at San Francisco. These descriptions (contained in a special confidential report to the government and in Wilkes's five-volume *Narrative*) influenced various Anglo-American boundary negotiations in the 1840s and stimulated subsequent official interest in California and the Oregon country.

The expedition also coincided with important new developments in transportation and technology; these, in turn, intensified the desire of Americans to subdue what Daniel Boorstin termed a "half-known country." The voyage struck the public mind less as an end in itself than as a means to several specific ends. In seeking reliable geographic data, the expedition created "a public purpose which the democratic society could properly patronize," as George H. Daniels so nicely put it. For the first time in American history civilian scientists utilized the navy to carry out scientific objectives. While the Lewis and Clark expedition of 1804–6 marked the first marriage of science and the military, the Wilkes voyage settled scientific exploration as a province of government, and it fixed the scientists' dependence upon the military for transport and auxiliary services.

An important step in the maturation of American science, this project—a sort of "floating doctoral program"—proved valuable both in training scientists (including some who did not make the journey) and in providing impetus toward the growth of scientific agencies. Yet if this ambitious undertaking in government-sponsored science presented great opportunity, it also posed problems. As a prototype of the close, uneasy alliance of government, science, and the military in the twentieth century, the expedition foreshadowed a patently modern concern: securing and maintaining cooperation between civilians concerned with "pure" science and regular naval personnel, whose scientific interests centered on improvements in naval technology and architecture. Of necessity, Wilkes spent much of his time mediating between civilian demands and the daily requirements of his sailors. Though he did not always succeed in reconciling those differences, he made sure they did not interfere with the objectives of the voyage. To this end, he ordered each officer to keep a journal, refused to become involved in shipboard politics, and sought to prevent the emergence of cliques. Wilkes was an indefatigable worker, and he personally supervised all developments in geodesy, magnetism, physics, meteorology, geography, hydrography, astronomy, and surveying. A hard taskmaster, he drove himself as hard as he drove subordinates.

Among its many other objectives the expedition sought to

protect whalers and traders in the Pacific by regularizing relations with aboriginal tribes through "wood and water" agreements and, when necessary, by punishment. Though usually restrained in his dealings with native peoples, Wilkes could, on occasion, use force; when he believed that power would have salutary effect, he acted decisively. Crew members once imprisoned a native chief implicated in an earlier murder of sailors from an American brig; on another occasion, after natives absconded with supplies pilfered from a disabled cutter, Wilkes destroyed their village; and on the island of Malolo, after the murder of two of his crew, Wilkes ordered two more villages razed. These early instances of gunboat diplomacy marked a step toward law and order and were designed to impress the natives with the consequences of harm to American visitors or vessels.

Wilkes also exercised quasi-diplomatic powers when he appointed agents to represent American whalers and traders at Upolu and the main island of Fiji. The two men earned their posts by aiding negotiations with native chieftains for the protection of visiting ships and crews (and for safeguarding the natives from the sailors), but because few American ships touched at these outposts the agents had little to do. Still, Wilkes's diplomacy, if such it was, represented an early attempt to establish international agreements with native chiefs in Samoa and Fiji. The accords illustrated the growing interest of naval commanders in protecting American overseas property and preserving international order and stability. Foreshadowing similar agreements between army officers and Indians after the Civil War, Wilkes's accords also anticipated executive agreements of the sort that naval commander William T. Truxton concluded with chieftains in the Gilberts, Marianas, and Marshalls in the 1870s.

Several episodes during the expedition, in New Zealand, Hawaii, and Oregon, brought Wilkes in contact with some of the main themes of nineteenth-century diplomacy. Like many of his countrymen, he had a full measure of Anglophobia, and events during the voyage exacerbated that sentiment, furthered his appreciation of the interrelatedness of political sovereignty and economic progress, and revealed him as an ardent advocate of Manifest Destiny.

The first of these incidents occurred in 1840 when Britain established a measure of sovereignty in New Zealand by negotiating the Treaty of Waitangi with approximately five hundred Maori chiefs, an agreement that ceded North Island to the crown. Wilkes, arriving in New Zealand only days after the signing, concluded that James R. Clendon, an Englishman who a year earlier had become the first American consul for the important post of the Bay of Islands, had used his diplomatic post to force the chiefs to agree. More concerned with his substantial landholdings than with defending American interests, Clendon resigned his post in 1841, but not before new import laws and tonnage duties severely damaged a profitable Yankee whaling and shipping trade. Among other things, the new regulations prohibited American whalers from hunting their favorite waters and curing their oil on North Island. In fact, between 1840 and 1841 the number of American vessels calling at the Bay of Islands dropped by 50 percent, and Wilkes estimated that the loss from the annual oil yield would reach three hundred thousand dollars. Terming the Treaty of Waitangi a disaster for the natives that transformed them into prey for "the hosts of adventurers flooding in from all parts," he concluded that Clendon's part in the accord emphasized the need for American citizens to serve as commercial representatives abroad.

Unwilling to involve himself in matters that might jeopardize the expedition, Wilkes adopted a realistic view of his nation's embryonic interests in Polynesia and did not contest the treaty. Nevertheless, Clendon's role in the agreement indicated a deficiency in American diplomacy: commercial connections proved a more powerful motive for becoming a diplomatic representative than either ability or sympathy for United States interests.

The expedition reached Hawaii in late September 1840, and Wilkes lauded the spirit of enterprise and level of civilization there. He also noted with interest the strategic potential of ports at Lahaina and Pearl River and the commercial future of such products as indigo, coffee, cattle, and sugar. The commander expressed surprise at how well local American merchants and missionaries got along with each other. He soon recognized that this cordiality signified less a community of interests than a defensive drawing together in the face of apparent British and French challenges to American commercial and religious interests. The years 1840 and 1841 witnessed a dramatic (though temporary) statistical increase in English commercial contact with the islands. Additionally in the eyes of several Protestant clergymen, France had embarked upon an aggressive Hawaiian policy. In 1837 and

1839, French naval officers forced King Kamehameha III to conclude treaties guaranteeing the diplomatic principle of extraterritoriality to French citizens, the free importation of French wine, and the toleration and protection of Catholicism. Although subscribing to the Protestant clergy's view that French wine would accelerate the spiritual and physical decline of sailors and natives alike, Wilkes did not share the missionaries' anti-Catholicism and saw no reason to take action beyond dispatching his impressions to Washington. Lacking specific orders, he did not accede to Kamehameha's proposal to renew and strengthen an agreement concluded a decade earlier with Captain Thomas ap Catesby Jones.

A theoretical devotion to global liberty and equality infused the rhetoric of many Americans in the mid-nineteenth century, but navalists did not always share these sentiments. Wilkes's rejection of a petition for a territorial constitution presented by American settlers in the Willamette Valley of Oregon seems to suggest that he responded to pragmatic rather than to ideological pressures. His demurrer demonstrated an appreciation of the dangers of premature involvement, which might threaten the national interest by engaging America in a situation it could not control. At that time, American interests in New Zealand and Hawaii did not warrant an active policy, but in the Pacific Northwest conditions differed. There, the questionable intentions of Britain's Hudson's Bay Company had made Oregon a contentious issue in Anglo-American relations, a fact reflected in instructions sent Wilkes to accord close attention to the Columbia River, the northwest coast, and San Francisco Bay.

As members of the expedition carried out scientific and surveying duties in the Puget Sound area in May 1841, Wilkes and a party of men journeyed to Astoria, where they encountered the remnants of the former headquarters of the Hudson's Bay Company. American settlers in the Willamette Valley had charged the company with "avarice, cruelty, despotism, and bad government," but Wilkes found the corporation's representatives, especially Sir George Simpson and Dr. John McLoughlin, helpful in providing aid and useful suggestions. Wilkes's praise of McLoughlin's facilities and of the hospitality offered by company officers at Vancouver contributed to the notion that he had succumbed to British blandishments while ignoring "the wants of the infant settlement of Oregon." This criticism, popular among Anglophobic settlers and subsequent local historians, missed its mark. Wilkes could, when necessary, subordinate his own Anglophobia to the demands of mission. In this case he recognized that without the aid of the company his expedition could not proceed as planned, particularly in the northernmost reaches of the Oregon country. Although the committee of five that presented its plans for a territorial constitution claimed to represent the sentiments of all Americans in the region, Wilkes refused to be drawn into the controversy. In fact, he suggested that the committee acted from selfish motives, hoping to induce a flood of new settlement and thus augment the value of their farms and livestock. The settlers, Wilkes concluded, should await a more propitious time when Washington would "throw its mantle over them."

Wilkes's dispassionate view of the Oregon question reflected his skill as a naval diplomat, although his actions belied his true feelings. The removal of the Hudson's Bay Company headquarters to Vancouver struck him as the portent of a glorious American future. Praising the agricultural and commercial potential of the Willamette Valley, he stepped forward as a naval apostle of Manifest Destiny. Sensing that he and his men "were not strangers on the soil," he explained that they "could not but take great interest in relation to its destiny, in the prospect of its one day becoming the abode of our relatives and friends."

Such sentiments, in fact, prevented Wilkes from filing a special report on Oregon until 13 June 1842, three days after he returned to New York. The forty-four-page document remained confidential because Navy Secretary Abel P. Upshur felt its release might threaten concurrent diplomatic negotiations between Secretary of State Daniel Webster and the British diplomat, Lord Ashburton. While Webster and his adversary had hoped to include the Oregon questions in their broad agenda, the return of the exploring expedition prevented its solution. A hint of the report's contents became public on 20 June when Wilkes presented a synopsis of his findings in a lecture at the National Institute in Washington. Scorning the mouth of the Columbia as a potential port, he reported the wreck of one of his vessels as it attempted to enter the river. "Mere description can give little idea of the terrors of the bar of the Columbia," he wrote. "All who have seen it have spoken of the wildness of the scene, and incessant roar of the waters, representing it as one of the most fearful sights that can possibly meet the eye of the sailor." This gloomy description contrasted with his enthusiastic assessment of more northerly harbors, upon which, he suggested, the future security and maritime prosperity of the United States depended. Lauding the safety of the Juan de Fuca Strait, Admiralty Inlet, Puget Sound, and Hood's Canal, he pointed out that no area in the world afforded "finer inland sounds or a greater number of harbors . . . capable of receiving the largest class of vessels, and without a danger in them that is not visible."

Even these views sounded mild when compared with the frankly expansionist tone of the confidential report. Wilkes argued that by surrendering disputed territory north of the Columbia the United States would forfeit a vast storehouse of natural resources that in time would provide "an extensive commerce on advantageous terms with most parts of the Pacific." The report also contained a strong argument favoring a 54°40′ boundary. Wilkes noted that a division along the forty-ninth parallel would decrease the value of much territory south of that latitude. Moreover, the nation that commanded northern waterways adjoining the Juan de Fuca Strait would control Vancouver Island and access into the heart of the Oregon country. In addition to pointing out the practical difficulties of locating a boundary along the forty-ninth parallel, Wilkes expressed concern lest the territory then occupied by the Hudson's Bay Company become a staging ground for brigands and Indians to attack Americans in the Willamette Valley.[2]

2. In his confidential report Wilkes sought to dramatize the fact that the Hudson's Bay Company had already moved "to secure permanent settlement in the area" by "asserting its rights to the soil north of the Columbia." In his view American procrastination would allow the company "to obtain such a foothold as will make it impossible to set aside British sovereignty in it." Clearly, Wilkes shared with many Americans a deep-rooted fear of British encirclement. John Quincy Adams, whose dislike of Britain Stratford Canning described as "ravenous," probably best personified this attitude, which was descended from an older New England doctrine of containing French and, later, English strength wherever possible. The need to stave off French Catholic encirclement figured prominently in the external affairs of the Massachusetts Bay Colony, while a subsequent anti-British animus motivated colonial leaders in the decade before the Revolution and influenced Benjamin Franklin's vision of a rising American empire. During the early 1840s, vigilance against what Adams had termed the " 'bastard liberty' of the British, with its inequalities and aristocracy," became an integral facet of America's move to the Pacific. This tendency in American thought, noted by Frederick Merk and Richard W. Van Alstyne, will be considered in greater detail in the author's forthcoming biography of Wilkes.

There is no way to determine the precise effects of the report and other expedition publicity upon subsequent American acquisition of Oregon and California, and certainly no evidence suggests that Wilkes's call for 54° 40′ contributed in any substantial way to the later cry for that boundary. Nevertheless, in late 1842, Navy Secretary Upshur made public the sections of the report setting forth the immense value of the western part of Oregon, stimulating what became a year later the "Oregon fever." Even Webster, who earlier likened Oregon to "a land of deserts, eternal snows, of shifting sands, and sagebrush, fit to be inhabited only by the jack-rabbit and the coyote," admitted that the inland waters adjoining the Juan de Fuca Strait contained all the good harbors between the Russian settlements and California.

Although Wilkes's confidential report did not mention California (an omission reflecting Washington's overriding concern for Oregon), his subsequent Narrative offered a glowing description of the strategic importance of San Francisco Bay. Located on a major trade route linking China, Manila, Hawaii, India, and ports in Mexico and South America, the bay promised to become "one of the finest, if not the very best in the world—sufficiently commodious that the combined fleets of all the naval powers of Europe might moor in it." Convinced that the near absence of Mexican authority at Yerba Buena signaled an imminent American windfall, Wilkes suggested that possession of both San Francisco Bay and the harbors of Puget Sound would strengthen American commerce by establishing a transpacific triangle.

While the exploring expedition marked the entrance of the navy into "honorable competition with the navies of the great maritime nations of Europe," the project also denoted an important new chapter in the opening of the West, producing a wealth of reliable information about topography, climate, commercial prospects, and navigational problems. Americans moving westward after 1842 no longer found it necessary to depend for information upon the earlier reports of Lewis and Clark and Lieutenant William Slacum, the fiction of James Fenimore Cooper and Washington Irving, or the sketchy, often contradictory accounts of mountain men and missionaries. Despite shipboard dissension and personal recriminations that led to a court-martial for Wilkes and widespread criticism in the press, the commander's report and *Narrative* must surely be accorded a significant part in transforming the context of the Oregon question.[3]

Charles Wilkes's Civil War career is too well known to require more than a brief recapitulation here, but during the conflict his definition of the national interest and the tactics he employed to advance it shed useful light on the perils of naval diplomacy at a critical juncture in American history.

His place in American diplomacy centers on the events of 8 November 1861, when on his own initiative he removed two Confederate envoys from the British mail packet *Trent*. Historians have assessed the importance of that event in many ways: from the vantage point of international law, as an example of the way public opinion complicates presidential decision making, as a chapter in Anglo-French diplomacy, as a way of measuring the temperature of British politics during the early Civil War. These and other interpretations have allowed readers to view from more angles than usual one of the most significant crises in American history.[4]

The delicate balance between military necessity and civilian responsibility has, of course, become an issue of vast significance in the twentieth century. In emphasizing this theme as it emerged during the *Trent* affair, historians have failed to stress an unexpected result of the incident. Ostensibly, Wilkes provoked a crisis that brought Great Britain to the verge of war; but the question turned on one variable: whether the Washington government would sanction the seizure. As even the most ardent Anglophobes

3. Frederick Merk, "The Oregon Question in the Webster-Ashburton Negotiations," *Mississippi Valley Historical Review* 42 (December 1956). As William H. Goetzmann demonstrates, however, neither Polk nor Secretary of State James Buchanan evidenced great interest in Wilkes's description of Puget Sound and San Francisco in 1844. See Goetzmann, *Army Exploration in the American West, 1803–1863* (New Haven, 1959), p. 103 and passim.
4. Lincoln and Welles found Wilkes next to impossible to restrain; his capacity to influence national policy resulted from the primitive communications network that left naval officers on their own for weeks at a time. Wilkes's freedom corroborates the observation that throughout the nineteenth century, and well into the twentieth, naval vessels often served perforce as independent, "floating embassies," supplanting distant or nonexistent State Department authority. See also the essay in this volume on Seward.

admitted, that possibility, despite the president's strong inclination to keep the Confederates, was extremely remote.

Many factors, including the problem of defending Canada, the fortuitous advice (and death) of the Prince Consort at the height of the imbroglio, and doubts concerning the motives of Napoleon III of France, militated against Britain entering the conflict. Consequently the martial bluster emanating from both sides of the Atlantic amounted to little more than a rhetorical equivalent of war. In light of these factors, Wilkes's part in the affair was somewhat ironic. What struck many contemporaries (and subsequent historians) as a *casus belli* became a strong force for peace. By establishing earnest diplomatic relations between the United States and Britain early in the war, the *Trent* incident created channels of communication that became invaluable during the ensuing years. Had the incident not occurred when it did, the parameters of Anglo-American relations would have remained uncertain; in November 1861, however, each nation found it necessary to assess publicly and soberly the motives of its adversary.

The *Trent* incident, which featured Wilkes in the combined roles of international lawyer and prize court judge, came at the nadir of Union fortunes and affected Northerners in a way similar to the Battle of Saratoga in 1777 and Jackson's victory at New Orleans in 1815. The overwhelming popular support offered Wilkes as reflected in the unionist denial that his act contravened the principle of maritime neutrality for which the United States fought France in the 1790s and England in 1812 focused attention upon Alexis de Tocqueville's warning, three decades earlier, that "foreign politics demand scarcely any of those qualities which a democracy possesses; and they require, on the contrary, the perfect use of almost all those faculties in which it is deficient." Tocqueville, to be sure, took the position of an alarmist. The nineteenth-century record of American diplomacy reveals a successful balancing of means with ends by leaders who hesitated to extend national interests into areas where the country might prove unable to exercise commensurate power.

The response of President Lincoln and Secretary of State William H. Seward to the *Trent* affair proved no exception to this general rule; yet the incident—and Wilkes's subsequent Civil War career—underlined the ease with which an isolated, impetuous naval officer might involve his country in a crisis. Wilkes's zeal

POLICEMAN WILKES, noticing by the last Number of *Harper's Weekly*, that the well-known Rogues, MASON and SLIDELL, were about to Pawn some of their late Employer's Property at Messrs. *Bull, Crapaud & Co.'s* Shop, kept a bright look-out for'ard, and nabbed them in the nick of time."

during the conflict resulted largely from his own ambition, thwarted during the preceding two decades by a series of frustrating experiences. While other naval explorers carried the flag to North Pacific, Asiatic, and Latin American waters, the commander of the famous exploring expedition had remained on shore, facing the indifference of President John Tyler's Whig administration, enduring a highly publicized court-martial, and waging a ceaseless battle with Congress for appropriations to finance projects connected with the voyage. Meanwhile, another blow fell when a British explorer, Sir James Clarke Ross, denied the validity of Wilkes's greatest accomplishment, proving the continental dimension of Antarctica, by claiming to have sailed directly over the "discovery." Wilkes's survey of California's Sacramento Valley also ended in a bitter dispute, after the famed "pathfinder" of the West, John C. Frémont, located mistakes in Wilkes's map, indicating that he had copied it from a discredited English chart.

Problems like these contributed to Wilkes's aggressive conduct and to his growing tendency to ignore the feelings of individuals and rights of nations with whom he dealt. Unable to accept criticism, he came into continuous conflict with others, including politicians, fellow officers, and enlisted men before and during the expedition; the Tyler administration upon Wilkes's return; fellow scientists and unsympathetic members of the Joint Congressional Committee on the Library as he prepared his *Narrative* and administered scientific collections during the 1840s and 1850s; the Navy Department during the Civil War; and, because of his contempt for international law while intercepting blockade runners and chasing Confederate commerce destroyers in the West Indies, with naval and diplomatic representatives of Britain, France, Spain, Denmark, and Mexico.

Wilkes's derring-do in the *Trent* incident led to his appointment in July 1862 to command the newly formed James River Flotilla, and subsequently, after a nine-day stint in charge of the Potomac River Flotilla, to head the West Indian Flying Squadron. In the first position he earned a reputation as a headstrong commander, on one occasion disobeying Navy Department orders to detach two men from his squadron and on several others entreating the department to allow him to combine his forces with those of General George B. McClellan's Army of the Potomac to storm the Confederate stronghold at Richmond. Even after General Henry W. Halleck ordered McClellan's troops to withdraw to defend Washington, D.C., Wilkes persisted, informing Navy Secretary Gideon Welles that the mundane tasks of reconnaissance did not satisfy his desire to turn the tide of conflict.

Wilkes's appointment in September to lead the Flying Squadron represented Lincoln's veiled warning to European nations, especially the British, to honor the requirements of maritime neutrality. The president and his advisers could count on Wilkes to follow an aggressive course; they had a fair idea of the lengths to which their agent might carry his attempt to capture the *Alabama*, *Florida*, and the numerous contraband carriers that slipped past the Union blockade. Soon, however, it appeared—especially to the British—that Wilkes had again exceeded instructions; in effect he had extended the blockade into West Indian waters. Believing, like Alfred Thayer Mahan, that the navy's major wartime duty consisted of locating and destroying the enemy, Wilkes disregarded Welles's counsels of caution and acted as though existing conditions excused breaches of the law or naval etiquette. Wilkes was convinced that European colonial officials had forfeited their rights as neutrals by aiding Confederate vessels, and he literally transformed Havana into a base of American operations as he searched for the Confederate cruisers. To extend the moderate capacity of his own vessels, he illegally established and employed coaling stations on French, Spanish, Danish, and British soil; to facilitate capture of blockade runners, he allegedly placed "sentinels" on British soil and ordered his ships to "hover" in the waters off the Danish port of St. Thomas; and to strengthen his overall command, he unilaterally detached vessels from the squadrons of David G. Farragut and C. H. Baldwin.

Wilkes's failure to capture the Confederate cruisers provoked widespread criticism of Welles and his department. Antagonism between the secretary and his ambitious underling increased after Wilkes charged that the department had discriminated against him by failing to provide the manpower and vessels required to execute his mission. Wilkes's assertion that these measures would have enabled him to capture the *Alabama* or *Florida* contained some truth; but the Union commander lacked specialized knowledge of the myriad reefs, inlets, and cays dotting Caribbean waters. This shortcoming, compared with the geographical expertise and nautical skill of his Confederate adversaries, contributed significantly to the futility of Wilkes's nine-month command.

In Welles's view, Wilkes exhibited less interest in capturing the cruisers than he did in collecting prize money from vessels captured while attempting to trade with the Confederacy. Although its scope made halting the contraband trade virtually impossible, the Flying Squadron upset the continuity of Confederate transactions, forced shifts in the bases of operation, and compelled Southern vessels to ply the Caribbean and Gulf waters with greater circumspection; but Wilkes's arrogant attitude and disrespect for maritime law (epitomized by his frequent use of neutral ports as bases from which to stalk suspected ships) made him a symbol of Anglo-American hostility. His detention of several British ships created legal and diplomatic squalls across the Atlantic, and his heavy-handed pursuit of duty left Englishmen aghast at the actions of a man whom the *Liverpool Mercury* described as "an ill-informed and violent naval officer."

Secretary Welles removed Wilkes from active duty in June 1863 as a diplomatic gesture toward Anglo-American amity that placed the administration in a favorable light. Having demonstrated its toughness by appointing Wilkes, it could now reap the rewards of conciliation by removing him. For Wilkes, however, the recall signaled a bitter end to a stormy career. The *Trent* affair was all but forgotten; Union victories at Vicksburg and Gettysburg would supply a new cadre of military heroes. His reputation tarnished by failure, his zeal unappreciated, Wilkes returned to New York, feeling that he had been sacrificed to Navy Department incompetence and British diplomatic pressure. There remained, however, a denouement, a second court-martial that convened in March 1864. The list of particulars had a familiar ring: Wilkes had disobeyed orders and engaged in conduct unbecoming an officer; by allowing publication of a letter critical of Welles's *Annual Report*, he had displayed insubordination; by falsifying his age and failing to provide a suitable explanation, he had disobeyed a general naval regulation and demonstrated disrespect toward his superiors. Judged guilty on all counts, the "hero of the *Trent*" received a public reprimand and a three-year suspension—a sentence that Lincoln later reduced. In July 1866, as the culmination of a stormy career, Wilkes achieved a lifelong goal when he was named rear admiral, albeit on the retired list.

Zealous in his execution of duty, imperious toward associates, and single-minded in devotion to God and country, Wilkes exemplified throughout his career attitudes characterizing the old navy. As those who served with him observed, duty addressed Wilkes in severe terms, and he in turn expected as much of subordinates as he did of himself. Like many contemporary navalists, he harbored an enduring faith in America's political, commercial, and spiritual mission—a mission, incidentally, in which he found a major role for himself. This egotism, especially in his later career, led him to make decisions based upon ambition and impulse, to disdain the delicate balance between military means and diplomatic ends, and to ignore naval etiquette when orders or regulations contravened what he defined as a proper course. Wilkes's major weakness lay in impulsive overconfidence. Sincere in believing that he could not err, he defined issues in black-and-white terms. This characteristic often led to disagreements with superiors. Navy Secretary Welles, despairing of Wilkes's contumacy while commanding the James River Flotilla, described the man perfectly as "very exacting toward others, but . . . not himself as obedient as he should be." Possessing ability "but not good judgement in all respects," Wilkes might "rashly assume authority, and do things that might involve himself and the country in difficulty."

His problems during the Civil War leave the impression that Wilkes's significance in diplomatic history lies in his unwarranted assumption of power over the formulation of national policy. Such an interpretation, stressing the danger in a "my country, right or wrong" attitude, is one-sided. As an explorer and scientist he demonstrated courage and ability; as a discoverer, surveyor, and cartographer, he contributed to growing national prestige. Given the primitive technology at his command during the late 1830s, his confirmation of the continental dimensions of Antarctica compares favorably with the complex systems supporting American space efforts during the 1960s. Similarly, rather than ending up in dusty archives, Wilkes's charts of Wake Island, the Makins, and Tarawa endured among the more reliable sources of information employed by the navy during South Pacific operations in 1943.

According to James Dwight Dana, who accompanied the exploring expedition and knew well its commander's acerbic tongue, Wilkes's conceit did not detract from his "wonderful degree of energy." Nor did Dana err when he confided to Professor Asa Gray of Harvard that one could find "no more daring or driving officer" in the navy. As Wilkes's son John stated after his father's death in 1877, the latter impressed acquaintances as "a fearless, energetic, and unflinching officer, never afraid to assume responsibility." Such characteristics, of course, tossed Wilkes into choppy waters as a wartime commander; yet they also contributed to his success as a scientist. His legacy included, quite understandably, the admonition that the national interest depended upon continued government support of scientific research and exploration. Wilkes's participation in organizations such as the American Philosophical Society, his writings on such diverse subjects as the Oregon Territory, meteorology, and the zodiacal light, and the impetus given by the scientific expedition to the development of the Smithsonian Institution and other governmental agencies all advanced the expansionist *Zeitgeist* that permeated the United States in the mid-nineteenth century.

The overall strategic importance of exploration during antebellum America necessitates revision of the diplomatic era traditionally described as dominated by young America. On the one hand, the All of Mexico movement, the Ostend Manifesto, and the ill-fated filibustering expeditions of Narciso López into Cuba and William Walker into Nicaragua illustrate some uncoordinated muscle flexing by an adolescent nation attempting to elbow its way into world politics. Offsetting these episodes in bumptious diplomacy, the government and the navy demonstrated their appreciation of the need to acquire systematic knowledge of the globe and its ports, products, and peoples. Matthew C. Perry's epochal voyage to Japan ranks as the best known of these expeditions; but other voyages, including one led by Lieutenant William F. Lynch to the Dead Sea area in 1847, another led by Lieutenant William L. Herndon and Passed Midshipman Lardner Gibbon to the Amazon River in 1851, and a third in 1853 led by Lieutenant John Rodgers to North Pacific waters off China and Japan, suggest that Manifest Destiny influenced spheres of activity far removed from the domestic emphasis on westward continental expansion.

Apart from his scientific work, Wilkes expressed his greatest concern for the international image of the navy. As his narrative of the scientific expedition made clear, he also appreciated Sir Walter Raleigh's dictum that "whosoever commands the sea, commands the trade; whosoever commands the trade of the world, commands the riches of the world and consequently the world itself." Although as commander of the project Wilkes in no way spoke as a captive of special economic interests, he did conceive of the Atlantic and especially the Pacific as oceanic highways rather than barriers. Anticipating the post–1865 vision of Secretary of State Seward, he believed that knowledge of the seas would consolidate control over global waterways. Even if the United States could not wrest maritime supremacy from Great Britain, the navy might stabilize maritime routes so that American political and commercial interests might profit. Well before Mahan systematically articulated the strategic variables that comprised global navalism, Wilkes stressed the continuing necessity of employing sea power in peacetime as an instrument of scientific, technological, and economic advancement.

Although Wilkes favored extending to aboriginal peoples the benefits of Anglo-Saxon, republican government and Protestant religion, his Anglophobia precluded kinship with the American naval aristocracy of the late nineteenth and twentieth centuries. Although he rejected Rousseau's characterization of the "noble savage" enjoying an idyllic existence in a Pacific paradise, several passages in his *Narrative* and "Autobiography" (especially those dealing with the expedition's transactions with native peoples), make clear that Wilkes often employed a yardstick of idealized American cultural values to measure the level of "civilization" of the aborigines he encountered. He agreed with most navalists who criticized American missionaries and commercial agents who failed to execute with sufficient verve their respective moral and material commissions.

As an explorer Wilkes exhibited what the historian Richard W. Van Alstyne has termed "a mariner's sense of distance from the United States." Wilkes's earnestness in stressing the economic and strategic potential of Puget Sound and the harbor at San Francisco presaged an American mercantile empire in the Pacific. In this sense the naval scientist possessed a "Pacific consciousness" long before Seward, the first great apostle of that doctrine. Wilkes's *Narrative*, although printed in limited number and written in a turgid style, made him a prophet. Not only in his belief that Oregon, California, and Hawaii would eventually fall under the dominion of the United States did he foresee future developments; he also predicted that San Francisco Bay and the Juan de

Fuca Strait possessed "everything to make them increase, and keep up an intercourse with the whole of Polynesia, as well as the countries of South America on the one side, and China, the Philippines, New Holland, and New Zealand on the other." From these sites would come "materials for a beneficial exchange of products and an intercourse that must, in time, become immense, while this western coast," he predicted, "is evidently destined to fill a large space in the world's future history."

While not a first-rate naval officer, nor, for that matter, a maker of American diplomacy in the same sense as Adams, Polk, or Seward, Wilkes certainly qualifies as a builder. Indeed, throughout his career he directed his primary interest toward progress in naval science and other utilitarian ends. His work in the fields of hydrography, geodesy, and meteorology augmented the safety of vessels traversing oceanic routes; his compilation of charts and surveys completed during the expedition facilitated coastal and international commerce; and his maps of California and the Oregon Territory increased the confidence of Americans migrating westward during the late 1840s and 1850s. Wilkes's career suggests, finally, that while the pseudoscience of Social Darwinism contributed heavily to the distinctiveness of the new Manifest Destiny of the 1890s (and to the *raison d'être* of the naval aristocracy), a genuine scientific concern formed a major component of mid-nineteenth-century expansionism.

BIBLIOGRAPHIC NOTE

Like many of his naval contemporaries, Charles Wilkes left scattered records pertaining to his life, which have come to rest in depositories across the United States and in several other countries. Surprisingly, there is only one full-scale biography of this controversial navalist: Daniel Henderson's *The Hidden Coasts: A Biography of Admiral Charles Wilkes* (New York, 1953), a volume that should be retitled "an essay in hagiography." Satisfactory in few areas, its unyielding tone of admiration leaves the impression that Wilkes still awaits his biographer. Wilkes's personal "Autobiography" in the Wilkes papers in the Library of Congress, the major source of primary materials concerning his career, reveals his driving ambition, egotism, and atrocious penmanship. Fortunately, a substantial portion of the manuscript is in typescript.

Turgid and overwritten, yet exhibiting its author's scientific and diplomatic interests, Wilkes's *Narrative of the United States Exploring Expedition during the Years 1838, 1839, 1840, 1841, 1842,* 5 vols. (Philadel-

phia, 1845), also indicates the ethnocentrism that colored his world view.
The only scholarly synthesis of the exploration is David B. Tyler's *The
Wilkes Expedition: The First United States Exploring Expedition (1838–
1842)* (Philadelphia, 1968), a solid study whose narrow focus nevertheless
ignores broad implications of the voyage. An important dissertation
suggesting the difficulty in Wilkes's attempt to reconcile his scientific
interests with political necessities, John E. Wickman's "Political Aspects of
Charles Wilkes' Work and Testimony, 1842–1849," Indiana University,
1964, also assesses the vicissitudes of John Tyler's Whig administration.
These sources may be supplemented by Record Group 37 (M-75), a
collection of twenty-five rolls of microfilm in the National Archives,
containing "Records Relating to the U.S. Exploring Expedition under the
Command of Lt. Charles Wilkes, 1836–1842," and a series of articles
marking the centennial commemoration by the American Philosophical
Society of that voyage. The latter are contained in the Philosophical
Society's *Proceedings* 82 (June 1940).

Contemporary accounts of the expedition include "The Exploring
Expedition," *North American Review* 56 (April 1843), 258–70; "The United
States Exploring Expedition," *North American Review* 61 (July 1845),
54–107; and "The Wilkes Exploring Expedition," *Edinburgh Review* 83
(April 1846), 431–52. Louis N. Feipel, meanwhile, reviews "The Wilkes
Exploring Expedition, Its Progress through Half a Century, 1826–1876," in
United States Naval Institute Proceedings 40 (September–October 1914),
1323–50; and Daniel C. Haskell summarizes the literature resulting from
the voyage in *The United States Exploring Expedition, 1838–1842, and its
Publications, 1844–1874: A Bibliography* (New York, 1942).

Several authors assess the developing relationship between science
and naval exploration during the 1840s W. Patrick Strauss, "Preparing the
Wilkes Expedition: A Study in Disorganization," *Pacific Historical Review*
28 (1959), 221–32, traces the comedy of errors that preceded the voyage.
George H. Daniels, *Science in American Society: A Social History* (New
York, 1971), A. Hunter Dupree, *Science in the Federal Government: A
History of Policies and Activities to 1940* (Cambridge, Mass., 1957), and
Dupree, *Asa Gray, 1810–1888* (Cambridge, Mass., 1959), analyze the
scientific, social, and political milieu in which the Wilkes expedition
occurred. Edward L. Towle stresses the nexus between scientific and
commercial objectives in naval planning in "Science, Commerce, and the
Navy on the Seafaring Frontier (1842–1861): The Role of Lieutenant M. F.
Maury and the U.S. Naval Hydrographic Office in Naval Exploration,
Commercial Expansion, and Oceanography before the Civil War," Ph.D.
dissertation, University of Rochester, 1966. Three studies that elaborate
upon themes related to the Wilkes expedition include John P. Harrison,
"Science and Politics: Origins and Objectives of Mid-Nineteenth Century
Government Expeditions to Latin America," *Hispanic American Historical*

Review 35 (1955), 175–202; A. Hunter Dupree, "Science vs. the Military: Dr. James Morrow and the Perry Expedition," *Pacific Historical Review* 17 (1953), 29–37; and William H. Goetzmann, *Army Exploration in the American West, 1803–1863* (New Haven, 1959). See also the same author's *Exploration and Empire: The Explorer and the Scientist in the Winning of the American West* (New York, 1966), especially chapter 7.

For accounts of the expedition's work in Pacific waters, readers may consult W. Patrick Strauss, "Pioneer American Diplomats in Polynesia, 1820–1840," *Pacific Historical Review* 31 (1962), 21–30, an article distilled from the same author's "Early American Interest and Activities in Polynesia, 1783–1842," Ph.D. dissertation, Columbia University, 1958. In *The American Frontier in Hawaii: The Pioneers, 1789–1843* (Stanford, 1942), Harold W. Bradley discusses Wilkes's Hawaiian visit against a background of threatening French and British interests.

The importance of maritime and commercial considerations in the expansionism of the 1840s is emphasized in Norman A. Graebner, *Empire on the Pacific: A Study in American Continental Expansion* (New York, 1955); and Richard W. Van Alstyne, *The Rising American Empire* (New York, 1960). Frederick Merk's *The Oregon Question: Essays in Anglo-American Diplomacy and Politics* (Cambridge, Mass., 1967) incorporates many of the author's previously published essays. An early study of Wilkes's importance as a publicist of the strategic and commercial advantages of the waterways of the Oregon Territory and of San Francisco Bay is provided in Helen Ramage, "The Wilkes Exploring Expedition on the Pacific Slope, 1841," master's thesis, University of California, 1916; while Wilkes's confidential report on the Oregon Territory is contained in the *Congressional Record*, 62nd Cong., 1st sess., 15–20 July 1911, 47: 2977–85.

Wilkes's activities during the Civil War have been the subject of two critical studies; the more notable is William W. Jeffries, "The Civil War Career of Charles Wilkes," *Journal of Southern History* 11 (August 1945), 324–48, a distillation of his master's thesis, under the same title, at Vanderbilt University in 1936. Less analytical, though still useful, is John S. Long, "The Wayward Commander: A Study of the Civil War Career of Charles Wilkes," Ph.D. dissertation, University of California, Los Angeles, 1953. The tense relationship between Wilkes and the Navy Department during the war is clearly manifest in Edgar T. Welles, ed., *The Diary of Gideon Welles*, 3 vols. (Boston, 1911). For bibliographic references to the *Trent* affair and related issues, the reader may consult the essay in this volume by Gordon Warren. One book, however, in which the treatment of the incident is perceptive in terms of Wilkes's personal motives, is Jay Monaghan, *Diplomat in Carpet Slippers: Abraham Lincoln Deals with Foreign Affairs* (Indianapolis, 1945). A recent article suggesting a new departure in *Trent* historiography, F. C. Drake, "The Cuban Background of the *Trent Affair," Civil War History* 19 (March 1973), 29–49, emphasizes the role of the American consul in Havana, Robert W. Shufeldt, in events preceding the capture of Mason and Slidell.

Important assessments of the navy during Wilkes's lifetime include Peter Karsten's provocative *The Naval Aristocracy: The Golden Age of Annapolis and the Emergence of Modern American Navalism* (New York, 1972), a work that provides the first critical analysis of the affluent Episcopalian milieu that produced the initial generation of modern navalists—officers devoted to Anglo-American rapprochement, the protection of American commerce, and their own professional interests. By stressing Navy Secretary Dickerson's original justification for the Wilkes expedition—as a venture "promoting the great interests of commerce and navigation," with science "an object of great, but comparatively of secondary importance"—Karsten perhaps overemphasizes the primacy of economic motivation behind antebellum naval exploration; and he fails to stress the degree to which science had become a contentious political issue in the years between 1825 and 1836.

Harold D. Langley, *Social Reform in the United States Navy, 1798–1862* (Urbana, Ill., 1967), discusses reform in the pre–Civil War navy. The emergence of the "new navy" in the 1890s should not obscure the importance of earlier developments. See Robert Seager III, "Ten Years before Mahan: The Unofficial Case for the New Navy, 1880–1890," *Mississippi Valley Historical Review* 40 (December 1953), 491–512; Charles O. Paullin, "Beginnings of the United States Naval Academy," *United States Naval Institute Proceedings* 50 (February 1924), 173–94; Harold and Margaret Sprout, *The Rise of American Naval Power, 1776–1918* (Princeton, 1946); Daniel J. Carrison, *The Navy from Wood to Steel, 1860–1890* (New York, 1965); and Bern Anderson, *By Sea and by River: The Naval History of the Civil War* (New York, 1962).

For a critique of "traditional" approaches to diplomatic history, see Alexander DeConde, "What's Wrong with American Diplomatic History?" Society for Historians of American Foreign Relations *Newsletter* 1 (May 1970), 1–16.

JAMES K.
POLK

and the Rewards of Rashness

David M. Pletcher

Beyond doubt the one-term president who left the deepest
imprint on American foreign relations was James K. Polk. In four
years he brought the United States into and out of a major
diplomatic crisis with Great Britain and fought a war with Mexico
in which the United States did not lose a single major battle.
Following his instructions, American diplomats negotiated treaties
that added to the national domain the present-day states of
Washington, Oregon, California, Nevada, Utah, most of Arizona
and New Mexico, and parts of several others. Polk's agents also
completed the annexation of Texas, an action that his predecessor
John Tyler had initiated. Between 1845 and 1849, while Polk was

This essay is based on the author's *The Diplomacy of Annexation: Texas, Oregon,
and the Mexican War*, which was written with the assistance of Fulbright and
Social Science Research Council fellowships and research grants from Hamline and
Indiana Universities.

president, the United States established itself as a second-rank power, one that Europe had to consult or at least consider in any international matters affecting North America, Central America, or the Caribbean.

Despite his importance, historians have treated Polk with remarkable inconsistency. Since he was a narrowly partisan Democrat, it is not surprising that early studies of his administration were mostly party tracts. By the end of the nineteenth century, Clay, Calhoun, and Webster seemed to loom over him so far that J. T. Morse, Jr., failed to include him in his American Statesmen series; but when Theodore Roosevelt began to reassert executive leadership in foreign relations and Woodrow Wilson again drew public attention to Mexico's shortcomings, Polk's tribulations and achievements appeared more relevant than at any time since 1848. In 1919 Justin H. Smith defended the Mexican War in a two-volume history packed with footnotes, which won a Pulitzer Prize and immediately became a classic. After that time no student of America's middle period could ignore Polk. In the early 1960s a poll of historians ranked him eighth in importance among presidents—just below Theodore Roosevelt and above Harry S. Truman.

Polk's manner and personality were partly responsible for his long obscurity. At the age of forty-nine, when he became president (the youngest man until then to hold the office), he was short, spare in frame, with long, grizzled hair brushed back over his neck. His thin face with its high cheekbones and set jaw usually wore a sad expression, sometimes relieved by a stiff smile on his thin lips. The features everyone remembered were his deep-set, piercing gray eyes.

The personality beneath this drab exterior was introverted, intense, narrow, and almost entirely humorless. Self-disciplined and methodical, Polk seldom relaxed; for one period of thirteen months he hardly went outside the city limits of Washington. Some contemporaries thought him devious, for he kept his own counsel more than most other politicians of that easygoing period. A clear and forceful, if not especially inspiring, speaker, he had a sharp memory for names, faces, and interests and was a shrewd but overly suspicious judge of men. Toiling upward through the rough, semifrontier politics of Tennessee, he had hitched his career to Jacksonian Democracy. By 1842 that career seemed to have reached its limits after undistinguished service as Speaker of the U.S. House of Representatives and governor of his state. Then, through energy, careful organization, and good luck at the deadlocked convention of 1844, Polk slipped into the Democratic nomination for the presidency—but only after humbling himself with the promise that he would serve only one term in the White House. Although opponents and some of his own followers belittled him during the campaign, an expansionist program and wavering opposition gave him a narrow victory.

Once elected, Polk was determined to be the master of his own administration. About four months after his inauguration, he started a detailed diary of his actions and thoughts, a remarkably revealing record that clearly shows how he moved toward his goal. Having patterned his career and convictions after his patron, Andrew Jackson, he believed that the president, the only official representing all the people, should dominate the government. More than any other Jacksonian Democrat, he accepted the grinding labor this power involved and mastered the problems and techniques of every executive department. At the same time, however, he was careful to share with Congress the responsibility for every policy that might prove unpopular.

Polk's relations with his cabinet reflected this combination of decision and caution. First, he chose a reasonably able group of professional politicians whom he could control. His secretary of state, James Buchanan, had a reputation as an outspoken Anglophobe and, like Polk, was a shrewd, calculating political manipulator; but he was timid and indecisive in action. While Buchanan's arguments supplied a useful foil in cabinet discussions, his policies did not often prevail over those of the president. Secretary of the Treasury Robert J. Walker affected foreign relations mainly through his low-tariff program, which Polk supported. The only other cabinet member to play a major role in foreign policy decisions was Secretary of the Navy George Bancroft, the New England historian, an ardent Jacksonian and nationalist whose expansionist ambitions exceeded those of Buchanan.

Having chosen his cabinet, Polk exacted of each member the written pledge that he would not campaign for the presidency while in office. At biweekly meetings he sought each man's advice on most important matters, especially on questions of foreign policy, but he made up his own mind. He delegated power reluctantly and demanded frequent and full accountings; Buchanan, for example, called at the White House for consultation nearly every day, bringing the latest dispatches for Polk to examine. When the secretary began his instructions to diplomats with "The President wishes . . . ," he was telling the literal truth.

Polk brought to the conduct of foreign relations no special knowledge or talent. Indeed, he felt little but contempt for diplomatic protocol, especially because he spoke no foreign language.[1] As a nationalist from mid-America, he felt a strong xenophobia, unmitigated by any sophisticated, cosmopolitan appreciation of European culture or institutions. If he entered the White House with any model for relations with Britain or Mexico, it was the one supplied by Jackson in the 1830s: blunt defiance of France for delaying the payment of American claims and the conniving mission to Mexico of Anthony Butler, who sought to obtain the sale of Texas through bribery.

In the midst of the Oregon controversy Polk gave various associates a rationalization of his stern, unbending policy toward Britain, the traditional enemy. This view is most succinctly expressed in a diary account of a conversation with a minor congressman: "I remarked to him that the only way to treat John Bull was to look him straight in the eye; that I considered a bold & firm course on our part the pacific one; that if Congress faultered [sic] or hesitated in their course, John Bull would immediately become arrogant and more grasping in his demands; & that such had been the history of the Brittish [sic] Nation in all their contests with other Powers for the last two hundred years." As he wrote to another man, Britain always took advantage of any nation that approached it for a favor. Polk did not bother to compose a corresponding characterization of Mexico, his other adversary; but his public references to the government and people showed that he held them in contempt, as hardly worthy of nationality. Such feelings could produce only an aggressive policy of bluntness and bluff: Take a bold stand; negotiate from real or apparent strength; assume what you cannot prove; make no concessions that might be interpreted as weakness; and keep your opponent off balance. Ideas of mutual interest and compromise formed little part of his thinking.

1. On one occasion, while receiving a newly arrived diplomat, he delivered a quite acceptable reply without waiting to have the man's presentation speech translated. Later he wrote in his diary that he had guessed in advance what would probably be said.

◇◇◇

When Polk took office, he inherited from John Tyler two major problems of foreign policy, both concerning American territorial expansion. At Tyler's urging, Congress had passed a joint resolution authorizing annexation of the independent Republic of Texas. Most Texans favored annexation, but their government was unsure of its proper course. Agents of Britain and France urged it to remain independent, in order to counterbalance the United States in the international politics of North America; President Anson Jones leaned toward this policy. Mexico, which still claimed Texas as part of its domain even after nine years of *de facto* Texan independence, threatened the United States with war if it went through with annexation. As soon as Congress passed the joint resolution, the Mexican minister called for his passports and departed, thereby breaking diplomatic relations.[2]

An older controversy with Britain had been smoldering for years on the northwestern frontier. Both Britain and the United States claimed title to Oregon, a region between the Continental Divide and the Pacific coast, stretching from 42° of latitude (the northern boundary of California) to 54°40′ (the southern boundary of the Alaska panhandle) and including present-day Oregon, Washington, and British Columbia. Treaties of 1818 and 1827 had established joint occupancy of the disputed area, with provision for termination by either party after a year's notice. At first the Hudson's Bay Company dominated Oregon, but by 1845 several well-defined, self-governing American settlements faced the company's trading posts along the line of the Columbia River.

Pressed by Congress, Tyler and his secretary of state John C. Calhoun had opened exploratory negotiations concerning Oregon; but Calhoun, seeing the progress of American migration, favored what he called "masterly inactivity" and let the negotiations lapse. Meanwhile the British foreign secretary, the earl of Aberdeen, had come to the conclusion that the fairest solution to the question would probably be division by a line along 49°, reserving for Britain the whole of Vancouver Island.[3] Aberdeen

2. Tyler's minister to Mexico remained at his post for a time, but he had stopped communicating with the Mexican government after a quarrel, and Polk recalled him as soon as he became president.
3. Vancouver Island extended south of 49° for perhaps one-fourth of its length. The British wanted the whole island for access to the straits south of it, which were

had not determined how to convince his prime minister, Sir Robert Peel, and the rest of the cabinet or how to broach the compromise to the United States without damaging Britain's negotiating position.

In addition to these two western territorial questions, the American desire for Upper California was almost certain to affect foreign relations during Polk's term of office. California was undeniably Mexican territory, to which the United States had no shadow of a claim, but distance and political confusion prevented Mexico from asserting its rightful control. The people of California were a mixture of Mexicans, Indians, Europeans, and Americans; their government was virtually autonomous. Also, New England traders had established firm economic connections between the Pacific ports of California and the east coast of the United States. During the early 1840s a few of the American emigrants to Oregon were straying off into central California; before long they would be establishing independent settlements, as in Oregon. By 1845 the Mexican hold on California had virtually disappeared, and Americans wondered whether the British would intervene there as they were trying to do in Texas.

As Polk was about to assume the presidency, he faced the first decision of his foreign policy: what to say about Texas and Oregon in his inaugural address. He devoted considerable space to Texas, congratulating the country on its approaching annexation and warning foreign powers not to interfere in this purely American problem. He might have passed over Oregon with the remark that delicate negotiations were still pending; but the Democratic campaign platform of 1844 had mentioned the "clear and unquestionable" American title to the whole territory, and westerners expected him to speak out. He therefore declared: "Our title to the country of the Oregon is 'clear and unquestionable,' and already are our people preparing to perfect that title by occupying it with their wives and children. . . . The world beholds the peaceful triumphs of the industry of our emigrants. To us belongs the duty of protecting them adequately wherever they may be upon our soil. The jurisdiction of our laws and the benefits of our republican institutions should be extended over them in the

---

more easily navigable than those to the north and east. In 1845 the Hudson's Bay Company established its headquarters on the southern tip of the island.

distant regions which they have selected for their homes. The increased facilities of intercourse will easily bring the States, of which the formation in that part of our territory can not be long delayed, within the sphere of our federative Union. In the meantime every obligation imposed by treaty or conventional stipulation should be sacredly respected." Undoubtedly Polk hoped that these assurances would satisfy the West without arousing the British. In the long run, he was wrong on both counts.

After his inauguration, the new president bent his attention to the annexation of Texas. Thinking he would secure Mexican acquiescence, he sent a special diplomatic agent to approach the Mexican government unofficially for a renewal of relations, hinting at possible payment of an indemnity for Texas. Meanwhile, he sent other agents to Texas to join Chargé Andrew Jackson Donelson (nephew of Jackson and Polk's personal friend) in urging the Texan government to accept the terms of the joint resolution. British and French diplomatic agents were also exerting their influence in favor of reconciliation between Texas and Mexico, and the British agent even persuaded the Mexican government to grant Texas formal recognition as an inducement to refuse annexation; but their actions came too late. By May, Texan public opinion was overwhelmingly annexationist; in June and July, the Texan Congress and a special constitutional convention accepted the joint resolution and voted to enter the Union.

The successful campaign of Polk's diplomatic agents in Texas drew the United States measurably closer to war with Mexico. By then Texas was claiming the Rio Grande as its southern and western boundary, on rather dubious grounds; without carefully examining the Texan claim, Polk committed himself to its support. Mexican leaders would recognize neither annexation nor the Rio Grande boundary and threatened to send an army across the river against the Texan frontier. Having promised to protect the Texans, Polk dispatched a naval squadron along the coast, and in mild-June he moved several thousand troops under Zachary Taylor from the Louisiana border to Corpus Christi on the Nueces River, at the northern edge of the disputed zone, with permission to move south if Taylor wished. At the same time, for good measure, he also sent private orders to Commodore John D. Sloat, commander of the Pacific squadron, that if Mexico attacked Texas and war resulted, Sloat should seize the principal ports of California.

Some historians believe that at this point Polk was consciously plotting war with Mexico. To be sure, the commander of the squadron protecting the Texan coast, Commodore Robert F. Stockton, was an ultraexpansionist with powerful political support at home. From certain inconclusive letters of his, it appears that he considered a preventive seizure of Mexican territory south of the Rio Grande, and President Jones of Texas later declared that Stockton proposed provoking a war. Without written orders from Polk or some other equally clear evidence, however, the "plot thesis" rests on surmise. Secretary Bancroft's formal instructions to Stockton were defensive; so were Buchanan's to Donelson; and other factors suggest that at this time Polk neither desired nor expected war with Mexico.

Perhaps the best reason why Polk should have wanted to stabilize the border question was that Anglo-American relations had taken a turn for the worse during April and May, thanks to the blunt passage on Oregon in his inaugural address. British observers failed to notice that the president had carefully respected the sanctity of treaties and that, in proposing to extend legal protection to American settlers, he was only following the example of the British government and the Hudson's Bay Company. They focused instead on his assertion of the "clear and unquestionable" American title, and, smarting at the prospect of defeat in Texas, the British press hurled insults and threats at the overbearing, aggressive Americans, arrogant in words and feeble in deeds. When questions arose in Parliament, Aberdeen passed them off temperately, but Peel bristled and declared that Britain also had "clear and unquestionable" rights in Oregon. Naturally the American press seized these statements and returned them with interest.

Behind the scenes the British government began unobtrusively to check fortifications along the Canadian-American border and also Channel defenses, in case France supported the American cause. At the same time Aberdeen encouraged a few moderates to disparage the value of Oregon in the press and sent instructions to Richard Pakenham, the British minister at Washington, to seek American terms or propose arbitration of the Oregon question. In a private letter Aberdeen suggested that Pakenham draw from the Americans if possible an offer of the 49° line and Vancouver Island, with the right to navigate the Columbia River, so that he might open cabinet discussions in London. Buchanan discouraged talk of arbitration but delayed a further reply for several weeks.

At this point both parties blundered. When Buchanan finally gave Pakenham a formal reply on 12 July, he indeed proposed the 49° line, conceding to Britain all of Vancouver Island although not navigation of the Columbia; but (undoubtedly at Polk's behest) he set forth the ramshackle American claim to the whole area—up to 54°40'—in a manner that made the compromise offer appear to be a gracious American favor. Outraged, Pakenham replied with a strong statement of the British claim and, carried away by his own rhetoric, rejected Buchanan's offer out of hand instead of referring it to London, as he should have done. Polk recoiled, certain that the wily British had tricked him into showing his cards without ever intending to compromise. After brooding over the rejection for several weeks, he had Buchanan withdraw the offer altogether at the end of August and intimated that if the British wished to negotiate, they must assume the initiative with an offer of their own.

Thus, in the first six months of his administration, Polk had widened the breach with both Mexico and Britain and limited his freedom of action in each case. With a little more understanding of diplomacy, he might have realized that Pakenham's behavior had opened the possibility of putting Britain on the defensive by giving Aberdeen a chance to explain and excuse his minister's mistake. The situation called for a Talleyrand's probing pen; instead Polk had used an eraser. The impasse over Oregon continued through the autumn of 1845, for neither Polk nor Aberdeen would move to reopen negotiations for fear of losing face and bargaining leverage. When the American press and public learned of Polk's stand, western expansionists took heart, for the administration now seemed disposed to carry out the party plank of pushing the boundary to 54°40'.

Still, the Mexican issue, at least, did not seem beyond settlement, for Polk's special agent in Mexico City and the American consul there reported throughout the summer that although government and people were furious at the American annexation of Texas, lack of funds and the uncertain loyalty of the army would probably prevent hostilities. Both men thought that the government would receive a special American commissioner to discuss the Texas question (presumably with the idea of granting Mexico a disguised indemnity for its loss). Polk seems to have understood the limited nature of the Mexican concession, but he determined to appoint a full minister plenipotentiary and reestablish formal relations, ignoring the Texas question and hoping that the minister could persuade Mexico to sell California. For this mission he chose John Slidell of Louisiana, a rising young politician with good manners and knowledge of Spanish who had had no previous association with Mexican affairs.

Before Slidell departed in late November 1845, however, news from the Pacific coast suggested that the California question might require more direct action in addition to negotiation for purchase. In mid-October, Buchanan received an alarming dispatch from Thomas O. Larkin, an enterprising American merchant at Monterey whom Tyler had appointed part-time consul to represent American interests. Larkin warned that Britain was apparently preparing to dominate California, for a new British vice-consulate had just been established at Monterey, probably to operate in conjunction with the Hudson's Bay Company. Also, there were rumors that Mexico was sending out troops, paid for by British money, to reassert authority. Larkin's report was three months old, and its contents were exaggerated or downright wrong; but Polk and Buchanan had no way of knowing this.

Without giving up plans for the Slidell mission, Polk added strings to his bow. First he drew up instructions for Larkin to propagandize among the Californians for annexation to the United States and for resistance against any British effort to establish a protectorate, a strategy that Larkin himself had long favored. These instructions Polk sent out with Commodore Stockton in the frigate *Congress*; but since that ship would need several months for the long voyage around Cape Horn, Polk selected a young marine lieutenant, Archibald H. Gillespie, to memorize the instructions and carry them in his head to California by way of a shorter route through central Mexico. At this point the expansionist Senator Thomas Hart Benton of Missouri seems to have suggested that Gillespie should also carry coded orders and private letters to Benton's son-in-law, the army explorer Lieutenant John Charles Frémont, then conducting a reconnaissance in eastern California and Oregon.[4]

4. These orders and letters have never come to light. Reports of an earlier Frémont expedition had already publicized the far West. Some historians have regarded the

While Polk stood his ground in the Oregon controversy and drew up instructions for Slidell, Larkin, and Frémont, he was also composing his first annual message to Congress, one of the most important documents of his whole career. In that message Polk said nothing of his hopes and plans for California; but he described the measures he had taken to protect Texas against Mexican aggression, traced the long history of American damage claims against Mexico, and reported that he had sent Slidell to restore diplomatic relations and to obtain Mexican payment of these claims. (The claims had also figured prominently in Slidell's instructions.)[5]

Concerning Oregon, the president described Anglo-American negotiations under Tyler, which he had attempted to continue, and placed the whole blame for their rupture on Britain: "The civilized world will see in these proceedings a spirit of liberal concession on the part of the United States, and this Government will be relieved of all responsibility which may follow the failure to settle the controversy." He called on Congress to provide an armed guard for emigrants to Oregon and make them formal land grants there, and he further suggested that it would be appropriate to give Britain the prescribed year's warning to terminate the joint occupation treaty.

After his discussion of Oregon, Polk reaffirmed "the principle avowed by Mr. Monroe"—the first important invocation of the Monroe Doctrine since its original declaration in 1823. This passage has an interesting history. Apparently Polk intended something like it for his inaugural address but deleted it at the suggestion of some adviser. During the summer he was much irritated to read a statement by the French prime minister, François Guizot, that France must play an active role in North American affairs in order to preserve "l'équilibre des forces"—which the American press translated as "the balance of power," a term embodying to Americans all the decadent, deceitful ways of

---

1045 expedition as aggressively intended from the beginning and have suggested that the orders and letters told Frémont to foment revolution in California. Unless the missing papers are found, a final settlement of the question seems unlikely.

5. Most of these claims arose from damage to American property during Mexican revolutions or from arbitrary acts of the Mexican government. A mixed commission (1840–42) had awarded about two million dollars to American claimants, but the Mexican government had stopped payments.

monarchical Europe. Guizot had been referring to Texas, for France had little interest in California and none in Oregon. Polk, however, intended his declaration to reinforce his analysis of the Oregon question and probably also to warn Britain off California.

The purpose of Polk's annual message was twofold, as far as it concerned foreign relations. In it he sought to explain his policy toward Mexico and Britain as favorably as possible, to demonstrate that he was trying to preserve the peace, whatever the adversaries might do in the future. Also, in the case of Oregon, he called on Congress for prompt, decisive action that would show government and country to be united behind him. Britain, he hoped, would then be compelled to break the impasse at a disadvantage and offer new terms, which he could treat as he chose. What he really accomplished was to limit his actions further by revealing too much of his ambitions to the Mexicans and by making Congress his partner in determining policy toward Britain.

Under the political circumstances of the day it was unrealistic to expect prompt, decisive action from Congress. After the bitterly fought election of 1844, a Whig minority sought revenge against the victorious Democrats. What was more important, during the last phases of the Texas question, expansionism had become entangled in the coils of the abolitionist movement; and the resulting confusion of personal ambitions, partisan loyalties, and ideological convictions made it impossible to predict anyone's actions. Dangerous lines of cleavage ran through the Democratic party, separating a group of western expansionists who cried "Fifty-four Forty or Fight!" and a Southern bloc led by Calhoun, who had put his whole heart into the campaign for Texas but now favored delay and compromise in Oregon.

The debate began in December 1845, soon after the reading of the annual message, and dragged on until late April 1846. It was immediately apparent that the critical issue was abrogation of the joint occupation treaty, since this action would remove the only legal safeguard against war over some trivial local incident. Polk wanted a simple, noncommittal statement advising the president to give notice of abrogation; western Democrats, especially in the Senate, wanted to add a shout of rude defiance that would effectively prevent any diplomatic response from Britain; and moderates at first opposed any notice at all. By February, however, Whigs and antiwar Democrats in the House of Representatives managed to pass a mildly worded resolution of notice, virtually inviting Britain to resume negotiations but shifting full responsibility for them to the president. After weeks of thunderous debate, which stirred the country to its depths, the Senate finally accepted the House resolution, as Calhoun and his bloc recognized that some sort of notice was necessary. The innocuous wording infuriated western extremists, who foresaw a compromise settlement and suspected (probably with reason) that Polk had encouraged the moderates in the last weeks of the debate rather than have the Senate adjourn without acting.

Deprived of his demonstration of national unity, Polk made no progress in negotiations with Britain during the winter of 1845–46. Aberdeen was well aware of conciliatory sentiment in the United States through editorials in the antiwar eastern newspapers and roundabout correspondence between businessmen, Whigs, and other Anglo-American moderates. Indeed, the foreign secretary probably underestimated the force of western expansionism pressing on Polk. Since Peel and the rest of the British cabinet insisted on regarding Oregon as a point of honor, Aberdeen continued his campaign of downgrading the area in the press. At first he hoped that Polk might change his mind and either offer terms or accept arbitration. During March and April, however, he reconciled himself to waiting until Congress passed a resolution that would enable Britain to reopen negotiations without loss of face. Meanwhile he dropped hints that Britain might send naval reinforcements to Canada if pressed too hard. (These hints undoubtedly helped induce Polk to favor compromise in the Senate.) Anglo-American diplomatic communications during the impasse were admirably maintained by the two ministers, Louis McLane in London and Richard Pakenham in Washington, who made as much sense as anyone could out of the complex situation.

While Polk's plans for settling the Oregon dispute were going awry, American relations with Mexico were also worsening. Slidell arrived in Mexico City in early December and found nationalists livid at the prospect of selling more territory and a moderate government clinging feebly to power. The foreign minister, unhappy at Slidell's inopportune arrival, refused to receive him on the grounds that his credentials were those of a full minister plenipotentiary rather than a temporary commissioner.[6] At the end

6. This distinction, which seemed like hair-splitting to Polk, actually had some reasonable basis, for if Mexico accepted full renewal of relations before negotiat-

of the month the nationalists had their way in a revolution, and an army leader, General Mariano Paredes y Arrillaga, became president.[7]

Since Paredes hoped for an Anglo-American war over Oregon, he was naturally no more willing to receive Slidell than his predecessor; the continued rejection confronted Polk with a dilemma just as the Oregon debate was approaching its climax in Congress. Undismayed, he advanced his position and took another strong stand. First he ordered Taylor at Corpus Christi to move his forces across the disputed zone and occupy the north bank of the Rio Grande, avoiding any offensive action against the Mexicans. Then, at the end of January he sent Slidell a message that if Paredes would not see him, "nothing can remain but to take the redress of the injuries to our citizens and the insults to our Government into our own hands." Some historians have interpreted the strong language to mean that Polk never expected Slidell to succeed and that the mission was merely an excuse for military attack. At the same time, however, Polk wrote to his brother that Paredes had probably exaggerated his anti-Americanism in order to gain power and that the order to Taylor was merely "a precautionary measure." It is reasonable to believe that he hoped Slidell would sign a treaty but was prepared to increase the pressure if he did not.

During March and April 1846, Polk's relations with both Britain and Mexico reached a turning point. In Texas, after weeks of preparation, Taylor led his army to the bank of the Rio Grande, where the soldiers built a fort within cannon shot of a Mexican border city, Matamoros, and waited to see if the garrison commander there would send troops across the river to challenge them. In Mexico City, Slidell, after reading Buchanan's January instructions, sent a final request for reception, received another refusal, and prepared to leave for home. In London, the British government was clearly waiting for action in Congress on the Oregon question; and in Washington, the congressional debate

---

ing, it would have little chance of any indemnity or other concession in return for the loss of Texas.

7. Slidell reported rumors that Paredes's party intended to establish a Spanish prince on a Mexican throne with British aid. This report was true, except that Spain was actually the instigator. The intrigue lasted from mid-1845 until the first American victories in May 1846.

was splitting the Democratic party and threatening Polk's whole legislative program. (At the beginning of May he told the Speaker of the House that if Congress tried to adjourn prematurely, he would forbid the action and force a showdown.)

Hitherto Polk had regarded war with Mexico as an unlikely possibility. At some time during April 1846, however, he seems to have concluded that a short, limited conflict on the Rio Grande might be the best way to reunite his party and perhaps also to impress Britain while bringing Mexico to terms. During this period he learned of Slidell's final rejection. On 7 April he discussed the whole matter with the cabinet, which agreed that he should send a message to Congress recommending that the United States take matters into its own hands; but he delayed action, first waiting for the end of the Oregon debate, then for Slidell's return to Washington, and finally for some sort of Mexican attack that would arouse congressional patriotism.

The crisis came during the weekend beginning 8 May. On Friday morning Slidell arrived in Washington from Mexico. After talking with him, Polk decided that he must appeal to Congress for action; but on Saturday morning he and the cabinet decided to wait several days longer, hoping for further news from the Rio Grande. Four hours later the adjutant general called at the White House with a dispatch in which Taylor reported that Mexican troops had ambushed one of his reconnaissance parties north of the river, killing or capturing most of its members. Taylor remarked laconically, "Hostilities may now be considered as commenced." Polk agreed; he spent most of Sunday composing a war message, and on Monday morning he sent it to Congress.

A cynic might have guessed that the message had been written on a Sunday, for it combined the self-righteous wrath of the Old Testament with the long suffering patience of the New. Polk emphasized the "liberal and honorable" terms, the "fair and equitable" principles, that the United States had displayed toward Mexico. He recited American claims and other grievances and elaborately justified Taylor's presence on the Rio Grande. At the end he drew together the strands of his indictment in words that were to serve as the text for a general debate lasting through the whole war: "The cup of forbearance had been exhausted even before the recent information from the frontier of the Del Norte [Rio Grande]. But now, after reiterated menaces, Mexico has passed the boundary of the United States, has invaded our territory and shed American blood upon the American soil. She has proclaimed that hostilities have commenced, and that the two nations are now at war. As war exists, and, notwithstanding all our efforts to avoid it, exists by the act of Mexico herself, we are called upon by every consideration of duty and patriotism to vindicate with decision the honor, the rights, and the interests of our country."

Congress received these stirring words with mixed feelings. Nearly everyone recognized the danger to Taylor's men and favored voting reinforcements and supplies, but the Whigs and Calhoun's bloc of Democrats opposed a formal declaration of war or any statement blaming hostilities on Mexico until they could investigate the circumstances surrounding Taylor's advance and the ambush. Without much difficulty administration forces in the House rushed through the desired war bill. When Calhoun and the Whigs sought delay in the Senate, Polk's supporters outmaneuvered them at every point, and the president pressured Thomas Hart Benton, a key figure, to swallow his doubts. In the end the Senate, too, passed the war bill by an impressive margin, but many Whigs voted for it unwillingly, lest their party incur the stigma of disloyalty to the flag and go to pieces as the Federalist party had done during the War of 1812.

For several months Polk's plans succeeded as never before. On the Rio Grande, Taylor put his troops out of danger by defeating a larger Mexican army in two battles, Palo Alto and Resaca de la Palma. Then he occupied Matamoros and, after receiving reinforcements, moved slowly up the Rio Grande and into northern Mexico. While he was doing this, Americans were carrying through the occupation of California. When Larkin received his new instructions from Lieutenant Gillespie, he set out quietly to propagandize among the inhabitants; but the explorer John Charles Frémont, in the interior, determined on more drastic action. After talking to Gillespie, he marched his band of explorers to a settlement of newly arrived American emigrants near the site of modern Sacramento; within a few days he had assumed the leadership of an independence movement, to found the so-called Bear Flag Republic. At this point Commodore Sloat of the Pacific squadron received news that war had broken out. Moving his ships to Monterey, he cautiously consulted Larkin, and then, seeing the success of the Bear Flag revolt, he occupied Monterey and the bay area. A little later Stockton and the *Congress* arrived;

Polk sent troops overland; and the combined American forces, regular and irregular, completed the occupation.

Meanwhile the United States and Britain were solving the Oregon problem. By early May the conciliatory wording of the congressional resolution on Oregon had made it possible for Aberdeen to renew negotiations. First, the foreign secretary persuaded the rest of the British cabinet to approve the offer of compromise terms—apparently after considerable argument, although no record of the proceedings has been found. Then he proposed to McLane a treaty dividing the disputed territory at 49°, with Vancouver Island reserved to Britain and navigation rights on the Columbia River to the Hudson's Bay Company. When Polk learned of these terms, he balked at the navigation rights but eventually agreed to submit the whole matter to the Senate. Buchanan and Pakenham quickly prepared a treaty, and on 18 June the Senate approved it by a vote of forty-one to fourteen.[8] While the coming of the war undoubtedly made both Polk and Congress more eager for a settlement, it does not seem to have played an important role in forming British policy. During June and July, Britain and the United States further improved their relations by lowering tariffs and thereby increasing their trade.

Success on the Rio Grande, in California, and in Oregon undoubtedly led Polk to expect a short war with Mexico and a quick treaty confirming the annexation of California and some connecting territory. The Mexicans, however, showed unexpected stubbornness and powers of resistance, favored by their formidable geography: a belt of semidesert in the north, mountain ranges in the center, and the fever-ridden Gulf coast. Polk put out peace feelers to Antonio López de Santa Anna, perennial president of Mexico but then exiled in Havana, who had already sent an intermediary to encourage Polk's aggressive policy and offer his help. Santa Anna hinted that he would negotitate if back in power. Polk granted him free passage through the American blockade. Meanwhile he had Buchanan write the government at Mexico City suggesting negotiations. Nothing came of either venture. The government bluntly refused to discuss terms, and when the

---

8. The treaty granted navigation rights to the Hudson's Bay Company and to those trading with it but specified that these must be entirely subject to United States law on the same basis as the rights of American citizens.

returned Santa Anna gathered his supporters and seized power, he ignored his assurances to Polk. Instead, he issued a call for troops and organized the defense against the Americans. Meanwhile Taylor had advanced beyond the Rio Grande and captured the city of Monterrey, only to see its defenders retreat into the dry lands to the south.

Polk resented these frustrations all the more because several forces were pressing him to make an early end to the war. One was the British government, which had discreetly inquired more than once about the possibility of mediation, an expedient that Polk firmly rejected. More important, the Whig opposition was gaining support for its antiwar campaign in all parts of the country and especially among Northern abolitionists, who were convinced that Polk, a Tennesseean, had started the war to obtain more slaveholding territory. (The fact that Calhoun also opposed the war impressed few abolitionists. By then they thoroughly distrusted him.) Just before Congress adjourned, Polk sought a special appropriation of two million dollars, in order that he might make a cash offer to Santa Anna if the Mexican leader showed any disposition to treat for peace. Abolitionists attached to the bill an amendment (the famous Wilmot Proviso) forbidding slavery in any territory acquired from Mexico, and the resulting debate widened the sectional split. Even though Polk finally obtained his money at the following session of Congress, his opponents had gained an issue and a useful device for harassment.

By the end of 1846, Polk had to choose between alternative strategies for fighting the war and obtaining a peace. One was to occupy all of northern Mexico as far south as Tampico and San Luis Potosí, establish a line of forts, and wait until the Mexicans gave up. The other was to seize Tampico and Veracruz, the principal Gulf ports, send an army west from Veracruz along the old Spanish road through the mountains, and if necessary occupy the central Valley of Mexico and the capital city. The first plan was obviously within American capabilities, for small detached forces had already marched almost at will through New Mexico and Chihuahua. It was the safer and less expensive of the two strategies; but it called for patience from the dynamic American people, already restive at the duration of the war. The second plan was much riskier, for it required a landing and long supply lines of a kind the American army had never before attempted. One lost battle might stimulate the Mexicans to hold out indefinitely, and a

MEDIATION AND PACIFICATION.

series of victories would surely arouse the American appetite for territory. Buchanan and most other moderates favored the defense line. Slidell, Benton (who now ardently supported the war), and other activists called for a central invasion.

For several months Polk postponed a final decision, although in November 1846, he authorized the army to make plans for the capture of Veracruz. (Tampico was occupied without Mexican resistance at the same time.) Meanwhile the president sent special agents into Mexico to inquire about the possibility of peace. In January 1847, a ray of hope appeared, for an emissary arrived at Washington to inquire about American terms, armed with letters from Santa Anna and other Mexican officials. Even today it is impossible to establish the genuineness of this demarche, but Polk must have felt that he had nothing to lose by exploration and sent the agent back to Mexico with a formal proposal for negotiations. The proposal never reached Santa Anna, who was in the north with his army. Instead, the acting government in Mexico City returned a demand to Polk that the Americans withdraw all forces from Mexican territory before negotiations would be considered. Furious at what he considered Mexican trickery, Polk committed himself to an invasion of central Mexico.

This invasion was entrusted to General Winfield Scott, the ranking officer in the army and an excellent choice. Polk suspected Scott's Whiggish political ambitions, but Taylor was a Whig, too—more popular and harder to control. Even after planning for the occupation of Veracruz had begun, Taylor advanced beyond Monterrey against orders and fought a largely useless battle at Buena Vista against Santa Anna, sending the Mexicans on a long retreat to Mexico City. There political conditions had degenerated into virtual civil war; but by a great effort of will, Santa Anna reorganized his battered forces and led them out toward the Gulf coast. By then Scott had landed about twelve thousand troops, bombarded Veracruz, and forced the city's surrender, so Santa Anna took up a strong position in a mountain pass, hoping to thrust the Americans back onto the fever-ridden coastal plain. In the most spectacular victory of the whole war, at Cerro Gordo, Scott managed to outflank the Mexicans and drove them back in disorder; then he occupied the large upland city of Puebla. Beaten for the second time in less than two months, Santa Anna limped back to Mexico City.

Since neither army had enough strength for further fighting, the war again entered a phase of inaction, and Polk decided on another peace feeler. This time he chose an orthodox, if minor, diplomat: Nicholas P. Trist, chief clerk (and de facto undersecretary) of the State Department. Trist was a protégé of Buchanan's, a certified Democrat (his wife was Jefferson's granddaughter), and a onetime consul at Havana who spoke fluent Spanish and knew Latin American ways. Trist's instructions concerned the territory to be demanded of Mexico and represented a compromise between expansionists such as Benton and moderates such as Buchanan. Trist was to obtain at least a boundary line up the Rio Grande and across southern New Mexico at about 32° to San Diego on the coast. For this he was to offer fifteen million dollars; but if Mexico would also cede Lower California or other territory, he might raise the price.

After an initial period of jealous bickering, Trist and Scott formed an effective team and tried every conceivable expedient, straightforward or devious, to bring the Mexicans to terms. First, they established a secure line of communications to the Mexican government through the British minister at Mexico City, who was eager to end the fighting. Then, at a hint from Santa Anna, they sent him a "sweetener" of ten thousand dollars and promised immediate payment of one million dollars upon signature of a treaty. When Santa Anna seemed to lose his nerve, Scott led his forces into the Valley of Mexico, defeated the Mexicans in two more battles (Contreras and Churubusco), and encamped just outside Mexico City. Trist then met a commission of Mexicans to discuss terms; but Santa Anna, torn between factions, rejected them. Finally, Scott, seeing no alternative, attacked Mexico City itself, drove out the government, and prepared for indefinite occupation. Santa Anna, thoroughly discredited, resigned and headed for exile again, while the Mexican Congress and the ranking civilian leaders straggled off to a provincial capital to reorganize. The war had reached another impasse.

Back in the United States the news of successive victories and continued Mexican resistance was having a predictable effect on the impatient American public. Opponents of the war continued to cite mounting casualty lists and appropriations, but they faced the arguments of a newly active group of ultraexpansionists, North and South, who proclaimed that the long war and its unexpectedly heavy expenses justified the United States' demand for more territory—even the annexation of all Mexico: "As we shall have no peace until she be annexed, let it come, even though force be necessary, at first, to bring her. Like the Sabine virgins, she will soon learn to love her ravisher." Opponents deplored such ruthless conquest as degrading to the American character and predicted that the "mongrel" Mexican people would corrupt American democracy. Expansionists replied with "Manifest Destiny"—God had provided an opportunity for the United States to regenerate Mexico.

Having undoubtedly learned a few lessons about expansionists during the Oregon debates, Polk reacted to the all-Mexico movement with caution. His cabinet discussions during 1847 show that he was not unalterably opposed to acquiring territory south of the Rio Grande and 32°; but with every Democratic politician jockeying for position in the presidential race of the following year, he did not want to sacrifice control of his party by committing himself prematurely. At first he preferred to leave negotiations to Trist, although the envoy's quarreling with Scott had much displeased him. When Polk learned of the futile dickering at Mexico City, however, he decided to take another strong stand and ordered Trist to abandon his efforts and come home. If the Mexicans decided to discuss terms, they could send a representative to Washington.

By the time this order reached Trist, in mid-November, the situation in Mexico had greatly changed, to the American advantage. The civilian government that had succeeded Santa Anna was moderate and favored negotiation. Although extremists to both right and left invoked patriotism to continue the war, the government gradually brought them under control. When Trist's recall order arrived, he feared that the promising opening for negotiations, if not exploited, might disappear and that Scott's troops would have to occupy central Mexico indefinitely, surrounded by an increasingly hostile population and fighting off guerrilla bands. After several days of hesitation, urged by many American army officers, friendly Mexicans, and Europeans, Trist decided to disobey his orders and stay. Even after that decision, he had to wait two more months for a settlement, since the Mexican commissioners were disposed to argue every point at issue. Finally, on 2 February 1848, they signed the Treaty of Guadalupe Hidalgo, carrying out the most important of Trist's instructions.

Through it the United States obtained Upper California and New Mexico in return for fifteen million dollars.[9]

Trist's courageous insubordination rescued the president from the impossible task of reconciling American and Mexican ultranationalists. The news of the treaty arrived just at the height of the all-Mexico movement, and Polk lost little time in submitting it to the Senate. Whatever his feelings about additional annexations, he could not deny that Trist had achieved the original goals of the war, and he had some idea of the dangers to be incurred in continuing it. Except for ultraexpansionists, the country received the treaty with a collective sigh of relief, and when the Senate had taken time to consider the alternatives, it approved nearly all the terms by a vote of thirty-eight to fourteen. The Mexicans accepted its few revisions without difficulty, and the American troops were soon on their way home. The president, however, never forgave Trist for disobeying orders and for a number of tactless comments in his dispatches about presidential actions and policies. He stopped the envoy's salary at the point of his recall, and Trist had to wait over twenty years for full payment—or, indeed, for any other recognition of his accomplishment.

During the last year of his administration Polk briefly considered other ways of acquiring territory on which he mistakenly suspected British designs. It was probably fortunate for the United States that this reconnaissance led to no action, for the southwestern annexations and the sectional arguments they aroused strained the national institutions to their limit. Soon after the war ended, the rebellious Mexican province of Yucatán sought an American protectorate and intervention in a destructive local Indian war. Polk submitted the proposal to Congress, which could not agree on what to do and dismissed the matter. During the summer of 1848 Polk instructed his minister to Spain, Romulus M. Saunders, to explore the possibility of purchasing Cuba, recently racked by rebellion. Saunders, however, bungled the job, and a trial vote in the Senate indicated that Congress would probably have rejected a purchase treaty anyway.

Farther south, in Central America, the influence of Britain was

9. The boundary west of the Rio Grande was drawn along the Gila River to its junction with the Colorado and thence straight to a point on the coast just south of San Diego, which was a bone of contention during the negotiations. The United States also agreed to pay $3.25 million of American claims against Mexico.

more overt; but the Polk administration had little success in countering it. To offset the longtime British consul and chargé d'affaires Frederick Chatfield, Polk sent Elijah Hise as chargé with instructions to encourage the reunion of the weak, feuding Central American states, negotiate commercial treaties, and report on British encroachments. Hise signed two commercial treaties and exceeded his instructions in contracting for perpetual canal rights across Nicaragua, but this treaty was never ratified. The succeeding Whig administration of Zachary Taylor made use of the new prestige the United States enjoyed in the Caribbean after the Mexican War; in 1850 it signed the Clayton-Bulwer Treaty with Britain, thereby somewhat stabilizing the situation in Central America on a basis of Anglo-American equality.

A final act of expansionism by the Polk administration was the treaty of 12 December 1846 with New Granada (Colombia), in which the United States assumed certain responsibilities regarding the Isthmus of Panama. In 1903 Theodore Roosevelt was to use this commitment to justify his intervention and "seizure" of the Canal Zone. The treaty of 1846, however, owed little to Polk's direction. Buchanan had instructed the American chargé d'affaires at Bogotá, Benjamin A. Bidlack, that he should negotiate a commercial treaty and guard against any European effort to obtain sole transit rights across the isthmus. After much pressure from the New Granadan government, Bidlack included in the treaty as Article 35 a long statement in which New Granada guaranteed to the United States that the isthmus would always be open and free to Americans. In return, the United States guaranteed the neutrality of the isthmus and New Granada's sovereignty over it.

When the cabinet saw these provisions, its members remarked doubtfully that the American guarantees seemed to violate the country's tradition against entangling alliances; but Polk submitted Bidlack's Treaty to the Senate. Busy with the Mexican War, that body delayed action for over a year, while New Granada kept a special envoy in Washington to lobby for the treaty. Finally, in June 1848, it was approved with almost no discussion. In this casual manner the United States laid one of the legalistic cornerstones of its future Caribbean policy.

How may one fairly appraise the expansionist policies that Polk followed toward Britain and Mexico? First, it seems clear that he placed too great reliance on bold talk and too little confidence in the possibility of compromise. Suspicious by nature, he was inclined to view each offer by his opponents as a trap or an attempt to exploit American good nature and weakness. Although anxious to negotiate from an appearance of strength, he did not seem to think it necessary to realize that strength by building up the army and navy. As a result, he slipped into the dangerous practice of bluffing. Perhaps he did not appreciate how little respect American military forces inspired abroad; the navy had been in decline since 1815, and the army had struggled to eke out victory over the Seminole Indians in Florida during the early 1840s. More likely he counted on distance, trade, and the vulnerability of Canada to deter Britain from action and despised the Mexicans as strutting boasters, weak and disorganized.

Secondly, beyond these basic attitudes, much of Polk's foreign policy was improvised from month to month in response to events. The statement on Oregon in his inaugural address was a pacifier to the West; Buchanan's offer to Britain, an attempt to draw the fangs of British criticis; and the withdrawal of that offer, a startled and indignant reflex. Similarly, in dealing with Mexico, Polk sought to renew relations in the hope of keeping peace during the annexation of Texas; but as soon as he realized the confusion of affairs in Mexico City, he advanced his goals to the purchase of California. During his first year in office, he regarded war with either adversary as an unlikely last resort. Indeed, he never showed much real concern over Anglo-American hostilities; but in March and April 1846, changed circumstances, especially divisions at home, led him to favor a short tactical war with Mexico. As that war lengthened, he made other political and military decisions required by events.

Thirdly, Polk's largely improvised policies suffered from the phenomenon that twentieth-century analysts have called "escalation." This is a process by which an initial set of decisions starts a chain of causes and effects, each more difficult to control than its predecessor, each widening the area of action and requiring increased forces and money. On inauguration day Polk had a fairly wide range of acceptable policies from which to choose. Some of his early actions and the pressure of circumstances gradually reduced this range. Eventually, when Scott captured Mexico City, Polk found himself boxed in, unable to move, for ultraexpansionists at home would not let him withdraw from central Mexico to a defensive line, and he lacked the resources or the desire to extend the conquest over the whole country. Inaction, too, posed grave problems, for a few small guerrilla victories might have revived the Mexicans' morale and enable them to cut Scott's long supply lines and isolate him in Mexico City.

Finally, one is forced to conclude that Polk's policies were much more hazardous than he realized, thanks to his overbold improvising, the phenomenon of escalation, and the small forces that the United States deployed in the field. Even assuming that Britain had no desire to fight its best customer, Polk could not be certain that a sense of honor over some uncontrollable local conflict in Oregon would not precipitate a general Anglo-American war. Mexico sent a series of appeals to Britain for aid, at one point offering in disguise the cession of California; but fortunately Mexico's revolutions and financial recklessness had so damaged its reputation that the British government showed little interest. Nevertheless, there seems slight doubt that a Mexican victory over Taylor on the Rio Grande would have facilitated a private loan from British bankers. A military stalemate would probably have led to British mediation, and the United States might have had to abandon its hopes for California indefinitely. Fortunately Taylor prevented a stalemate at the outset; but even after more than a year of American victories and Scott's capture of Mexico City, there arose the prospect of an extended occupation—a grave prospect, as we now know, in view of the sectionalism and discord within Polk's United States, not to mention the disastrous French Intervention of the 1860s.[10]

Assuming that Polk was taking long chances as the leader of a tumultuous people and a little-tried army, could he have reduced

10. Between 1861 and 1867 French troops of Napoleon III defeated the Mexican armies of Benito Juárez, occupied most of central Mexico, and tried to establish a puppet empire under Archduke Maximilian of Austria. Juárez had to retreat into far northern Mexico, but his sympathizers kept up constant guerrilla warfare which gradually wore down French strength and made the venture dismayingly expensive. Since the United States would not recognize the puppet empire and European complications demanded attention, Napoleon finally had to withdraw his troops. Juárez retook Mexico City and had Maximilian executed.

these chances through some other line of action? An arguable alternative to bold tactics against either Britain or Mexico was the policy that Calhoun had recommended for Oregon: "masterly inactivity." This policy rested on two assumptions: the continuous, irresistible force of American western migration and the chronic involvement of most of Europe's strength in Old World affairs. At his inauguration, Polk might have refused direct comment on Oregon, while canvassing with Britain the possibilities of a negotiated settlement and carrying through the annexation of Texas. Having offered a compromise line at 49°, Polk should have waited for a formal reply from Aberdeen. If an agreement had been reached during 1845, Polk might have announced it in his annual message, forestalling western resentment with a *fait accompli*; if not, he could still have fallen back on the westerners' arguments.

In any case, Polk should not have proceeded against Mexico before settling the Oregon controversy. There was no need for haste; posting Taylor at Corpus Christi, in the western edge of effective Texan settlement, would have provided sufficient protection with a minimum of provocation to Mexico. As for California, careful analysis of British policy in Europe and the Western Hemisphere should have reassured Polk that Britain had few designs on that prize. Why not allow American settlers to occupy the province, keep American warships cruising off the coast, and see whether or not the Californians would repeat the history of Texas? During some later European crisis (such as the revolutions of 1848 or the Crimean War of the mid-1850s), the United States would have been free to open negotiations with an independent Californian government, which by then might have observed the prosperity of Oregon under American rule.

Perhaps war might have been avoided altogether. At worst, it would have been postponed until a more favorable moment, and, with the United States already occupying Texas and California, any fighting would have been defensive and limited to border areas. Mexicans, of course, would have resented the loss of California under any circumstances, but they had no means of retaining it, and this course would have spared them the humiliation of a foreign army in their capital. Most important to the United States, a policy of more gradual, peaceful expansion would undoubtedly have avoided many of the bitter debates in Congress and the press that widened the alarming gap between North and South.

No one can develop with certainty an argument from "contingent history." Nevertheless, a brief, cautious consideration of Polk's alternatives suggests that his policies, though brilliantly successful, risked too much and aroused hatred and division that gradualism might have minimized. Too impatient to allow time for American migration to take effect, Polk also assigned too small a role to diplomacy—until the last stage of each controversy, when Louis McLane ended the British crisis and Nicholas P. Trist the Mexican War by negotiation.

BIBLIOGRAPHIC NOTE

The principal manuscript sources on which this essay is based are the official foreign affairs archives of the United States, Great Britain, France, Spain, and Mexico; and the private papers of the policy makers involved. The most important private collections are those of James K. Polk, James Buchanan, George Bancroft, Louis McLane, Nicholas P. Trist, Sir Robert Peel, the earl of Aberdeen, and Valentín Gómez Farías.

Among published collections of documents the most important are two sets edited by William R. Manning: vol. 3 of *Diplomatic Correspondence of the United States: Canadian Relations, 1784–1860*, 4 vols. (Washington, D.C., 1940–45), and *Diplomatic Correspondence of the United States: Inter-American Affairs, 1831–1860*, 12 vols. (Washington, D.C., 1932–39), especially vols. 7, 8, and 12. Also useful for the last stages of Texan annexation are George Pierce Garrison, ed., *Diplomatic Correspondence of the Republic of Texas*, Annual Report of the American Historical Association for the Years 1907, 1908, 3 vols. (Washington, D.C., 1908–11); Ephraim Douglass Adams, ed., *British Diplomatic Correspondence Concerning the Republic of Texas, 1838–1846* (Austin, n.d.); and C. T. Neu, "The Annexation of Texas," *New Spain and the Anglo-American West: Historical Contributions Presented to Herbert Eugene Bolton*, 2 vols. (Los Angeles, 1932), 2:71–102. Many valuable documents concerning the negotiation of the Oregon treaty, the Mexican peace treaty, and the New Granadan treaty of 1846, as well as the texts of the treaties, are contained in vol. 5 of David Hunter Miller, ed., *Treaties and Other International Acts of the United States of America*, 8 vols. (Washington, D.C., 1931–48).

Tyler's and Polk's messages to Congress and Polk's inaugural address may be found in vol. 4 of James D. Richardson, ed., *A Compilation of the Messages and Papers of the Presidents, 1789–1897*, 10 vols. (Washington, D.C., 1896–99). Congressional debates are reported in volumes of the *Congressional Globe* for the appropriate sessions and years. A unique and indispensable published source is *The Diary of James K. Polk during His*

Presidency, 1845 to 1849, edited by Milo Milton Quaife, 4 vols. (Chicago, 1910). It is safe to say that no other nineteenth-century president has left such a detailed and revealing record of his thoughts, to say nothing of cabinet meetings and other official actions. Private papers of other major figures have also been published, the most significant being those of James Buchanan, John C. Calhoun, Daniel Webster, Thomas O. Larkin, Zachary Taylor, Antonio López de Santa Anna, and Manuel Crescencio Rejón. Among newspapers consulted the most important are the *New York Herald, Sun,* and *Evening Post,* the *Washington Union* and *National Intelligencer;* the *London Times; Le journal des débats* (Paris); and *El Siglo diez y nueve* (Mexico City).

The most recent secondary account of Polk's diplomacy, from which most of this article is derived, is David M. Pletcher, *The Diplomacy of Annexation: Texas, Oregon, and the Mexican War* (Columbia, Mo., 1973). This contains an amplified bibliography. Charles Grier Sellers is engaged in producing a multivolume biography of Polk, mainly political in emphasis, of which only two volumes were available for this essay: *James K. Polk, Jacksonian: 1795–1843* (Princeton, 1957) and *James K. Polk, Continentalist: 1843–1846* (Princeton, 1966). Frederick Merk has compiled his many articles on Oregon into a convenient book, *The Oregon Question: Essays in Anglo-American Diplomacy and Politics* (Cambridge, Mass., 1967). Other works of his pertinent to Polk's diplomacy (and written in collaboration with Lois Bannister Merk) are *Manifest Destiny and Mission in American History: A Reinterpretation* (New York, 1963) and *The Monroe Doctrine and American Expansionism, 1843–1849* (New York, 1966). These books emphasize press opinion. A shorter survey of the question, attractively written, is Norman A. Graebner, *Empire on the Pacific: A Study in American Continental Expansion* (New York, 1955).

Two older, large-scale secondary works on the subject, longtime classics but now partly superseded, are Justin H. Smith, *The War with Mexico,* 2 vols. (New York, 1919), and George Lockhart Rives, *The United States and Mexico, 1821–1848,* 2 vols. (New York, 1913). Smith's documentation is the more impressive of the two, but Rives has produced a much more balanced narrative. There are no new detailed Mexican monographs worth mentioning. An account by a contemporary of the war which contains some material of value is José María Roa Bárcena, *Recuerdos de la invasión norteamericana (1846–1848),* 3 vols. (reprint edition, México, 1947). The best study of U.S.-Colombian relations is E. Taylor Parks, *Colombia and the United States, 1765–1934* (Durham, 1935), chap. 12.

The "plot thesis" concerning the annexation of Texas, referred to in this essay, was first advanced with scholarly support in the articles of Richard R. Stenberg, especially "The Failure of Polk's Mexican War Intrigue of 1845," *Pacific Historical Review* 4 (March 1935), 39–68. It has been recently revived with elaborations in Glenn W. Price, *Origins of the*

War with Mexico: The Polk-Stockton Intrigue (Austin, 1967). For fuller comment on this thesis see Pletcher, *Diplomacy of Annexation,* pp. 197–200, 269–71. Concerning the historiographical quarrel over the role of John Charles Frémont see Merk, *Monroe Doctrine and American Expansionism,* pp. 124–30; and Pletcher, *Diplomacy of Annexation,* pp. 285–86. On claims against Mexico see Clayton Charles Kohl, *Claims as a Cause of the Mexican War* (New York, 1914). On the Spanish monarchist plot in Mexico, 1845–46, and Trist's negotiations of 1847–48 see Pletcher, *Diplomacy of Annexation,* pp. 357–60, 362–63, 442–43, 540–50.

Department of State

IMPERIAL DREAMER:
WILLIAM HENRY SEWARD

and American Destiny

Gordon H. Warren

No man faced greater challenges as secretary of state, possessed fewer qualifications for the task, or matured more fully in office than William Henry Seward. Dogged during his first term by the Civil War and the menace of European intervention, then hindered throughout his second by Reconstruction and the executive-congressional struggle, Seward learned to move carefully to save the Union and further his dreams of American empire. The secretary's remarkable success with both goals surprised detractors because nothing in his past had indicated qualties of statesmanship. He was a New York State lawyer unversed in international law, a politician ignorant of the manner of negotiation, and he did not even want to be secretary of state. All his life he reached out for the presidency, but it always eluded him.

Born in a little town in southern New York in 1801, Seward came from English, Irish, and Welsh stock. His paternal grandfather had taken part in revolutionary events and transmitted a

195

faith in republican principles to Seward's father. The latter, a doctor and merchant, had occupied a sort of middle tier of state politics as a postmaster, county judge, and legislator. Encouraged by his father to attend Union College, Seward graduated after acquiring a Phi Beta Kappa key, and proceeded to study law in several firms before accepting a junior partnership in the Auburn office of his future father-in-law, Judge Elijah Miller.

Politics soon attracted the young lawyer whose party mobility—Democratic-Republican to Albany Regency to National Republican to Anti-Mason—reflected a changing set of attitudes as much as local pressure. A keen appreciation of public opinion marked his entire career, and it is sometimes difficult to discern whether principle, practicality, or expediency influenced decisions.

Political groupings in New York tended to follow socioeconomic patterns. Progressives, composed mainly of small farmers, laborers, and skilled craftsmen, supported movements for social justice and democratic reform. Conservatives, usually from the less numerous wealthy mercantile and agrarian interests, relied upon liberal defections to maintain voting power. Seward's professional and social connections often clashed with his republican beliefs, yet he and many conservatives joined the Anti-Masonic movement that swept New York in 1828. As state senator representing the new party, he favored rechartering the Bank of the United States, penal reform, direct election of mayors, and state aid for railroad construction projects. The organization's narrow voter appeal, along with Democratic inroads and new issues, convinced its leaders to dissolve in 1834 and then hammer together an assortment of contradictory elements called the state Whig party. Arm twisting by Thurlow Weed brought Seward the Whig gubernatorial nomination that year. He lost by eleven thousand votes, and promptly retired from politics—always his initial reaction to defeat. For the next four years he kept up a visible practice of law and, maintaining interest in public affairs, supported the Whig dogma of protection, internal improvements, and a national bank. This tactic paid off in an upset election to the governorship in 1838; he became the first non-Democrat to hold that office in forty years. Two terms in Albany marked him as a reformer interested in building a national reputation. By expanding the state's transportation network of canals and roads, advancing education, and taking advantage of popular currents, he hoped to achieve higher office and thus escape the factionalism of New York politics.

While in office he never championed a cause that violated his principles, but he often concealed beliefs that lacked popular support. A characteristic mixture of idealism and opportunism appeared in his treatment of such issues as temperance, immigrant education, and slavery. Thousands of teetotaling converts inspired him to take the pledge, which he broke after leaving office, but his efforts to promote immigrant education arose less from political reasons than from a desire to strengthen the American system. His position on the slavery question perhaps best illustrates his adroit matching of principle to public opinion. He always opposed slavery as a moral and political evil, detrimental to prosperity and America's world image. Still, in the 1838 campaign the candidate declined to endorse black suffrage or jury trial for runaways. Then, as antislavery sentiment quickened, Governor Seward refused to surrender fugitive slaves or extradite alleged slave stealers, and approved British handling of the *Creole* incident.[1] His antislavery stance attracted nationwide attention in the early 1840s, just as the McLeod affair[2] brought foreign notoriety, and revealed an embryonic approach to international relations: firmness in public, conciliation in private.

Seward was a fascinating public character. "I am an enigma, even to myself," he admitted in an unguarded moment, a remark fully supported by contemporary opinion. One observer praised his "ill-disguised contempt both for party obligations and popular applause," while another said he believed in "majorities, and . . . nothing else." His subtlety (critics called him devious) has perhaps been exaggerated. Like any politician he acted artfully at times because indirection served him better. When he spoke his mind it

---

1. In November 1841 slaves on board the *Creole*, an American vessel en route to New Orleans slave markets, revolted and sailed the ship into the British port of Nassau in the Bahamas. The British refused to surrender the slaves to American officials.

2. In 1840 New York authorities arrested a British subject, Alexander McLeod, for allegedly taking part in the *Caroline* raid (an incident during the 1837 Canadian rebellion when a group of pro-British Canadians destroyed an American vessel for illegally bringing munitions into Canada). London protested to the Tyler administration, which brought pressure on Governor Seward to release McLeod. Upholding New York State prerogatives, he refused; but he assured Washington that he would pardon McLeod if convicted. The court acquitted him.

usually hurt him; and he loved to talk. His conversations, as young
Henry Adams marveled, would "inspire a cow with statesmanship." Charming, well read, well traveled, and cosmopolitan, his
monologues made commonplace observations sound brilliant. A
sociable disposition let him relax at parties where, with a big,
black cigar and a drink in hand, he entertained everyone with
stories and delightful confidences.

Seward did not seek a third term in 1842 because his devotion
to reform and internal improvements had antagonized so many
voters. He returned to law and public speaking, determined to
forsake office. The governor left the statehouse at a good time;
Democratic victories, personal feuds, and philosophical differences among New York Whigs in the 1840s undermined both the
party and Seward's career. When not absorbed in cases ranging
from homicide to patent rights, he campaigned for Whig candi-
dates and spoke on the popular topics of revolution, war, and, of
course, slavery. His support for Ireland's independence struck
some people as "impertinent interference," but he thought more
of Irish votes than conservative opinion. The outbreak of war with
Mexico, supposedly provoked by the Democrats' commitment to
southern expansion, persuaded him that slavery had become the
overriding issue. Seward was able to oppose Polk's "bastard war"
for moral reasons while supporting the president's firm stand on
settling the Oregon boundary dispute because he felt it would be
popular with voters.

Then office beckoned again; this time it was the Senate.
Controversial remarks linking the growth of American empire with
expulsion of European colonies from North America nearly prevented his election in 1848. A low profile on some matters helped
ensure his political comeback because, as Edwin L. Godkin put it,
his safety lay in silence.

Seward's Senate years in Washington coincided with the
finale of the great sectional rivalry that had plagued the Union for
two generations. The junior senator from New York, unable to
keep a freshman's silence, pushed into the battle waged by
Calhoun, Webster, and Clay and gained fame overnight for his
ability to turn a snappy phrase. As governor he had defended state
prerogatives against federal interference; now, upset by Southern
attempts to preserve the Mexican cession for slavery, he emphasized Congress's broad constitutional powers of exclusion. Seces-

sion threats rarely alarmed him, even during the winter of 1861, when he labeled disunion an "antiquated superstition" fit only to frighten children. He believed that necessity, nature, and mutual benefit had made the Union indestructible.

If delivery of speeches rather than their content determined a senator's influence, Seward might have gone unnoticed. Not even close friends called him an orator. Rasping along in a low monotone, apparently unconcerned whether anyone listened, his opening remarks in 1850 on Clay's compromise plan overwhelmed everyone. Then, as he warmed to the topic, slashing Calhoun, correcting Webster, the senators stirred. They began to sense a moment in history. He attacked all legislative compromise as betrayal of principle and branded Clay's proposals as immoral devices to rescue a temporary institution. Calling for gradual compensated emancipation, he invoked a "higher law" than the Constitution. Providence had chosen the United States to spread the benefits of republican government.

Internal disputes over slavery broke up the Whig party in the mid-fifties and Seward, normally willing to trade party allegiance for personal advancement, drifted into the Republican camp. During the fall of 1858 he gave several speeches including one at Rochester in which he described the free labor-slavery struggle as an "irrepressible conflict." Though nothing distinguished this discourse from previous addresses, "irrepressible conflict," like the catchphrase "higher law," caught public imagination and sounded more sinister than Lincoln's "house divided" speech. The unfortunate words concealed a natural moderation, and people failed to realize, as Major L. Wilson concluded, that "Seward's radicalism was more rhetorical than real." Seward never erased his radical reputation and, notwithstanding efforts by friends to explain his statements at the 1860 Republican convention, "Old Irrepressible" was defeated.

Seward contemplated retirement until friends, personal ambition, and a flood of speaking invitations dissuaded him. On a western circuit that fall he virtually ignored the Republican platform, speaking instead on slavery and a favorite theme, American expansion. At St. Paul he predicted that Russian fortifications in North America would become outposts of the United States. He had preached the "American gospel" for years and this latest address sounded familiar.

Seward, with a near-mystical belief in Manifest Destiny, had asserted in 1846 that Americans were destined to roll in "resistless waves to the icy barriers of the north, and to encounter Oriental civilization on the shores of the Pacific." He preferred to see America expand peacefully rather than by war (though he did accept the conquered provinces of Mexico). Peace would guarantee domestic prosperity and cultural and economic progress, and would attract adjacent peoples wanting protection of their property and freedom. Subscribing to what might be called the "fruit-drop" theory of expansion—the United States need not fight for land but merely had to wait for contiguous territories and offshore islands to drop like ripened fruit into its lap—Seward relied upon political, physical, and economic laws of gravitation to create an empire. A disciple of John Quincy Adams, he argued that the decay of Spanish power in Latin America and Canadian disputes with Britain presaged absorption of these colonies into the Union. Yet while Adams opposed acquiring territory hospitable to slavery, Seward usually persuaded himself that any new lands would expand, not contract, the area of freedom. Canada appeared "already half-annexed," with Cuba being drawn by "constant gravitation" and Mexico by the influx of American capital and emigrants. A nation must expand "commensurately with its resources and advantages," and the force of attraction exerted by larger bodies upon smaller ones made America's growth unavoidable. The popular application of scientific principles to international politics and the comparison of nations to inorganic matter, according to Albert K. Weinberg, conveniently justified territorial aspirations. The spread-eagle style of oratory came naturally to Seward, who denied that either man or nature could raise a barrier to American expansion.

While he accepted Manifest Destiny he did not trust fate. The federal government had a responsibility to smooth the way for the "three wheels of national greatness": agriculture, industry, trade. It should sponsor internal improvements to speed produce to market and raise tariffs to encourage manufacturing. Above all the nation must advance commerce and "command the empire of the seas, which alone is real empire." He called for a navy to protect American merchant ships, treaties to facilitate overseas investment, subsidized steamship lines to challenge British maritime supremacy, surveys of the Arctic and Pacific to broaden trade with East Asia, and he dreamed of a transcontinental railroad that would carry immigrants to the unsettled West and commodities to the Pacific coast. The nation that produced, manufactured, and sold the most goods would be the greatest power. So "multiply your ships," he commanded, "and send them forth to the East." Commerce, the "god of boundaries," would decide upon the Pacific, its islands, and continents whether the United States or Europe controlled the world.

Like Jefferson, Seward wanted to create an empire for liberty. The idea of mission had powerful appeal to generations of Americans. Since the Puritan migrations they had assumed that the New World must one day settle accounts with the Old. The Republic, Seward declared, was "a living offence" to Russia, Austria, and other despotic powers; Britain's "imperial drumbeat and the frown of royal battlements" endangered republican principles. The time of reckoning had come, but there would be no war. America's destiny, he proclaimed, was to "renovate the condition of mankind," to carry the spirit of republicanism abroad, to uplift the degenerate populations of Asia and Europe. The ships that took American produce to Pacific markets would carry the democratic creed.

If Seward had intended his expansionist speeches to distract voters from sectionalism, he failed. After November 1860, extremists on both sides contributed to a postelection constitutional crisis. Most Republicans, including Lincoln and Seward, doubted the secessionists' resolution, and overestimated the ability of Southern unionists to restrain them. Seward attempted to defuse the situation over the next four months by not opposing the Crittenden Plan for protecting slavery, preventing enactment of a "force bill," and encouraging delegates to the Washington Peace Convention. When conciliatory tactics did not succeed, he proposed that the North try to frighten the South into submission.

The president-elect, according to Seward, adopted a pose of "masterly inactivity" and supposedly left party leadership to Seward who soon developed an exaggerated opinion of his own influence. He feared to leave Washington for even three days lest the nation disintegrate in his absence. Before the new administration took office he was comparing the president to a hereditary monarch and telling everyone that Lincoln wanted him to be prime minister. About a month after officially taking his post as secretary of state, in the well-known memorandum of 1 April 1861, "Some Thoughts for the President's Consideration," he accused Lincoln of having no policy to deal with secession, offered to assume responsibility, and recommended defense measures as well as an aggressive foreign policy to rally the South in defense of the Union. Angry at Spain's annexation of Santo Domingo and the projected conquest of Haiti, he suggested that Lincoln demand explanations from Spain and France, and, if they replied unsatis-factorily, that he convene Congress to declare war. Lincoln should ask Russia and Great Britain to explain what their policies would be during an American civil war, and he should send agents to Canada, Mexico, and Central America. Lincoln filed the memoran-dum, but its contents leaked. Seward's "foreign war panacea" alarmed diplomats, particularly the British minister to the United States, Lord Lyons, who thought that the New Yorker would be a "dangerous Foreign Minister."

Lyons had all sorts of reasons to worry. Before entering the State Department, Seward had established a reputation among the British for nationalism and opportunism. They could point to the McLeod affair, expansionist speeches aimed at Canada, and a curious episode that occurred during the past campaign when Seward had attended a dinner party at Albany in honor of the Prince of Wales who was then touring America. On this occasion he allegedly remarked to the duke of Newcastle, Britain's colonial secretary and the prince's escort, that he intended to insult Britain to strengthen his own position, but that London should not interpret his remarks as a prelude to war, especially since the British could not afford to fight the United States. Seward denied the conversation, and more incidents followed. In late January, the minister from Bremen, Rudolph Schleiden, hinted that higher tariffs might induce trading nations to favor the South. Rolling his eyes heavenward, Seward stunned the diplomat when he said, "If the Lord would only give the United States an excuse for a war with England, France, or Spain, that would be the best means of re-establishing internal peace." Seward told the British minister early in March that if a European power aided South Carolina, he would "pitch in" to the offending nation and thus heal the Union. Later in the month at the British legation he embarrassed Lyons by denouncing foreign criticism of a new system for collecting customs duties in Southern ports. Then in April came an attack

NAUGHTY JONATHAN.

"YOU SHAN'T INTERFERE, MOTHER—AND YOU OUGHT TO BE ON MY SIDE—AND IT'S A GREAT SHAME—AND I DON'T CARE—AND YOU SHALL INTERFERE—AND I WON'T HAVE IT."

upon Canada's alleged lack of neutrality. Word of Seward's fulminations spread through Washington, and the chairman of the Foreign Relations Committee, Senator Charles Sumner, decided that the shock of losing the presidential nomination had driven Seward mad.

Seward's motivation, however, was method, not madness. The new secretary of state believed that two factors would deter European intervention in the Civil War; Union victories and a manifest readiness to declare war upon any nation siding with the Confederacy. When Charles Francis Adams, minister to Great Britain, attempted to gloss over Seward's bellicosity, the secretary warned, "You could do no greater harm, than by inducing an opinon that I am less decided in my intercourse with the British Minister than I am reputed to be or less determined to maintain the pride and dignity of our Government." Seward, however, gambled that no government would risk war, that European nations could not submerge their rivalries long enough to act in concert. He cultivated a lunatic image to keep Europe off balance.

Lord Lyons's outward demeanor remained coldly correct toward Seward, who represented the sort of American politician so disgusting to him; inside he was seething. He concluded that the secretary viewed foreign relations as "safe levers" for manipulating public opinion. He recommended to Prime Minister Lord Palmerston that he put Canada in a state of defense, reinforce squadrons in the West Indies, the Atlantic, and the Pacific, and pursue a common policy with France toward American problems. The British government accepted all of his advice.

At about the time Lyons sent these recommendations, Seward drew up a document designed to reinforce his admonitions against interference. Britain and France seemed about to "try to save cotton at the cost of the Union," and the secretary of state sent to Adams in London his Dispatch Number Ten of 21 May 1861. This vigorous instruction, which Seward liked to describe as a "bold remonstrance," contained reckless phrasing. Fortunately for Anglo-American affairs he first showed it to Lincoln, and the president, with Sumner's enthusiastic approval, toned it down. Even if the softened version had been communicated it "might have made a war in five minutes," or so the American minister's son Henry thought. Seward had wanted Adams to indicate that Washington demanded acceptance of the blockade, intended to treat captured privateers as pirates, and considered official or unofficial contacts between the British government and the so-called Confederacy tantamount to a breach of diplomatic relations. Hostilities might ensue between the United States and "one, two, or even more European nations," but Great Britain, not the Union, would be responsible for war. "War in defence of national life is not immoral," he concluded, "and war in defence of independence is an inevitable part of the discipline of nations." At Lincoln's insistence Seward had marked the instruction confidential and not for communication, only to publish it, for all the world to see, in the annual *Diplomatic Correspondence* series[3] he intiated in the autumn.

Unknown to the secretary when he drafted Dispatch Number Ten, Britain already had recognized Confederate belligerency by announcing neutrality the day before the American minister arrived in London. When the news reached Washington Seward did not retaliate, but he commented that the neutrality proclamation questioned the Union's right of self-defense. The administration, he tried to persuade Lyons, harbored no ill will, a statement that diplomat found hard to accept. At this juncture Lyons's dispatches, going beyond criticism of Seward, lacked balance. Page after page carried attacks upon the secretary's character, habits, motives. In the spring of 1861 nothing could sway the British minister's deep conviction that America, with Seward in charge of foreign policy, presented a serious danger to British interests. The secretary learned indirectly of Lyons's attitude from Adams, who wrote that London officials had been stiffened, not frightened, by talk of war. Embarrassed, Seward explained that his "emphatic and sometimes, perhaps, impassioned remonstrances" against Confederate recognition resulted from a "profound solicitude to avert foreign war."

The British and French governments thus could store up unflattering impressions, complicating Seward's problems in the *Trent* affair of late 1861, a situation for which he possessed at least partial responsibility. The affair contained all the ingredients of high melodrama: Caribbean seas and Confederate agents, screaming ladies and gallant officers, the Christmas season and a royal

3. U.S. State Department, comp., *Papers Relating to the Foreign Affairs of the United States, 1861-68,* 19 vols. (Washington, D.C., 1862–69). This was the forerunner of the series now entitled *Foreign Relations of the United States.*

funeral, imperious demands and an eleventh-hour retreat. Throughout the tense weeks of the crisis Seward revealed much about his approach to foreign affairs. No Civil War incident brought more clearly into focus the secretary's abilities and disabilities.

On a dark night in mid-October 1861, James M. Mason and John Slidell, the designated Confederate commissioners to the British and French courts, had slipped past the Federal blockade off Charleston Harbor and steamed toward Cuba where they expected to take passage for Europe. They spent two weeks in Havana before boarding, on 7 November, a British mail packet named the *Trent* which would take them to St. Thomas. The next day Captain Charles Wilkes of the U.S.S. *San Jacinto* stopped the vessel, removed Mason, Slidell, and their secretaries, and allowed the *Trent* to resume its voyage. After a search for precedents, Wilkes had decided that international law justified the arrest of the diplomats as "embodiment of dispatches." He had instructed his first officer, Lieutenant Donald Fairfax, to seize the *Trent*, but Fairfax refused because a seizure would have inconvenienced the passengers, delayed shipment of mail and specie to merchants, and weakened the Union cruiser's part in the anticipated Federal attack on Port Royal, South Carolina. Wilkes thereupon took only the Confederate commissioners and embroiled his government in a controversy of the first magnitude.

The deed raised important questions concerning neutral rights and belligerent obligations: whether Wilkes erred in removing Mason and Slidell, whether he should have taken the *Trent* as a prize, leaving the men aboard, and brought it before an American tribunal to determine if the vessel had violated neutrality by carrying the commissioners. Hardly anyone, including the United States attorney general, seemed to think so. Lincoln kept silent, and Seward, pleading illness, refused public comment, although Secretary of the Navy Gideon Welles reported him to be jubilant. The administration had decided not to risk public disapproval with a premature surrender of the agents and to await London's reaction. The Mason and Slidell affair, Seward predicted in a masterpiece of understatement, "will try the British temper."

If it was a typical Seward move to test British resolution, his adversary refused—perhaps typically also—to back down. The British government, press, and public regarded the *Trent* incident as an insult to the national honor. "The people are frantic with rage," an American living in London wrote Seward, "and were the country polled, I fear 999 men out of 1,000 would declare for immediate war." When Palmerston asked crown law officers for an opinion they responded that international law permitted a belligerent to stop and board a neutral vessel such as the *Trent* and conduct it to the belligerent's port for prize proceedings if there were suspicion of neutrality violations, but the law forbade the removal of any passengers. Wilkes's action was "illegal and unjustifiable." Over the next days the government prohibited export of war materials, began sending eleven thousand troops and tens of thousands of weapons to Canada, drew plans to blockade Union ports, strengthened the North American fleet, and, in a note composed by British Foreign Secretary Lord Russell, demanded that the Lincoln administration apologize and release Mason and Slidell within one week after receiving the protest. This, then, was the harvest of Seward's belligerence; Britain saw the *Trent* affair as his long-desired pretext for war.

At first Seward seemed to continue his usual truculence. Over a month passed after the capture before London papers arrived on 13 December bearing news of war preparation. Peace editorials sprouted, and provocative resolutions lost popularity in Congress. Everyone grew suddenly quiescent—everyone, that is, except Seward. At a cotillion on the sixteenth, where war crisis dominated the conversation, he startled other guests by crying out: "We will wrap the whole world in flames! No power [is] so remote that she will not feel the fire of our battle and be burned by our conflagration."

Then he began to back off. The secretary's defiance accomplished nothing. Three days after the party, Lyons called at the State Department to deliver Russell's ultimatum. Suspecting trouble, Seward persuaded the minister to describe the note's contents informally, to give him a copy unofficially, and, when Lyons mentioned the deadline, to postpone formal presentation of the demands until 21 December. Soon after Lyons returned to the legation the secretary rushed over to ask what would happen if, at the end of a week, his answer rejected the ultimatum or proposed further discussion. "I could not accept it," the minister warned. On the twenty-first Seward complained that since other duties had prevented him from studying the note he needed another two days. Lyons agreed, stipulating that he would not accept delay after 23 December.

Lincoln and Seward were at an impasse, and only gradually came out of it. The president had composed a document that called for extensive discussion of the *Trent* and other issues—touching even the British position throughout the Civil War—and submission of the whole affair to arbitration. Knowing that London would never consent to arbitrating a question of national honor, Seward stalled Lyons for four days while he argued with Lincoln. The minister, keeping his promise, finally gave notification on 23 December, thereby setting noon of 30 December as the deadline for a reply. Seward read the dispatch to Lincoln, who remained oblivious to the consequences of keeping Mason and Slidell. "I will never give them up," he said. Seward frowned. "Then I shall be obliged to ask you, Mr. President, to write the reply to Earl Russell for the strength of the argument from our own past policy, so far as I can see, is in favor of a compliance with his demands." On Christmas Eve a cabinet meeting debated the *Trent* crisis. Lincoln continued to push for arbitration and though Seward tried to object he suggested they both draw up answers and compare points. The cabinet met on Christmas morning to hear Seward read Russell's note and a draft reply. Four hours of debate ensued. Members seemed more disposed to surrender Mason and Slidell on the ground of avoiding another war than upon the real issue involving a flagrant violation of neutral rights. They grudgingly approved Seward's reply, and the secretary incorporated their sentiments into the final copy. He polished his draft, read it to the Foreign Relations Committee, and presented the document to Lyons on 27 December, three days before the deadline's expiration.

Seward had functioned as a peace-keeper during the *Trent* crisis once he realized the depth of British anger. He had argued the British case in cabinet, noting that Wilkes's act violated international law and American traditions. Confronted then with the impossible task of satisfying London, salvaging national honor, and preserving his reputation, Seward had written a paper that cheapened the high principles upon which he had urged surrender. He informed the British that Wilkes had a legal right to stop and search the *Trent* and then, quoting an admiralty judge, Sir William Scott, out of context ("You may stop the ambassador of your enemy on his passage"), claimed that the captain could have lawfully captured Mason, Slidell, and their dispatches as contraband of war. Having justified the seizure, Seward groped for an excuse to repudiate it. If Wilkes had involuntarily released the *Trent*, he commented, the United States was entitled to keep the prisoners; yet by voluntarily freeing the vessel he waived any claim. Wilkes's inadvertency constituted an illegal act for which Britain deserved reparation. Seward might well have stopped at this point but he had other purposes and another audience in mind, so he continued. If the Union's security had required the commissioners' detention, he said, they would not have been surrendered despite their illegal capture. Seward surrendered the men for the wrong reasons, indulging in what Lincoln liked to call the "horse-chestnut" style of argument, a "specious and fantastic arrangement of words by which a man can prove a horse-chestnut to be a chestnut horse."

However illogical his note, Seward deserves credit for ending the war crisis at considerable risk to his personal popularity. He also improved his reputation in London. Lyons's dispatches had convinced Russell and Palmerston that he meant to provoke a conflict. When the *Trent* affair, a perfect clash of neutral and belligerent rights, passed without hostilities, they questioned Lyons's interpretation. "I do not believe that Seward has any animosity to this country," Russell declared. "It is all buncom."

Henry Adams best defined Seward's approach. "The foreign policy of Mr. Seward," he wrote, "was, in principle, simple enough, although his expedients were innumerable. His intention was always to avoid war, but always to gain his objects; and he achieved astonishing success." While Seward avoided war over the *Trent*, the tone and phrasing of his note indicated a higher regard for domestic political reaction than for international goodwill.

Before Seward took office his old mentor Thurlow Weed had counseled that since a secretary must be popular with the people to be successful, Seward must cultivate a style that would please the public. Never forgetting that advice, Seward, more than any predecessor, wrote dispatches with an eye to public opinion. He frequently published his instructions in newspapers and, as mentioned, originated the *Diplomatic Correspondence* series. Publication did not endear him to foreign ministers who realized that he worded dispatches to appeal to his own public. "You are I believe aware," Russell wrote Lyons upon receiving the 1861 volume, "that Adams never read me any of those long, vainglo-rious & insolent dispatches which Seward has laid before Con-gress."

Contrary to the general belief that Seward became less volatile as he acquired experience and submitted to Lincoln's guidance, the secretary's bellicosity persisted for a long period after the *Trent* affair. The confident, almost cocky tone permeating his dispatches was designed to bolster the morale of Northerners at home and abroad. Seward believed that "to betray apprehen-sion would be to betray the Union." When the government's future seemed darkest he sounded most optimistic. Recognizing that tidings of military reverses coupled with hostile foreign judgments depressed American diplomats, the secretary oozed confidence in his dispatches. To one minister discouraged by a second defeat at Bull Run, Seward exhorted, "The United States must demand under all circumstances of their representatives in foreign countries what the old Romans required of their Generals, even when defeated, never to despair of the Republic." He did not despair. Through a series of crises that arose with numbing regularity—mediation offers, commerce raiders, a French expedi-tion to Mexico—he affirmed his faith in the inevitable triumph of the Union, "the chief security of nations."

An example is his behavior over the possibility of European mediation, which issue kept relations between the United States and Europe in turmoil for two years. From the war's onset the governments of Great Britain and France had acted jointly upon the question of deterring Washington from attacking either power. Both nations recognized Confederate belligerency in 1861, the British in May, the French in June. Seward ignored their common policy, hoping that Northern victories and his pungent language would deter any unpleasant move such as an offer to reconcile sectional differences by mediation. Fearing that recogni-tion of Confederate belligerency would lead to recognition of independence, he let it be known that he viewed recognition as equivalent to an alliance, and therefore a declaration of war. When France and Britain complained about curtailment of trade he retorted that the American stake was larger. He rejected the first offer of mediation in June 1861, warning that foreign intervention would produce "new and injurious consequences." He had a special message for Britain. The empire, an "aggregation of divers communities," might someday undergo strain. "Would it be wise for her Majesty's government, on this occasion, to set a dangerous precedent or provoke retaliation?" A master of counterattack, he predicted a speedy end to the war if only the European powers withdrew their recognition of belligerency.

Confederate victories nonetheless had fostered a belief in European chancelleries that the American Civil War, so disruptive to international trade and peace, should be humanely resolved by mediation. Lord Russell felt strongly about the matter and, encouraged by that tireless schemer Napoleon III, hatched a plan. He proposed to Palmerston in August 1862 that the British government, in consultation with Russia, Prussia, Austria, and France, should offer mediation to Washington with the intent of recognizing Southern independence if mediation failed. Seward, whose agents had reported an impending change in British policy, fired off a barrage of threatening notes to Adams which were not read to Russell but naturally appeared in the published correspondence for 1862 a few months later. Failure of foreign powers to respect American sovereignty, the secretary wrote, would lead to "a war of continents—a war of the world." It would unite the feuding sections. Fortunately there was to be no mediation. British cabinet members viewed Russian cooperation as essential to the plan's success; but when the enthusiastic French, acting as cosponsors, raised the idea at St. Petersburg in the autumn of 1862, they received a blunt refusal. If Russia and America had antithetical systems of government, they also possessed common enemies, and the czar valued American friendship. Seward's well-known determination to wage war against any power that intervened in behalf of the Confederacy undoubtedly played a part, along with Confederate defeat at Antietam.

The secretary soon ceased to worry about intervention and concentrated on saving the Union merchant marine from foreign-built commerce raiders. Since the Confederacy lacked shipbuilding facilities, it secretly negotiated contracts with British firms to supply vessels and then, obeying the letter of Britain's Foreign Enlistment Act of 1819, armed, equipped, and manned the steamers in the West Indies and elsewhere for careers of destruction. British authorities would not prevent their sailing unless furnished with incontrovertible proof of a belligerent destination. Minister Adams, consular officers, and a company of fumbling spies spent hours securing affidavits of the suspected vessels' destination, but London officials rarely found the evidence overwhelming. Seward accused the British of condoning open piracy and urged Congress to pass a bill authorizing the issuance of letters of marque. Since the Confederacy possessed no maritime commerce, and privateers preyed only on merchant vessels, the proposal was aimed squarely at Britain. Seward wrote in the summer of 1863 that the United States was drifting toward a war with Great Britain, all because its government would not enforce the neutrality law. Why, he asked, did the British insist on setting precedents when one day they might be at war and the United States at peace? Lawyerlike, the secretary prosecuted Britain in the pages of *Diplomatic Correspondence* by publishing scores of Adams's affidavits and intercepted Confederate letters relating to purchase and outfitting of vessels.

The commerce raiders never really endangered the Union war effort, but they did constitute a costly nuisance for which Seward rightly demanded compensation. He pressed for postwar payment of the so-called *Alabama* claims, tying their settlement to negotiation of a naturalization treaty designed to protect Irish-American Fenians from arrest when they visited Ireland. Seward considered canceling the claims in return for cession of Canadian territory, yet he realized that the British government would not accept such terms. The new American minister to London, Reverdy Johnson, finally signed an arbitration convention in early 1869 which incurred the Senate's displeasure for not containing a British apology or reference to indirect claims; however, Charles Sumner, who led the opposition, attacked the treaty because of his dislike of both Britain and the administration rather than because of any objection to the convention's provisions. Unable to arrange a satisfactory agreement, Seward at least laid a solid foundation enabling his successor, Hamilton Fish, to negotiate the 1871 Treaty of Washington.

Almost throughout his years as secretary, Seward also had difficulty with Napoleon III and devoted valuable time to coaxing French troops out of Mexico. The Maximilian affair originated partly in Mexico's suspension of foreign debt payments in 1861 and the Convention of London of that year in which France, Spain, and Britain agreed to undertake a joint expedition against the Juarez regime to force resumption of financial obligations. Seward had tried to guarantee the Mexican debt by supporting a loan of sufficient proportion to stave off creditors, with Mexico's northern provinces attached as security. The Senate rejected this perhaps bald-faced land grab, and when the powers invited American participation in the joint expedition Seward could only speak of Mexican political and territorial sovereignty. Declining association on these grounds, rather than mentioning the Monroe Doctrine (designed to prevent such invasions), he avoided antagonizing the allies. Seward's Mexican policy, Weed later observed, "breaks no eggs." Having discarded his foreign war idea the secretary saw no point in gasconading about Mexico while locked in a death struggle at home. British and Spanish troops left Mexico early in 1862 but the French, hypnotized by dreams of empire, installed the puppet emperor Maximilian and stayed until 1867. Seward informed Napoleon that popular sympathies toward Mexico made it difficult to enforce American neutrality laws, and that American security depended upon "continuance of free republican institutions" throughout the Americas. Except for occasional perfunctory objections the secretary then let the matter lie.

The State Department's cautious policy toward the Mexican intervention infuriated congressmen mindful of public reaction against a challenge to the Monroe Doctrine. In the spring of 1864 the House resolved that the United States government would not "acknowledge any monarchy erected in America upon the ruins of any republic, under the auspices of any European power." Seward privately described the resolves as passed with "more patriotic zeal than discretion" and assured Paris that the president contemplated no drastic change of policy. Far from adopting a firebrand attitude on every question, Seward thus often served as a brake to popular enthusiasms. Yet increasing public dissatisfaction and Confederate losses led him to publish his dispatches to France— sometimes before they reached Paris. The Civil War ended with almost a million Union soldiers under arms and, although the armies rapidly demobilized, fifty-two thousand troops massed on the Texas border. In September 1865, Seward signified that French evacuation would promote international peace and Franco-American friendship, and in December he induced President Andrew Johnson to warn Napoleon that continued good relations with the United States rested upon his troops taking French leave. The secretary then stated that Americans resented a foreign army overthrowing a republican government and "establishing upon its ruins" a foreign monarchy; significantly, Seward was using virtually the same language as the House resolutions passed two years earlier. Napoleon, perhaps remembering the relationship between discretion and valor, took the hint and agreed to withdraw from Mexico by the spring of 1867, leaving the Hapsburg Archduke Maximilian to his fate.

Seward's handling of the Mexican question typified his cautious approach to matters not directly affecting the Confederacy's status. "This government," he had declared late in the war, "has learned something of the value of concentration of purpose." The specter of Anglo-French mediation had nurtured in him an astonishing respect for the status quo. He maintained strict neutrality during the Italian civil war of 1862, declined to offer mediation of Latin American disputes unless asked, refused to recognize revolutionary governments lacking public acceptance, and condemned "sedition or rebellion against the imperial authority" in China. The man who had praised Hungarian revolutionaries in 1851 later wondered if the great maritime states should form a latter-day Holy Alliance to crush insurrection.

His conservatism appeared in other ways. While he pressed claims at London, he instructed representatives in Italy, Argentina, Santo Domingo, and Brazil to urge no redress of damages collectible only by force. As hostilities between North and South waned, European governments expected the Washington regime to undertake wars of vengeance. Seward's dispatches implied that eventuality, but he repeatedly said that he meant commercial, not political, reprisals. The United States, he wrote, believed in the principle of nonintervention and fielded no armies to wage aggressive war.

To be sure, he liked to keep foreigners uncertain. He suggested international expeditions to chastise Japan and Korea, an inconsistency for someone who defended Mexican sovereignty. His disavowal of postwar territorial ambitions did not impress diplomats acquainted with his desire to restore national prestige. The secretary of state, they thought, was most dangerous when he appeared agreeable.

Apart from surmounting the problems of foreign relations connected with the Civil War, Seward deserves a prominent place in American history because of his attempt to extend the national boundaries and foster commercial opportunities. Richard Van Alstyne has correctly stated that Seward was "the central figure of nineteenth-century American imperialism." For Africa and Asia, the Antilles and Alaska, he pushed a staggering variety of projects to strengthen his nation in competition with colonial, big-navy powers. A vision of American Manifest Destiny prompted him to rhapsodize:

> Our nation with united interests blest,
>   Not now content to poise, shall sway the rest;
> Abroad over Empire shall no limits know,
>   But like the sea in boundless circles flow.

Mr. Seward, Henry Adams once remarked, "was seldom satisfied with a small policy." All his life he shared the popular conviction that all of North America must fall under American control and worked to achieve that end by peaceful means.

Russian America became part of Seward's grand design. He had long coveted Russian territory, and Confederate raids on Union vessels in the Arctic seas confirmed his feeling that national security made ownership of the region desirable. American warships would secure coaling stations; the merchant marine would compete more effectively in the China trade. The secretary's attitude toward Russia had changed, of course; the alchemy of *Realpolitik* had transformed the czarist government from a "despotic power" in the 1850s to a "good friend" in the 1860s. Delighted at the rapprochement and worried about the unprofitable colony's weakness, the czar instructed his minister in Washington to unload Alaska on the United States. Seward quickly signed a purchase treaty and submitted it to the Senate. When that body appeared more interested in opposing Johnson administration measures than in extending American boundaries, the secretary of state undertook a program of public education, stressing that failure to ratify would insult America's only European friend. The Senate approved, but not for another year did a cantankerous House appropriate over seven million dollars for Seward's Icebox. Acquisition of Alaska fitted nicely into his Pacific policy because it facilitated communications and trade with East Asia, or the "Far West" as he viewed it. Elated at a deal comparable to the Louisiana Purchase, he bragged that if he could live another thirty years he would give to the people "possession of the American Continent and the control of the world."

The secretary spent his last two years in office working to secure territory. He planned to dot the Caribbean and Pacific with a network of ports serving American naval vessels and the merchant marine. He would link the two regions by a canal across the isthmus of Panama (the great American route) to cut transportation costs, strengthen defenses, and blunt British influence in Central America. Tackling the canal project first, the secretary negotiated a right-of-way through Colombia in defiance of the Clayton-Bulwer Treaty and then, believing that the popular mind would have to be conditioned to the idea, insisted on a survey to determine construction costs. Before the survey could begin, however, the Colombian Senate refused to ratify the treaty, setting the stage for a more violent settlement forty years later.

Undaunted by failure, Seward embarked upon a quest for island outposts. His tactics showed ingenuity if nothing else. In the Pacific he attempted to acquire the Hawaiian Islands by signing a generous reciprocity treaty to dispose the residents toward annexation. The Senate tabled it, and the Hawaiian kingdom promptly undertook negotiation of treaties of amity and commerce with Russia and Prussia. Resenting Hawaii's unseemly haste, Seward issued a general confidential circular stating that it would be "incompatible" with American interests to let the islands fall under the "jurisdiction, protection or dominating influence of any foreign power." He thus extended the Monroe Doctrine overseas. Although no minister ever presented Seward's circular, the Hawaiian mission did not succeed.

Closer to home he worked to fulfill an old American desire for Caribbean possessions. The dual problems of chasing down Confederate raiders and transforming the United States into a world power had convinced Seward that his government must acquire harbors in the West Indies or yield maritime supremacy. He experienced heartbreaking defeats. After negotiating a treaty in the autumn of 1867 for purchase of the Virgin Islands he could not persuade the Senate that it would be in the national interest. His standard attempt to rally public opinion failed, and not for another fifty years did title pass into American hands. Paralleling the Danish West Indies negotiations was a long-simmering effort to lease or buy the Bay of Samaná from Santo Domingo, but revolution cut short the lukewarm dickering. By the time the Senate had rejected the project as well as a suggestion to annex the whole island, plans to acquire St. Bartholomew, Culebra, and

Culebrita also had gone aglimmering. During his final days in Washington Seward realized that he would never see the American flag wave over Caribbean territory; yet he could remark with pardonable pride that "the country is not less now, but is larger than I found it when I entered my last public office."

All the while the secretary had been caught in the turmoil of rebuilding a shattered nation, and the failures of the Johnson administration had a good deal to do with the failures of his imperial plans. Intent upon humiliating Johnson, Radical Republican senators voted down nearly every measure originating in the White House or cabinet. Seward wooed key members, but could overcome neither their hatred for President Johnson nor their desire to reassert congressional prerogatives. His efforts to rally public opinion likewise collapsed. After the Civil War people wanted to return to business as usual. Then, too, they found the political struggle in Washington more interesting, Reconstruction problems more demanding, domestic expansion more pressing than Seward's summonses to greatness. Appeals to patriotism, destiny, even avarice scarcely budged a people seeking to avoid new challenges. The public mind, Seward sadly concluded, refused to entertain "the higher but more remote questions of national expansion and aggrandisement." His dreams turned to dust.

Seward had entered the State Department expecting to use it as a stepping-stone to the presidency. Throughout Lincoln's administration he sought to function as a prime minister, a shadow president, directing the business of government while other cabinet members, in his eyes, served as bothersome if necessary clerks. Cordially disliked by his colleagues, he had the support of both Lincoln and Johnson because they valued his political expertise and popular support. The secretary gradually abandoned his presidential hopes after realizing that, in his preoccupation with foreign relations, he had lost touch with voters and party leaders.

During the years 1861–69 Seward did not make policy in a vacuum, however. Although the flamboyant secretary cultivated the impression that he carried American diplomacy in his coat pocket he always solicited other opinions and weighed domestic

and foreign considerations before arriving at a decision. He then
ran a gamut of presidential, cabinet, and congressional criticism.
Lincoln usually backed the secretary but occasionally, as in the
matter of issuing letters of marque, deferred to the informed views
of Navy Secretary Gideon Welles. Seward also had to cope with
Senator Charles Sumner who, according to David Donald, moni-
tored State Department activities at Lincoln's request and became
an indispensable guest at diplomatic dinners. While close supervision affected neither the tone nor content of Seward's dispatches,
it sometimes helped him avoid mistaken actions.

The ordeal of conducting diplomatic affairs during the Civil
War provided Seward with a lesson in the limits of power. He soon
realized that "bold remonstrances" offered scant value if unsupported by force, which was often difficult to apply. In foreign
relations, as in politics, Seward knew when to advance and, above
all, when to retreat. The *Trent* affair proved to be his most
educational experience. In its aftermath, having previously ignored the Royal Navy's awesome firepower, he became almost
contrite. He avoided giving offense and to Welles's intense disgust
refused to press certain flagrant British violations of neutrality.
Seward exercised commendable restraint in handling Britain's
failure to detain commerce raiders. Lord Palmerston, himself an
expert practitioner of brinkmanship, conceded that he had "acted
fairly by us." While his Civil War diplomacy was perhaps not as
"masterful" as Alexander DeConde believes, he does merit accolades for steering the nation around the most perilous diplomatic
shoals since revolutionary days.

As secretary of state, Seward looked both to the past and the
future. A preserver rather than an innovator of foreign policy, he
elaborated the hemispheric aims of Thomas Jefferson and John
Quincy Adams. Uninterested in solving problems created by the
decline of Turkey, the rise of Prussia, and the stagnation of France,
he believed his country's interests to be in the Western Hemisphere and Asia. The policies he pursued in these areas revealed a
healthy mixture of idealism and realism, as well as a significant
amount of opportunism. He had glimpsed the value of a two-
ocean navy supported by a system of strategically placed bases in
the Caribbean and Pacific to facilitate trade and bolster security.
He foresaw the day when East Asia, not Europe, would be the
world's theater of rivalries. China with its millions of potential
customers had long attracted American entrepreneurs, and Seward

by purchasing Alaska hoped to acquire a bridge to Asia. The precursor of late nineteenth-century imperialists, a high priest of expansionism, the secretary anticipated Alfred Thayer Mahan's arguments for a large navy, extensive commerce, and overseas bases. Seward's vision, his aspirations and not his deeds, marked him for greatness. It was his misfortune to head the State Department during the Civil War and, in his second term, an antiexpansionist, antiadministration period. He nonetheless followed policies that led to the emergence of the United States as a world power in the twentieth century.

Over a public career spanning four decades, controversy swirled about William H. Seward. Contemporaries either admired or disliked the man; no one was neutral. Few knew him well enough to see him as history now does; they tended to observe only his loquacity and showmanship. As governor, senator, and secretary of state, he took stands on slavery and sectionalism that made more enemies than friends. A deep respect for public opinion often influenced but never warped his judgment. Surely, despite his unpreparedness for high office, despite his bombast and occasional errors of judgment, despite all that contemporaries found difficult, if not obnoxious, he was, one must say in the retrospect of a century, a great secretary of state.

BIBLIOGRAPHIC NOTE

The most important source of information on William Henry Seward is the collection of his papers in the Rush Rhees Library at the University of Rochester. They comprise one hundred fifty thousand public and personal items, including one hundred thousand letters chronologically arranged and indexed by correspondent. British opinion of Seward and reaction to his policies appear in the papers of Lord Russell and the records of the Foreign Office; both collections are housed in the Public Record Office in London. Lord Palmerston's papers at Broadlands contain thousands of letters, many of which refer to Seward.

Seward's *Autobiography*, 3 vols. (New York, 1877–91), edited by his son Frederick, contains little useful information except on the secretary's early years. George E. Baker, ed., *The Works of William H. Seward*, 5 vols. (Boston, 1884), contains his major speeches and essays. The fullest published documentary record of Seward's diplomacy appears in the volumes for 1861–68 (his successor did not compile a volume for 1869) of *Foreign Affairs of the United States*. Additional information on some diplomatic incidents appears in U.S. War Department, comp., *The War of the Rebellion: A Compilation of the Official Records of the Union and Confederate Armies*, 130 vols. (Washington, D.C., 1880–1901), and U.S. Navy Department, comp., *Official Records of the Union and Confederate Navies in the War of the Rebellion*, 30 vols. (Washington, D.C., 1894–1914). Roy P. Basler, ed., *The Collected Works of Abraham Lincoln*, 9 vols. (New Brunswick, N.J., 1953–55), sheds light upon the relationship between the secretary and the president.

The standard biography of Seward is by Glyndon G. Van Deusen, *William Henry Seward* (New York, 1967). He correctly portrays his subject as a remarkable administrator, a practical statesman, and a dreamer, but perhaps exaggerates Seward's alleged Machiavellianism. In *The American Secretary of State: An Interpretation* (New York, 1962), Alexander De-Conde shows how Secretary Seward "expected to govern as a prime minister, to direct the entire government in the President's name." Seward's attitude, as Van Deusen relates in *Thurlow Weed: Wizard of the Lobby* (Boston, 1947), derived partly from the machine politics of New York State where officeholders twitched when party bosses pulled the strings.

Joseph G. Whelan's dissertation, "William Henry Seward, Expansionist," University of Rochester, 1959, is a full account of the philosophy and results of Seward's expansionism. He presents Seward as an economic determinist, political idealist, and international realist. In the prewar years, Seward favored expansion to achieve domestic political balance, while strategic motives explained his post-1861 projects. In a dissertation entitled "William Henry Seward: A Study in Nineteenth Century Politics and Nationalism, 1855–1861," University of Rochester, 1965, Walter G. Sharrow traces Seward's attempt to counter sectionalism with a program of nationalistic legislation. Although Seward was instrumental in making the Republican party a reform movement, according to the author, he cannot be regarded as a radical on slavery.

Seward's views on the nature of the Union and the politician's role in expansion have been explored in several works. Paul C. Nagel, *One Nation Indivisible: The Union in American Thought, 1776–1861* (New York, 1964), illustrates how Seward attempted to "translate reverence for Union into a matter of American morality" and argued that technological advances would cement far western states to the federal government. In "The Repressible Conflict: Seward's Concept of Progress and the Free-Soil Movement," *Journal of Southern History* 37: 533–56, Major L. Wilson points out that Seward conceived of the statesman's task as not to resist but to give orderly expression to the "popular passion" for territorial acquisition. Albert K. Weinberg's *Manifest Destiny* (Baltimore, 1935) places Seward in the mainstream of those Americans who marshaled every conceivable theory to establish a rationale for expansion. Richard W. Van Alstyne, *The Rising American Empire* (New York, 1960), emphasizes the secretary's grasp of the historic directions of American imperialism.

Numerous scholars have examined carefully the policy of the State Department toward Great Britain. Ephraim D. Adams pioneered such research with *Great Britain and the American Civil War*, 2 vols. (New York, 1925), which describes hectic Anglo-American relations, the British response to Seward, and the trials of the American minister. The latter's relationship with Seward is set forth in greater detail in Martin Duberman's *Charles Francis Adams, 1807–1886* (Stanford, 1960). The dangerous issue concerning the construction of Confederate commerce raiders in British ports is treated in Frank J. Merli, *Great Britain and the Confederate Navy, 1861–1865* (Bloomington, 1970). Merli demonstrates that despite the State Department's concern the vessels were a costly nuisance, but no real danger, to the Union war effort. An excellent account of American violations of neutral rights and Seward's twisted interpretations of international law is Stuart L. Bernath, *Squall across the Atlantic: American Civil War Prize Cases and Diplomacy* (Berkeley and Los Angeles, 1970). The difficulties of policing a long border, violations of Canadian neutral rights, and the perils of loosely supervising Confederate activities in Canada emerge in Robin W. Winks, *Canada and the United States: The Civil War Years* (Baltimore, 1960).

An illustration of the impact of personalities and domestic politics upon international affairs appears in David Donald, *Charles Sumner and the Rights of Man* (New York, 1970), which reveals the senator's petty obstructionism and egocentric notions. The Union's relations with France have been examined in two works. Lynn M. Case and Warren F. Spencer, *The United States and France: Civil War Diplomacy* (Philadelphia, 1970), conclude that despite numerous crises, especially the Maximilian affair, Franco-American relations benefited from the Civil War because American power and democratic ideals impressed the common man in France. Daniel B. Carroll's *Henri Mercier and the American Civil War* (Princeton, 1971) treats with admirable understanding the French minister's relationship with Seward and his opinion of the Union.

For an understanding of the complexities of French policy in the Maximilian affair, one must consult the excellent work by Alfred Jackson Hanna and Kathryn Abbey Hanna, *Napoleon III and Mexico: American Triumph over Monarchy* (Chapel Hill, N.C., 1971), a work that incorporates the results of many years of research in numerous archives scattered over the United States, Mexico, and Europe. Calm and judicious, this work fills a long neglected gap in mid-nineteenth-century diplomacy. In smaller compass there is the well-done account of this incident in Henry Blumenthal's *France and the United States: Their Diplomatic Relations, 1789–1914* (Chapel Hill, N.C., 1970).

HAMILTON FISH

and American Expansion

James B. Chapin

As secretary of state, Hamilton Fish should have been an anachro-
nism. At sixty-one, one of the oldest men yet appointed to that
office, he came to it a dozen years after the collapse of his political
career. His selection by President Grant in 1869 was almost a
matter of chance, a sudden grab by an inexperienced president
desperate to save face. Contemporaries regarded Fish as an honest
if limited man of sound Republican sympathies, but one who was
out of touch with the vital concerns of the time. He himself might
have agreed with such assessments, for he wrote Charles Sumner

For extended treatment and full documentation of the views expressed in this essay
see the author's 1971 doctoral thesis at Cornell University, "Hamilton Fish and
American Expansion." A Samuel Fels Fund Dissertation Fellowship provided
financial assistance for the research upon which this essay is based. All quotations
in this essay, unless otherwise identified, may be assumed to be from the Hamilton
Fish collection at the Library of Congress.

223

that he was going to Washington to "undertake duties for which I have little taste, and less fitness."

Fish's service as head of the State Department was an unexpected climax to a political career otherwise typical of a number of upper-status Whigs whose expectations had been blighted by the political realignments of the 1850s. He had been born early enough to benefit from the lingering politics of deference, but too late for such politics to keep him in office for a lifetime. An unfriendly newspaper summed up the remarkable ease of his life by noting that circumstances, rather than toil or talent, had propelled him forward: "Few men have been more the favorites of the blind goddess than Hamilton Fish."

Born into the upper classes of New York City, Fish was descended from Stuyvesants and Livingstons on his mother's side; his father, Nicholas Fish, attended King's College (Columbia) with Alexander Hamilton and was one of the conservative Whigs who rode the tide of the American Revolution in hopes of taming it. Nicholas Fish served as a lieutenant-colonel under Washington, the first adjutant general of New York, founder of the state branch of the Society of the Cincinnati (the revolutionary officers and their male descendants), a Federalist alderman from New York City, and chairman of the Columbia University Board of Trustees. He was also a major banker, land speculator, and landowner.

He had declined Alexander Hamilton's request to serve as a second in that fatal duel with Aaron Burr; but when Fish had a son in 1808, he named him after his dead friend and endowed him with both wealth and social position. Hamilton Fish graduated from Columbia with highest honors and went on to study and practice law in a series of aristocratic firms. He specialized in legal advice to large property holders and seldom appeared in court. His profession reflected his status, as did his marriage to Julia Kean, descendant of John Kean and Lewis Morris. His father's death in 1833 left him financially secure, and the bequest of his uncle Petrus Stuyvesant in 1847 left him independently wealthy. He never again worked for a living. Throughout his life, Fish belonged to a small group of wealthy New Yorkers, sons of leading Federalists, a bourgeois aristocracy of men who combined wealth, power, prestige, and a unified outlook on social and economic problems; they believed that they were the upper classes of New York City and that the Whigs represented their interests as the Federalists had before.

The New York State Whigs appear to have been a coalition of a rural, liberal group from western New York (which came to the party from the Jeffersonians by way of Anti-Masonry) and a conservative and more urban faction (many of whom were old Federalists). Although the Whigs were the party of the "positive liberal state," to use Lee Benson's phrase, the upper-class city Whigs were less concerned with moral reform than with the power of the state to maintain order and build empire. Many recent historians have stressed the connection of the Whigs with evangelical religious morality, but Fish's group had no such associations. He himself regarded New England as a "nursery of vagaries and fanaticisms," and he hated the "remote philanthropy" of the Yankees, "their booriah-boola-gah enterprises, their frequent fanaticism and pharasaical assumptions."

A dull and dignified man who shared the ideas of his circle and had no desire to transcend them, all his life Fish identified with the principles of his party, desiring no other epithet than Whig. To him that designation implied devotion to the Union and to the great objectives of liberty and stability. Whig principles, he once told George Sumner, were enduring; they did not depend upon transient issues or the vagaries of government. They were, he said, "the principles of law and order, of the rights of persons and property, of personal liberty and social restraint, without which our republican institutions must cease to exist."

As time changed, however, such principles found varied expression. American politicians, then as now, easily slid from conservative to liberal rhetoric and back as occasion demanded; but it seems safe to say that Fish well fitted Louis Hartz's definition of a conservative—he was, after all conserving a liberal world view. In the 1840s and early 1850s Fish defended the right of petition, voted against the gag rule, supported the Wilmot Proviso, expressed his "unequivocal" opposition to the extension of slavery, and thought his generation might fulfill a noble destiny by thwarting oppression, extending freedom of thought, and vindicating personal liberty.

After the collapse of the Whig party, however, Fish looked forward to a new union of the nation's conservative elements, and by the outbreak of war in 1861 was describing himself as a conservative, "the guardian of order, of law, and of *instituted* liberty." Moreover, he felt it necessary to distinguish between that liberty and a natural one. The former was "fixed, established, appointed, enacted, settled, prescribed"; and by definition it excluded "that liberty which many claim in a state of nature."

Although Fish's rhetoric changed with his political circumstances, he consistently held to a Whiggish philosophy of the nature of man and to a Whig version of economic progress that bordered almost on a technological utopia. To these he joined an imperial conception of the past and future of America. His thought was imitative, shaped in the mold of the historical-minded imperialism of a John Quincy Adams or a William Henry Seward. Later, his official pronouncements put him squarely in the Hamiltonian Whig tradition. As a conservative he naturally thought in historical terms, and many of his state papers began with an appeal to precedent. He identified a common vision of society running from the Federalists to the Whigs, and then on to the Republicans. He recognized and applauded the farsighted vision of the Founding Fathers, who at the nation's infancy had predicted its glorious future, seeing that its institutions, authority, and peaceful influence would one day occupy the entire continent of America. The sense of himself as a natural leader of a society born to greatness remained with Fish for his entire life.

Raised at a time when upper-class status and involvement in politics still went together, Fish became politically active immediately upon graduation from college. In the 1830s he worked behind the scenes; in the next decade he ran for office. Though checkered with occasional defeat, his career was still remarkably fortunate: a fluke win of a Democratic congressional seat in 1842, followed by a crushing defeat in 1844; a race for lieutenant governor of New York in 1846 and another loss; a second run for the same office in 1847 and victory; election as governor in 1848, and then as a United States senator in 1851.

Fish prospered in the political circumstances of the 1840s, when both parties in his state were badly divided. He gained all of his electoral victories when the Democrats split. In the Whig party, he served as a figure capable of avoiding similar splits; he was an amiable, wealthy, and moderate man who did little while in office, but who accepted the lead of the Seward-Weed organization.

These qualities served Fish less well in the next decade. The Kansas-Nebraska Act of 1854 changed the face of politics. Without the ability to marshal public support either through oratory or organization and afflicted with timidity and self-doubt in dealings with politicians and voters, Fish had the wrong kind of abilities for the politics of the 1850s. In quieter times he might have fitted Into the Senate "club" by virtue of wealth, social position, conservative temperament, and amiability. In the politics of mass realignment he was singularly ineffective.

Although he voted some 79 percent of the time with Seward, Fish made a point of defining his views as a conservative alternative to the "radicalism" of his senior colleague. Such definition was left to his correspondence; he failed to speak publicly, and during six years in the Senate never made a formal speech. He was defensive enough on this matter by 1855 to make it clear that his failure to speak owed more to timidity than to reasoned opposition to "agitation." Although he wrote much of riding and controlling the wave of public feeling, he never explained how this could be done by a man without an organization who did not speak to the public. In fact, his naturalistic metaphors of "currents" or "waves" of public opinion seem to have reflected his thought; public opinion was *there*, like the sea, not something shaped, altered, and changed, but only sometimes disturbed by the "winds" of "agitation" before settling down once more to its fixed bed.

When the Seward Whigs went over in a body to the Republicans in 1855, Fish was not informed. He spent a year in futile attempts to revive the old party, for he did not want to join either of its successors, the Americans or the Republicans. In the end, he endorsed the Republican ticket in 1856, listing the chief issues as slavery—not as an abstraction "but as a question of right and of political power"—and the government's foreign policy. "Shall peace and justice, or violence and outrage, be its policy?" he asked.

After the election Fish wrote of the Republicans: "There is not and cannot be much sympathy between them and me. I was compelled to act with them at the late election because there was no other place to go to." He had no chance of reelection to the Senate; in 1851 Weed had wanted to conciliate conservative Whigs by nominating a man acceptable to that wing of the party, but in 1857 the conservatives were Americans, Fish was a laggard and unwilling supporter of the Republicans, and the group that Weed had to conciliate was the ex-Barnburner Democrats.

For a politician, Fish had been a remarkably sheltered man; he had had to do little for his success and rarely moved in circles beyond the class of his birth. Although personally amiable, he never showed any particular empathy for those in less fortunate circumstances. He showed special talent for routine administration. A natural bureaucrat, concerned with the precise discharge of duty and the exact balancing of books, he was a perfect executive, according to the limited Whig conception of what an executive should be: a man who carefully, punctually, and completely handled minor matters.

Fish naturally moved toward the middle of any group in which he found himself. This, indeed, explains the apparent changes in his political views, which tended to shift as the men around him changed—from his conservative New York City set, to the Albany politicians led by Weed, to the Senate, back to New York, and finally to Grant's Washington. He may have seen himself as a great compromiser, but he did not serve that function well. His conception of politics was too rigid, he himself too sheltered and timid, his knowledge of men too limited for him to unite a divided party or a divided country. George Templeton Strong, who always disliked him, once wrote, "If you want to know which way the wind blows, throw up Hamilton Fish." There was an element of truth in that mordant phrase.

After his forced departure from electoral politics, Fish played an active role in attempts to institutionalize his class's claim to status. He served as president of the Society of the Cincinnati, of the St. Nicholas Society, of the Union League Club, of the New York Historical Society, and of the Board of Trustees of Columbia University, and was perhaps the leading lay member of the New York Episcopalian church. He began what appears to have been an attempt to model his life-style on that of the English Whig aristocracy that served as a social and political model for his class, including a two-year tour of continental Europe and building a five-hundred-acre country estate at Glenclyffe. As a member of the most exclusive group in the nation's largest city, Fish stood at the peak of American society.

To Fish, the only important part of the sectional question lay in the destruction of the *political* power of the slave interest. Having no interest in a social reconstruction of the South, he wanted the necessary political climate to put Whig conceptions into practice. (Since these conceptions centered on government support for the development of bourgeois capitalism, they spelled doom for the slave interest in any event.) So he unenthusiastically supported Lincoln in the 1860 election, arguing that the issue of

governmental power over slavery in the territories had to be
settled once and for all. After Lincoln's victory, Fish advocated
compromise with the South; if the new administration were
willing "to concede all that the most extreme Southern men ask,
(except for the reopening of the Slave trade) Slavery would never
again be aggressive in the legislation of affairs of the country."

Fish reacted to the war itself like a panicky conservative. He
volunteered his services to the Union, serving as chairman of the
New York City Union Defense Committee in 1861–62. He took a
soft position on Reconstruction terms but an extreme position on
the war itself: "The exemplary punishment of a few disloyal men,
the hanging of a few spies, and the shooting of a few deserters
would have a most salutary influence." By the end of 1862 he had
lost all faith in the national government. ("God protect us—this
Administration certainly cannot"), and he spent the rest of the war
morosely grumbling about the drift of affairs. Reluctantly and late
he adhered to the Lincoln ticket in 1864. After the war, despite his
distrust of Seward, he felt that Andrew Johnson was "proving
himself to be a first-rate President" and attended a mass meeting
supporting his veto of the Freedman's Bureau Bill.

Under pressure of the 1866 elections, Fish backed away from
Johnson and eventually endorsed the regular Republican ticket;
but by now his political influence was small. In 1868, however, his
prospects changed.

After the war Fish had befriended U. S. Grant, who was
lionized by New York society as the great hero of the Civil War.
The general had visited Fish several times in the years 1865–68. Fish
felt that he could support Grant more freely and more consistently
than he had any presidential candidate since 1852, and he made
substantial financial contributions to the general's campaign. After
the election a few people suggested that Fish might become a
cabinet member, but most thought that he would receive one of
the major diplomatic appointments.

Grant's initial selection of advisers surprised the nation, giving
perhaps the first indication that he was not to be a good president.
After some ill-considered and unfortunate choices, the cabinet
had to be reconstructed. The original selection for secretary of
state, Elihu Washburn, a congressman from the president's home
district, had no apparent qualifications for the post beyond his
early fostering of Grant's military career. The choice for the
treasury post raised other difficulties. Grant wanted the millionaire

New York importer A. T. Stewart, who was ineligible for the office under a 1789 statute that Congress, under Senator Sumner's leadership, refused to repeal. Washburn served for only five days and Stewart not at all, so the president had two important positions that had to be filled on rather short notice. So it came about that Fish received a sudden and rather offhand letter from Grant stating, "I have thought it might not be unpleasant for you to accept the portfolio of the State Department." The appointee's immediate attempt to decline met with the news that the Senate had already approved his appointment.

Fish's career as secretary of state falls naturally into three periods: the first, lasting some fourteen months, a period of failure for him and for the administration in general; the second, lasting nine months, marked by a remarkable reversal of political alliances that secured Fish a place in power and in history; the third, covering the remaining six years of his service, showing no substantial change either in American foreign policy or in Fish's position within the administration. Thus, the first two years of Fish's service outweigh in importance the rest of his term.

The key to understanding the changes in this period is the struggle between two groups in the Republican party. Their nature is difficult to define precisely, but almost every observer of the time (and since) recognized their existence. The following tendencies (or self-definitions) might define the spectra of differences: British or other European role models vs. self-conscious American-ism, educated men vs. practical men, political amateurs vs. political professionals, respectability and/or honesty vs. success, old money vs. new money, reformers vs. regulars ("Stalwarts"). Although a cluster of linked attitudes rather than a single clear line defined the differences, their reality was as obvious (yet as hard to define) as the reform-regular struggle that has split the Democratic party in our own time.

Grant's historical identification with the "spoils system" has tended to obscure the fact that many of his early appointments went to those identified with the older elite: Fish as secretary of state, E. R. Hoar as attorney general, Jacob D. Cox as secretary of the interior, David Wells as special commissioner of revenue, John Motley as minister to England, Moses Grinnell as collector of the

New York port. Grant made a crucial decision during 1870, abandoning his original appointees and casting his lot with the "Stalwarts." Hoar, Cox, Wells, Motley, and Grinnell all lost their jobs; only Fish survived.

This abrupt—and often overlooked—change in Grant's policy clearly resulted from the failure of the president's attempt to annex the Dominican Republic, which was thwarted by the strong opposition of the chairman of the Foreign Relations Committee, Senator Charles Sumner, and many others of the old elite. Faced with the choice between his old friend Sumner and the president, Fish survived by using his position to help destroy Sumner. In doing so, he not only survived, but turned his defeats into victories; he took advantage of the split with Sumner to settle the greatest foreign policy crisis facing him, the *Alabama* claims controversy, and made himself an indispensable figure in the administration.

Fish's reputation as secretary of state rests largely on the *Alabama* claims settlement.[1] The other aspects of his tenure—the attempt to annex Santo Domingo, the inglorious policy toward the Ten Years' War in Cuba, the policy of drift punctuated by failure in the Far East—are hardly the stuff of which reputations are made. The one expansionist triumph of Fish's term, the Hawaiian

---

1. During the American Civil War, the Confederate States of America succeeded in building a number of naval cruisers in British shipyards. Subsequently armed outside crown jurisdiction, these ships did tremendous damage to Northern commerce. The most famous of these raiders, the *Alabama*, in a twenty-two-month cruise after its escape from Liverpool in 1862, destroyed over sixty American ships and drove many more to the safety of foreign registry. Union diplomats always claimed that the failure to prevent the building and dispatch of such ships—Sumner liked to call them "pirates"—constituted a breach of proper neutral conduct on the part of the queen's ministers, and as the war in America wound down, efforts to force Her Majesty's government to admit culpability and pay damages intensified, and the efforts dragged on for years. Americans found the Johnson-Clarendon Convention of 1869 unsatisfactory because it lacked an apology and an admission of guilt by the British; the Senate rejected it by an overwhelming vote. Before the final adjudication of the claims by the Geneva arbitration of 1872 (provided for in the Treaty of Washington negotiated by Fish in 1870–71) both the United States and Great Britain felt it necessary to revise the rules of neutrality and to incorporate three rules of proper neutral conduct into the Treaty of Washington that Fish signed on 8 May 1871. For a recent extended discussion of the British response to Southern shipbuilding, see Frank J. Merli, *Great Britain and the Confederate Navy, 1861–1865* (Bloomington, 1970).

Reciprocity Treaty of 1875, is not treated at all in the massive standard biography of Fish by Allan Nevins.

Uncritical acceptance of Fish's account of his role in the settlement of the *Alabama* business and of the reasons for his split with Sumner has obscured the important question of what terms Fish himself originally set for settlement. Until September 1870 his terms included a British withdrawal from Canada. In later years this stipulation was laid at Sumner's door, and he was blamed for all the difficulties of Anglo-American relations in 1869–70. Indeed, Fish cleverly shifted the grounds of his split with Sumner from the inglorious question of Dominican annexation to the higher ground of peace with England. Almost every major American political figure in the post–Civil War period shared Sumner's desire for Canadian annexation, however.

When Fish came to power, the Dominion of Canada was less than two years old. Its mere existence challenged the long-standing American dream of continental empire, but there was much evidence that the jerry-built Canadian union might not survive. The new government had not yet established control of any area west of Ontario, and it faced widespread opposition inside areas already incorporated. The Canadian economy had suffered badly from America's refusal to renew reciprocity, with exports to the United States dropping from a duty-free $48.5 million in 1866 to $25 million in 1867, on which duties of some $3.5 million had to be paid. The Maritime Provinces, already least favorable to the confederation, suffered worst of all. The new government took half their revenues to Ottawa, and returned little, while the new Dominion tariff wiped out their chief source of income and reduced imports. Anti-Confederationists swept the Nova Scotia elections in 1867, and despite the defection of their leader Joseph Howe, a series of by-elections in early 1869 showed that they retained considerable strength. This anticonfederation sentiment was concentrated in the economic elite of Nova Scotia and New Brunswick, who were most closely tied to the United States economy.

Under these pressures, the Canadian government was desperate for reciprocity. Since the Americans were unresponsive to their demands, they directed pressure against the weak point in the United States, the fisheries.[2] Canada doubled the license fee for

2. In the peace treaty of 1783, Americans had received the right to fish off the coasts of Canada and Newfoundland, and throughout the nineteenth century this

U.S. fishing in 1867 and again in 1868; in 1870 it abolished all licenses and took active steps against American fishermen. Ironically, these moves financially injured groups in America who were favorable to the Canadian position, but did not affect those hostile to reciprocity.

The connection between the *Alabama* claims and Canada was not obvious, and the British steadfastly resisted linking the two questions. Charles Sumner brought the idea of trading the claims for Canada to center stage in a speech on the Johnson-Clarendon Convention in April 1869. This convention, a last-minute stab by the unpopular outgoing administration at solving the claims issue, was doomed in any event (the Senate rejected it by a vote of fifty-four to one). Sumner's speech did not directly mention the exchange of Canada for the claims; the Massachusetts senator rather gave a huge assessment of the damages owed to America, the so-called indirect claims, charging Britain with the entire cost of two years of the Civil War, more than a billion dollars—a sum that by implication could be met only by the cession of Canada.

Contrary to popular belief, Sumner did not originate the idea of trading the claims for Canada; indeed, such an arrangement had already been formally proposed by the Minnesota legislature, and six days before Sumner's speech, John Hamilton (son of Washington's secretary of the treasury and a close friend of both Fish and Grant) had already written Fish that, following the expected rejection of the Johnson-Clarendon Convention, the best American course would be a simple statement of American claims, after which "the territorial acquisition [could] be brought in as an ultimate relief for the difficulties."

"right"—an economic prize of considerable importance—became a frequent source of friction as the United States sought to extend it and the British and Canadians to restrict it. The Reciprocity Treaty of 1854 had given Americans extensive privileges in Canadian waters, but when that treaty lapsed an earlier, more restrictive convention of 1818 again became operative, and Canadian efforts to impose restrictions on American fishing vessels stirred up considerable animosity, especially in New England. The dispute over fishing rights, reciprocity, and the San Juan boundary in the Pacific Northwest were all intertwined with the negotiations over the claims for damage done by Confederate ships, and are usually given the generic title of *Alabama* claims or the Treaty of Washington negotiations. That treaty extended American rights in exchange for a cash award to the Canadians. A three-man commission, after much dickering, awarded Canada $5.5 million in 1877.

Fish's reply to Hamilton showed that his mind ran along similar lines. He wrote that the difficulty lay in the instructions to be presented by the new minister to England (Sumner's man, John Motley, who was to replace the discredited Reverdy Johnson). The private claims were not large but were hard to handle separately; America's real grievance, the national claim, was difficult to specify: the hasty British recognition of the Confederacy's belligerency and other hostile acts had prolonged the war by at least a year, but the bill for such offenses would be difficult to draw up. "The value can never be paid in *money*. It may be compensated by a territorial concession, but *to suggest this to Great Britain is to assure* its refusal." Perhaps accepting Hamilton's idea, Fish decided to let the problem lie, planning later to resume negotiations in Washington. This decision was followed by the cabinet as well; the United States would do nothing to settle the issue, and hope that economic pressure (refusal to grant reciprocity) combined with dissent inside the Dominion and British desire to withdraw troops from Canada would resolve the situation in America's favor.

In the first of his articles entitled "The Session" for the *North American Review* in April 1869, Henry Adams expressed confidence that an American consensus had emerged, noting that the conviction that the "whole continent of North America" would eventually fall under control of the United States was "absolutely ingrained in our people." He further asserted that a British offer to cede Canada in exchange for the claims would find immediate assent in the Senate and that the senators would give their consent "without giving a second thought to international law or establishing any new principle whatever." An impartial observer watching the actions of the senators and reflecting upon their behavior might well conclude that "territorial aggrandizement" lay at the back of their minds, "that these claims were to be reserved and used to lead or force England into a cession of territory." The acute Adams hinted that a prudently managed foreign policy might achieve the desired result, for an independent Canada would be "safer from violence" than it had been under British rule.[3]

3. In the postwar period a group of extreme Irish-American nationalists, the Fenians, conducted a numer of raids on Canadian territory and by their efforts created serious Anglo-American friction, for the British believed that these raids had the connivance, if not the direct support, of American officials. Since many of the Fenians were protesting British policy in Ireland, an independent Canada would presumably eliminate the border raids.

Keenly aware of their weakness in North America, the British recognized that their vulnerability hampered negotiations with Washington. On one occasion, in late March 1869, Prime Minister Gladstone told his foreign secretary, Lord Clarendon, that the "indefensible" Canadian border "made poor John Bull content to exhibit to Americans a submissiveness such as he has never to my knowledge shewn to any other people upon earth." That weakness made the British eager for settlement, especially as the prospect of a Franco-Prussian war came closer—but they were not prepared to give up Canada as the price of settlement with America.

In July, the Canadian minister of finance, Sir John Rose, passed through Washington en route to London and had several days of discussion with Fish. Though Rose wanted a new reciprocity treaty between America and Canada, the secretary of state told him that the time was not ripe either for reciprocity or for settlement of the claims. Although Sumner's speech denouncing the Johnson-Clarendon Convention was not to be interpreted as a demand for damages, Fish described it as a "fair expression" of the American sense of grievance; the next step, he said, would be up to Her Majesty's government.

Consensus on Canada did not prevent disagreement in the American camp. Fish later claimed these differences showed that Motley and Sumner wanted war with England, while he struggled for peace. The evidence does not support his claim. The first disagreement came over a memoir that Motley had presented to Fish as a suggestion for the instructions that would accompany him to London. (The two men later disagreed about how this memoir came to be written, and they could never subsequently agree about who had asked whom for it.) Fish rejected Motley's memoir, but not because of its strong position of indirect claims (a principle fully accepted by Fish and advanced three years later In the American case at Geneva) or because of his hostility to England, but rather because of a disagreement over the right of nations to recognize belligerency. Sumner and Motley felt that the hasty British recognition of Confederate belligerency in May 1861 was the key event justifying the large American claims. At that juncture, however, Grant and Fish were wrestling with the problem of whether or not to recognize Cuban belligerency in the revolt against Spanish rule; they did not wish to inhibit their own maneuverability by any broad statements that might later constrict their freedom of action.

The instructions eventually entrusted to Motley were a compromise between the views of Fish and Sumner, written by that jack-of-all-diplomatic-trades, Caleb Cushing. When Motley first presented the American position to Clarendon in June 1869, however, he used language that followed Sumner's view rather more closely than it did that of Grant or Fish. Though he had technically exceeded his instructions—a rather serious diplomatic fault—at the time he received only a mild rebuke, and nothing more was heard of the matter until a year later, when the administration dredged it up to justify its abrupt dismissal of Motley.

At this time, the summer of 1869, Fish's muted criticism of Motley did not affect his relations with Sumner; but the two men did have a disagreement: Fish did not want to make any further statement of the American position, while Sumner argued that America should make a statement of its case *"so that England may see its extent."* Only then, when Great Britain had seen the enormity of its crime, when it had recognized the extent of America's "massive grievance," would it be "ready for the remedy": departure from North America. Finally, Fish agreed to a restatement of the American position and asked Sumner to draft it, but the latter, pleading overwork, declined and suggested that the task be entrusted to Cushing. The new instruction, Number 70, was sent at the end of September. Later, after breaking with Sumner, Fish argued that there were "wide differences and broad distinctions between those instructions and Mr. Motley's paper." Few contemporaries agreed.

When Number 70 was published at the end of the year it led to a breach between Fish and Clarendon. Despite a formal protest by the British minister in Washington, Sir Edward Thornton, Fish refused to publish the foreign secretary's "observations" on Number 70. Clarendon, who had responded so softly to what the administration later called Motley's "warmongering," was deeply wounded by the September dispatch, considering it "offensive." American refusal to publish his observations sealed his break with the secretary of state.

Earlier, on 6 November, Clarendon had written Fish that the British regretted the absence of concrete suggestions for settlement in Number 70. Her Majesty's government could not "make any new proposition or run the risk of another unsuccessful negotiation" without some definite proposal from America. Fish would make no such overtures; he wanted Canada. He told cabinet colleagues that the British might part with the Dominion if the Canadians so requested, but they would not surrender the province "as satisfaction for any claim." Fish wanted to keep Canada a private matter to avoid stiffening British backs. For example, on 23 December 1869, when Thornton again asked for American terms for a settlement of the claims, Fish declined to give any. The subject then turned to the threat of a new Fenian invasion of Canada, and Fish suggested that a British withdrawal from there would "remove the pretext" for the Fenian threats, while permitting immediate settlement of the *Alabama* claims.

Two days earlier, Fish had told a delegation of midwestern Republican representatives that "the pressure of the existing commercial relations is increasing the feeling for annexation. . . . England is believed willing to allow the Provinces to separate from the mother country. . . . We wish not to retard the growing feeling in favor of annexation." Fish had two new reasons to anticipate annexation: the rebellion of the *métis* (French-Indian half-breeds) in the Red River (the Riel Rebellion) and a petition from British Columbia requesting it. On 6 January 1870, Fish discussed the petition and the rebellion with Thornton, suggesting that these matters presented an opportunity for Great Britain to separate itself from Canada. He hinted heavily that "the removal of the British flag would render easy the settlement of all other questions between the two governments."

By the spring of 1870 Fish had made clear to the British that settlement of the claims depended upon withdrawal from Canada. Though not formally expressed this position was repeated many times in private communications between the two governments. For instance, on 12 March, Fish's assistant secretary, J. C. Bancroft Davis, wrote Sir Curtis Lampson, deputy governor of the Hudson's Bay Company, to propose that the British grant Canadian independence, adding the none-too-subtle hint, "Why could not this change be accompanied by a settlement of differences which now appear too far apart to settle any other way?" Fish later stated the matter even more clearly; on 14 June he told Thornton, "You may depend upon it that twenty-four hours after Canada is independent, you and I will be able to settle the *Alabama* question as easily as possible." Two weeks later he wrote Horace Greeley asking him to devote some space to the idea of Canadian independence, adding that "annexation must follow independence very soon."

Fish based his policy on several misapprehensions. He thought a policy of delay would lead to a settlement; instead it led to trouble. He entertained what Thornton once called the "delusive expectation" that the British would grant Canadian independence. He believed that a policy of pinpricks (ranging from refusing Canadian reciprocity to denying the use of Sault Sainte Marie to British troops on their way to the Red River would speed withdrawal. By the fall of 1870, however, American hopes foundered on the rock of British and Canadian resistance, a resistance that could have been overcome only by a willingness on the part of the United States to bluff, to use its own forces, or to support the use of force by Red River rebels or Fenians. Such willingness might not have meant war, but it would have required steely nerves and a gambler's temperament. Fish had neither, and never thought Canada worth a split with England. (Indeed, he once wrote that the *Alabama* dispute was unfortunate because it weakened England's power in world affairs.)

It is possible to pinpoint within a week Fish's change of policy. As late as 18 September he was still suggesting that "the best solution would be independence," only to meet with Thornton's standard response: "It is impossible to connect the question of Canadian independence with the settlement of the *Alabama* claims." Eight days later, the two men had another conference. Fish began in his usual way, by complaining about the fisheries, but then he suddenly shifted his tone: "Disclaiming any official character or purport in the suggestion, I asked whether Great Britain would settle all the questions pending between the countries at once. . . . That if the United States abandoned their opposition to arbitrating the *Alabama* claims, Great Britain might agree to the American claim of the San Juan boundary line. All commercial claims to be referred to arbitration. The inshore fisheries to be opened to American vessels, and in return a more free trade be allowed in certain articles between the United States and its [Great Britain's] colonies." Fish had suddenly dropped Canadian independence as a requirement of settlement, as well as abandoned his long-standing position that the next gesture must come from the English.

He had received two important communications in the week

between these two conferences with Thornton. On 19 September a letter from the American consul at Vancouver told him that annexationist sentiment in British Columbia had passed, and that the province was about to join the Dominion. A second letter from Representative Benjamin Butler, dated 25 September, complained bitterly of Canadian policy on the fisheries and hinted that his constituents might take matters into their own hands: "The Springfield rifle, loaded at the breech, is the only negotiator." These letters indicated not only that there was little chance of picking off any portion of the Dominion, but also that continued postponement of agreement might lead to war.

Four other factors pushed Fish toward a settlement. First, the death of Lord Clarendon at the end of June 1870 removed from office one of Fish's enemies and replaced him with the amiable "Pussy" Granville. Secondly, pressure for settlement of Civil War damages was mounting. The claim holders included many important economic and political figures who were becoming impatient with the continued postponement of settlement. The "new" Grant administration being created in the fall of 1870 was especially vulnerable to interest group pressure, and when Fish brought his new idea before the cabinet in October he began by mentioning "the desire of many parties interested in the *Alabama* Claims to have that question settled."

A third important influence on the course of Anglo-American relations was the great American war debt. During 1870, the administration decided to refund this massive amount at a lower rate of interest; any refunding would necessitate the cooperation of the English financial community, and this militated against any trouble with England. Sir John Rose listed the American debt first among factors pushing the United States toward settlement. Immediately after Fish told the cabinet of his January 1871 discussions with Rose, Secretary of the Treasury George Boutwell announced that refunding the debt could begin.

The fourth and most important factor—the split between Grant and Sumner—was somewhat fortuitous. Enraged by the defeat of his treaty for Dominican annexation, and feeling betrayed by Sumner's part in senatorial rejection of the treaty, Grant fired Motley as minister to England; this in turn enraged Sumner, who began to pressure Fish to take his side. Fish took exactly the opposite course, answering Motley's complaints by publishing the so-called Moran letter in which he blamed Motley's disobedience of orders (rather than Sumner's opposition to the Dominican treaty) for his dismissal and attacked Sumner by calling him "one who uses the words and assurances of friendship to cover a secret and determined purpose of hostility." This letter ended a twenty-year friendship.

As a result of his speech on the Johnson-Clarendon Convention, everyone identified Sumner with the idea that Canada was a fair exchange for the claims. This identification was sealed in the eyes of the British by a private memorandum that Sumner wrote for Fish on 17 January 1871 repeating the idea that settlement should wait until the British withdrew from the continent; Fish immediately showed the memorandum to Rose. He was able to use Sumner as a universal bogeyman, scaring Grant on the one side and the British on the other.

Most importantly, by joining in the assault on Sumner, Fish allied with the Stalwarts. His conference of 14 January with Senator Zachariah Chandler showed that both men knew what they were doing. Chandler, who had played a leading role in the removal of Fish's erstwhile friends, Cox, Motley, and Hoar, and who just six months earlier had fiercely attacked Fish, now stated that he no longer sought war with England or annexation of Canada, and that he no longer opposed Fish's retention of his post. In other words, in return for Fish's attack on Sumner and for his toleration of the activities of Chandler's friends within the administration, Chandler would support Fish on foreign policy, an area that was not for him of first importance. Fish would lend a touch of respectability to the otherwise raffish new administration, while Anglo-American reconciliation would strengthen Grant among the "independent" voters most likely to defect in 1872.

Settlement of the *Alabama* claims prevented the last real attempt of the United States to absorb Canada. On almost every other issue, however, Canadian interests were sacrificed to Anglo-American reconciliation. Fish did not impose his will on the claims problem. The events of 1869–70 narrowed and defined the alternatives, and suggested the shape of the 1871 settlement. The United States demanded a settlement of the claims and of the fisheries, and would not concede reciprocity; the British would give in at all points except the independence of Canada, and so compromise terms were reached. The American government nearly threw away even this victory by the inclusion of the "indirect claims" in the American case at Geneva, and Fish's later

THE APPLE OF DISCORD AT THE GENEVA TRIBUNAL.

THE LAST SCENE OF THE WILLIAM TELL TRAGEDY.

Harper's Weekly, 5 October 1872

willingness to accept an unfavorable arbitrator in the fisheries dispute and to allow the three rules of neutrality to be abandoned leaves it a moot point whether his earlier course had been a result of cleverness or of weakness. In either event Fish's importance in 1870 was simply that he was realistic. While Sumner and Grant tore each other to pieces over annexation of the Dominican Republic, Fish kept his eye on Canada and Great Britain. Sumner and Grant weakened themselves politically and damaged their historical reputations, while Fish secured a place in power and in history.

Fish's career was overshadowed by that of Seward. As in the case of his predecessor, the rise of the Whig party in New York in the 1830s had shaped his politics. Influenced by many of the same men, they shared a belief in Whig expansionism. At every step of his career, however, Fish proclaimed that he differed from Seward. In practice these proclaimed differences often turned out to be temperamental rather than ideological. Both believed in the Whig creed of orderly progress, though Fish perhaps stressed the order a bit more than the progress. A genial, expansive, and optimistic man, Seward had made his own way up; Fish, on the other hand, was born at the top of American society, never felt at ease with those who were not at his own level, and spent much of his life defending an established social position.

The relative success of Fish's service in the State Department demands explanation. The change in type of job alone explains part of the difference. He had always been a better bureaucrat than a legislator and worked better in small groups than in large ones. His success was not simply a matter of changing position or adapting to circumstances, but of adapting to a different time in American life. His term of office coincided with the Reconstruction Era. The Civil War, which in many areas had less impact than is commonly assumed, crucially affected the foreign policy and self-image of America. Before the war, Southern interests had always greatly influenced foreign policy. Afterward, foreign affairs became the private preserve of the northeastern metropolitan elite. Fish himself was one of the first representatives of this new breed. In a sense, he marked the beginning of the "establishment" in foreign policy, of the old-family, Ivy League–educated men who were to dominate this area of American life for the next century.

The effect of the Civil War on America's self-image can hardly be overstressed. It seems clearly to have marked the change from a revolutionary to a conservative power. Revolutions directed at the American state had no appeal, and in the face of such a revolution, the state became a positive moral good. It was no coincidence that the reputation of Hamilton began to rise, and that of Jefferson to fall, after 1860.

Meanwhile, important areas in the rest of the world were moving toward the left. The United States had welcomed the 1848 revolutions in Europe, and men like Fish and Calhoun who had opposed them had been a small minority. The Paris Commune of 1870–71 called up a far different reaction. Fish was not alone in his abhorrence of this social movement; almost every opinion maker and politician in the country shared it. Even more striking was the lack of enthusiasm of many Americans for the Cuban revolution. The Spanish revolutions of 1868 and 1873 won greater support because they seemed in the tradition of bourgeois democracy rather than radical revolution. It was now acceptable for a Caleb Cushing to express doubts about even this kind of revolution. If it was impossible to introduce capitalist parliamentarianism into backward nations, and if the only choice was between revolution and reaction, there was no question which the new American leaders would choose.

Fish, who in the 1850s had seemed so out of date, was in the 1870s far more relevant to the new realities of an increasingly conservative America. In a cabinet discussion early in 1870, he even expressed hostility to the principle of asylum. It helped revolution, he argued, and tended to encourage and convert into revolution "every change of political power, [and it] retards civilization and the establishment of a recognized stable government." It is difficult to think of an earlier secretary of state who might have said the same thing. Ironically, Fish's apparently outmoded conservatism made him more relevant to later American history than the "advanced liberals" of his own day.

In stressing the anachronistic aspect of Fish, his biographer Nevins saw him as a magnificent monument from the American past, whose essential world view was cast aside by the men of 1898. One might argue instead that the men of 1898 carried out many of Fish's ideas more effectively than he ever could have. The failure of Nevins and other historians such as Ernest May to see the continuity between Fish and the 1890s has resulted from their tendency to see the history of 1865–1900 as a consistent struggle between imperialists, and anti-imperialists, with one side triumphing in the 1870s and the other victorious in the 1890s. A close study of congressional roll calls and speeches during the years 1865–75 shows that no imperialist–anti-imperialist dichotomy existed at that time; positions on one expansionist issue did not predict positions on other such issues.

Certainly Fish himself could not qualify as a member of either side of this simple dichotomy. He continued the American pattern of expansion into new areas before there was immediate economic or social reason for possessing them, anticipating the future needs of the American political economy. A mere list of places where America intervened militarily during his tenure would serve as an outline of future theaters of American action: Hawaii, Korea, Mexico, Panama, the Dominican Republic.

The American empire, so far from being "accidental," was a conscious intellectual creation. Throughout his public life Fish thought in terms of past and future expansion, and was heavily influenced by the English model. His personal life-style closely resembled that of the English aristocracy, and like other Whigs he was keenly aware of English "free-trade imperialism." He wrote enviously on how the English could gain empire without responsibility, and then proposed steps by which the United States could achieve the same end.

For instance, in his 1870 message to the Senate on Latin American trade, intended as a major statement of policy, he praised the Senate for stating that "close relations of geographical continuity and political friendship" justly entitled the United States to a share of Latin American trade, and for regarding "the commercial and the political relations of the United States with the American states of Spanish origin as necessarily dependent upon each other." After a discourse that traced America's rise to greatness (with particular praise for John Quincy Adams and Henry Clay), he tied the no-transfer principle[4] to the Monroe

4. In his first annual message to Congress on 6 December 1869, the president (in a passage furnished by Fish) said that the United States had no disposition to interfere with the relations between Spain and its colonial dependencies in the New World, believing that Spain and other European powers holding colonies in the Western Hemisphere would find it in their own interests to establish such

Doctrine: "It looks hopefully to the time when, by voluntary departure of European governments from this continent and adjacent islands, America shall be wholly American." Toward the end, in a cool statement, he presaged the more famous Olney Fiat:[5] "The United States . . . occupy of necessity a prominent position on this continent, which they neither can nor should abdicate, which entitles them to a leading voice, and which imposes on them duties of right and of honor regarding American questions, whether those questions affect emancipated colonies, or colonies still subject to European domination."

Fish set forth many of his ideas on the Caribbean policy of the United States in a letter to Colonel Alexander Hamilton, Jr., on 13 March 1870. Beginning with an acid portrayal of British colonialism—which he saw as selfish but successful—Fish noted that the British system nonetheless created benefits for the mother country by securing self-sustaining colonies that were forced to pay tribute to British trade and help fight Britain's wars. He then elaborated his own views. While favoring the independence of Cuba he did not think its people fit to become citizens of the United States, especially since adoption of the constitutional amendments giving blacks equal rights. (He thought the Negroes in Cuba "less educated, less civilized than those who were lately slaves in our Southern States.") The protectorate was his chosen tool for expansion: "My plan looked to independence with a certain guardianship or trusteeship over the Cuban duties, which [would] have enabled a certain training to be extended to the people." He argued that Santo Domingo—"the key to the Gulf"—would be a better acquisition than Cuba because it had equal potential for cultivation, fewer people, and provided a needed "harbor *outside* our Coast line" to protect the proposed transisthmian canal.

---

colonies as independent members of the family of nations. He then went on to say, "These dependencies are no longer regarded as subject to transfer from one European power to another."

5. During the course of an Anglo-American dispute over the boundary of Venezuela in 1895, Secretary of State Richard Olney made a famous—and much quoted—statement of America's position in Latin American affairs: "Today the United States is practically sovereign on this continent, and its fiat is law upon the subjects to which it confines its interposition. Why? . . . It is because, in addition to all other grounds, its infinite resources combined with its isolated position render it master of the situation and practically invulnerable as against any or all other powers."

Annexation of the island would also compel an early Spanish surrender of its "insular possessions on the Gulf."

Fish would have liked an autonomous Cuba under terms that would have guaranteed American control of the island. Spanish unwillingness to leave the island prevented such a settlement, but the Platt Amendment achieved it three decades later.

Fish proposed a similar solution to the Dominican crisis in May 1870, but Grant's obsession with annexation and his unwillingness to compromise with Senators Sumner and Carl Schurz defeated that plan. The latter two equally supported American domination of the Caribbean, but wanted a West Indian confederation under the protection of the United States.[6] This liberal paternalism matched the pattern that Sumner had already tried to establish for the American Negro.

Fish's failures in Canada and Cuba resulted from control of those areas by powers that would not sacrifice their interests to the United States. In the Dominican Republic, American policy failed because the question of annexation became embroiled in domestic struggles within the Republican party. Fish faced no such problem in Hawaii, however; there his plan of American economic control of the island succeeded. In the Pacific, Americans had more options and fewer restrictions on their maneuverability than in the Caribbean. In the Hawaiian Islands no other power was prepared for an open confrontation, and no powerful, concerted, domestic opposition existed to the expansion of American influence there. In such circumstances the United States could keep a warship on permanent station at Honolulu, indulge in direct military action to prop up a friendly regime, and even contemplate a military occupation to protect the citizens and interests of America. Hawaii was so far removed from American concerns that a policy of military intervention in the islands (much like the

6. Schurz's own vision of American empire was shown in his praise for the German settlements in eastern Europe: "Colonies not political, but colonies commercial, which protect themselves, regulate themselves and feed German commerce of their own motion, without imposing upon the mother country the remotest political responsibility." (*Speeches, Correspondence and Political Papers of Carl Schurz*, vol. 2, edited by Frederic Bancroft [New York, 1913] p. 117.) Here was the clearest imaginable statement of an old American liberal chimera: the invisible hand translated into international affairs; a self-regulating system in which every other nation would of its own volition serve American national interests.

administration's support of Baez in the Dominican Republic)
aroused no significant public or congressional protest.

In the 1870s a majority of Congress opposed both annexation
and establishment of protectorates, but was more willing to
consider the former than the latter. Fish knew that the greater
sophistication of "informal empire" would not win for it any
popular support, recognized that protectorates violated the sacred
principle of "no entangling alliances," and understood that
existing political alignments and attitudes would make it difficult
to conduct any subtle policy. Indeed, he knew that it would be
extraordinarily difficult to conduct any policy requiring congressional approval.

The beauty of a reciprocity treaty with Hawaii was that an
economic negotiation could cover political motives. Fish saw a
future that "might extend the jurisdiction and limits" of the
nation, one that would require "a resting spot" on the ocean
between the Pacific Coast and the "vast domains in Asia, which
are now opening to Commerce and Christian Civilization." Like
his minister in the islands Fish believed that reciprocity would
"bind these islands to the United States with hoops of steel." He
negotiated a treaty that provided free entry of Hawaiian sugar into
the United States in exchange for the reciprocal free importation
of virtually all American products, an arrangement that on balance
quite naturally worked to America's advantage.

Fish told the president that he would not negotiate a treaty
unless assured of all-out administration support; then, armed with
that assurance, he set about getting the treaty through Congress.
The Senate Committee on Foreign Relations was informed of the
danger that Hawaii's entire sugar crop might go to British
possessions and that in the future the islands might look to New
Zealand, Australia, and Canada for economic and political support.
The secretary's spokesman hinted—and given the prevailing Anglophobia of many Americans it was a clever ploy, well calculated
to touch a responsive chord—that the island kingdom might well
become an appendage of the British Empire. Senators were
reminded of the "grave importance" of reciprocity and that
"political supremacy in the islands must inevitably follow commerce." After the addition of a new article forbidding Hawaii to
lease bases to other powers or to sign reciprocity treaties with
them, the Senate passed the treaty on 18 March 1875 by a vote of
51 to 12. Even more difficult was the task of getting the enabling

legislation through the House (which traditionally opposed such treaties as an infringement upon its prerogatives). It took nearly a year of lobbying, support of House leaders from both parties, threats that England might take over the islands, and timely financial inducement to get a 115–101 vote from the House in 1876.

The effect of the treaty was to make the islands dependent upon a sugar monoculture, controlled by large American capitalists, and dependent upon the American market for an outlet for its only product. "The reciprocity treaty of 1875 was a perfect example of a commercial and economic negotiation dictated by political motives. It was designed primarily to extend American influence over the islands and only secondarily to secure economic benefits. The annexationist-minded Grant administration was aware of the prevailing anti-annexationist feeling in the Congress. Hence, there was achieved through the execution of a commercial instrument the substance of a policy that would have been defeated if brought to an open fight on the floor of the Senate. This convention prevented any European power from gaining a political foothold in Hawaii, and at the same time—from the commercial point of view—rendered the archipelago a significant appendage of the United States."[7] That triumph in Hawaii was the only real expansionist success of an administration that had been forced to abandon plans for expansion in the Caribbean and in Canada. For the success of the Pacific venture Fish deserves much credit.

Henry Adams wrote that Fish's reputation was the only one not ruined by association with Grant. The separation of the secretary from the "mess in Washington" has probably been overstressed. Involved on the periphery of several unsavory episodes, he proved himself neither moral enough nor strong enough to do much about them. Although he often complained to Grant, he could not even control patronage in his own department. A sign of the administration's decay after 1872 was that Fish came to be thought of as the "strong man" of the government. Whatever his faults, he was one of the few men left aboard the sinking ship who cared more for policy than for plunder. Fish had

7. Merze Tate, *The United States and the Hawaiian Kingdom* (New Haven, 1965), p. 42 and passim.

convictions, but only rarely carried them into practice. His timidity and lack of strength in enforcing his beliefs often limited his control of foreign policy and generally rendered his policies ineffective. However clearly he defined his principles, in practice he often seemed the plaything of stronger forces and stronger men.

In any survey of American policy during the period, it rapidly becomes clear that the most characteristic feature of American policy under Fish was inconsistency. Purposes were not clearly defined, ends and means were not matched, government lacked the personnel and organization to follow consistent lines of policy toward other nations. Many monographs treating the relations of the United States with other countries during this period stress the weakness of American policy, but almost all, influenced by Nevins, absolve Fish.

All politicians blame their blunders and mistakes on outside forces but few have had their claims so fully accepted by historians as Fish. Grant, Sumner, and Congress have absorbed the blame for the wavering policies of the United States. All deserve criticism, but it is still clear that Fish dominated most areas of foreign policy, and that American policy in many areas under his control showed the same weaknesses as policy in more contested areas.

Fish's historical importance was not that of a man who made history, but of one who responded to it. His main political assets were durability and adaptability. He was not an original man, but reflected the prevailing ideas of the American elite of his time. Although as secretary he might be judged "good in planning, poor in execution," he was not out of date. He had the ability of the true conservative to move with change without abandoning the past. With his roots in the old Federalism of his namesake, he lived long enough to see the beginnings of the new Federalism of the age of William McKinley. Fish's career benefited from the increasing conservatism of bourgeois liberalism, as it became less a triumphant march to the future and more a defense of existing institutions and arrangements of power. He was perhaps the first American secretary of state to define himself as an antirevolutionary, but he was not the last.

BIBLIOGRAPHIC NOTE

The central source for study of Fish is, of course, the massive collection of Fish manuscripts in the Library of Congress, particularly the manuscript diary he kept for his eight years in the State Department. Indeed, the very amplitude of Fish documentation, particularly of the inner affairs of the Grant administration, has somewhat naturally tilted the history books in his favor; most events are seen through his eyes. The Grant papers do not tell us much of this enigmatic man, who still remains one of our more mysterious presidents. The Library of Congress also contains the papers of most of the other significant politicians of the Grant era, with the major exception of Charles Sumner, whose papers can be found in the Houghton Library at Harvard.

No volume of *Foreign Relations* was published for 1869, and the volumes published for the other years of Fish's term are of low quality. Most of the significant published documents having to do with American foreign policy under Fish can be found in the *Executive Documents* of either the House or the Senate (some, on Cuba, were not published until the 1890s).

Just as the Fish diary dominates manuscript materials of Fish's life, so Allan Nevins's massive Pulitzer Prize–winning biography, *Hamilton Fish* (New York, 1936), has dominated secondary materials for nearly forty years. It remains what Matthew Josephson called it: a "literary monument raised by pious hands." With appendices, it comes to more than nine hundred pages. It is a remarkable work with one flaw: too-close identification with the subject. This is particularly obvious in the treatment of Fish's break with Sumner. This impressive work dominated other secondary works until recently. Thus, although C. C. Tansill, in *The United States and Santo Domingo, 1798–1873* (Baltimore, 1938), carefully redressed the balance as to Fish and Sumner, few historians seemed to note it. Sumner's side of the story seemed to reach historians only with David Donald's equally impressive *Charles Sumner and the Rights of Man* (New York, 1970).

There has yet been no book published on Grant's political career to replace William B. Hesseltine's *U. S. Grant: Politician* (New York, 1935), which is somewhat out of date. In some ways the book that still best describes Grant's Washington (as it struck a young aristocrat who knew its leaders) is *The Education of Henry Adams* (Boston, 1918).

The chapter on "Conservatives and Moderates," in Eric Foner's *Free Soil, Free Labor and Free Men* (Oxford, 1970), is an excellent account of Fish and those like him in the years before the Civil War. Modern historians have been keenly aware of the postwar cleavage in the Republican party. Ernest May, in *American Imperialism: A Speculative Essay* (New York, 1968), speaks of division between "cosmopolitans" and "non-cosmopolitans," and uses this division to explain the debate on American policy toward the Dominican Republic and indeed the whole course of American foreign policy from 1865 to 1900. Irwin Unger, in *Greenback Era* (Princeton, 1962), writes of a "hard-money elite," which closely resembles in its membership May's cosmopolitans. Ari Hoogenboom, *Outlawing the Spoils* (Urbana, Ill., 1968), writes of the "better sort" who were thrown out of power in 1870–71 and as a result became civil service reformers. (Hoogenboom is one of the few historians to realize the importance of Grant's new tack in 1870.) Each of these historians seems to be attempting to define the same cultural and political division.

There are numerous books covering America's relations with one country or another during this period. Some recent books treating various aspects of American-Canadian relations are P. B. Waite, *The Life and Times of Confederacy* (Toronto, 1962), a good account of the perilous early years of Canada; Donald Warner, *The Idea of Continental Union* (Lexington, Ky., 1960), detailing nineteenth-century plans for the union of Canada and the United States; Brian Jenkins, *Fenians and Anglo-American Relations during Reconstruction* (Ithaca, 1969), which is stronger on the Seward period than on Fish; and Alvin Gluek, Jr., *Minnesota and the Manifest Destiny of the Canadian Northwest* (Toronto, 1965), a nice little work detailing American designs on the Canadian Northwest.

In a recent article Doris W. Dashew treats the connection between the claims and territorial expansion: "The Story of an Illusion: The Plan to Trade the *Alabama* Claims for Canada," *Civil War History* 15 (December 1969), 332–48. Sumner's part in the claims has been superlatively examined in David Donald's recent biography, cited previously. The *Alabama* claims are a vast subject in themselves, but there is really no recent satisfactory work on them. [Frank J. Merli has work in progress on this subject.—EDITOR]

JAMES GILLESPIE BLAINE

Department of State

The Ideologue as Diplomatist

Lester D. Langley

The world in which James G. Blaine died in 1893 and the world
into which he had been born in 1830 were profoundly different. In
the sixty-three years of his life, the American people had rounded
out the continental domain and fought a civil war. The America of
his youth was principally an agrarian society, and its political
leadership, dominated by Andrew Jackson, Henry Clay, John C.
Calhoun, and Daniel Webster, dealt largely, though not altogether,
with domestic issues. At the time of his death America possessed
political magnates less intellectually imposing but no less motivated by awareness of domestic tensions and prospects of
American greatness in world affairs. Their society was as much
industrial as agricultural, and their analyses of foreign policy and

This essay is based in part on Professor Langley's study of U.S-European rivalry in
the Caribbean.

253

prescriptions for America's role in the world were products of the political and economic stresses of the preceding thirty years.

In shaping the principles of American foreign policy James G. Blaine played a large role, both as ideologue and practitioner. The sectional stresses that led to the creation of the Republican party and to the Civil War had molded his mind. He dominated the postwar political scene as no other presidential candidate since the era of Clay, Calhoun, and Webster. A later generation of textbook writers would rate Blaine as just another Gilded Age politician, identifying him with unsavory political maneuverings. Yet, in his own way, Blaine contributed more to the shaping of American foreign policy than any individual of his generation, with the exception of William H. Seward.

Like Seward, Blaine felt strongly about America's place among the great powers. Both men proposed far-reaching policies for the advancement of United States economic and political influence in the Western Hemisphere, Seward with plans for acquisition of the Danish West Indies, Blaine by efforts in the Pan-American movement. In both minds the intellectual justification for American hegemony in the hemisphere stemmed from the moral and political "superiority" of the Anglo-Saxon peoples. Seward found it natural to expand his "higher law" antislavery arguments of the 1850s by applying such precepts to the ills of Latin America; Blaine shared his predecessor's assumptions and coupled them with an often expressed pity for the degradation of the Latin American polities, with their backward societies and bickering governments. Both secretaries of state encountered an obstinate Congress that momentarily thwarted their Latin American policies.

In the Pacific and Far East, too, the parallels between the strivings of Seward and Blaine are remarkable. Though never accomplishing so awesome a territorial acquisition as Alaska, Blaine nevertheless continued Seward's basic Pacific policies. Seward tried to bring Hawaii closer to American annexation in his 1867 proposals for a reciprocity treaty, and in 1881 Blaine brought the islands within the scope of the Monroe Doctrine, contending that, for moral and economic reasons, Hawaii's future was tied to that of the United States. Seward and Blaine anticipated John Hay's Open Door notes in their belief that the western Pacific was a gateway to the Asian market. Like Seward, Blaine was a transitional figure in American diplomacy, articulating an imperial plan but never accomplishing the grand task.

◇◇◇

Like other Americans during the Age of Jackson, Blaine was a migrant, though he migrated east, or more precisely northeast, from southwestern Pennsylvania to Maine. At the age of ten, his family sent him to the home of Ohio relatives, where he was tutored by William Lyons, uncle of Queen Victoria's minister to the Lincoln government. He returned to Pennsylvania and entered Washington College. In 1847, at age seventeen, he graduated, sharing highest honors in his class of thirty students, an indication of Blaine's intellectual talents (and, of course, the limitations of the curriculum). For the next six years he taught, first in the Western Military Institute near Lexington, Kentucky, then at the Pennsylvania Institute for the Blind. In his spare time he studied law, often the chosen profession for a young man who wanted to advance; but he soon gave it up. On the last day of June 1850, he married Harriet Stanwood, descendant of a well-known Massachusetts family. One branch of the Stanwood family had established roots in Maine, and this connection provided the opportunity for Blaine to begin his journalistic ventures in that state in 1854.

In Maine, Blaine served with two newspapers, the *Kennebec Journal*, which he partly owned, and the *Portland Advertiser*. There was little in Blaine's journalism career that could be called preparation for the secretaryship of state or any diplomatic post, though as newspaper editor he soon displayed a literary and political interest that the successful newspaperman should cultivate. He also possessed a remarkably retentive mind, capable of recalling many names and much information. In an age when most people intimately associated public speaking with political popularity, his oratorical skills were an obvious asset. (Years later, Blaine could work crowds into a frenzy with his "perfidious Albion" orations yet still charm his dinner guests, who sometimes were British diplomats, with his discourses on literature, history, and culture.)

During these years—years of sectional antagonism and political realignments—Blaine's political attitudes developed and matured. His family voted Whig. Blaine idolized Clay, whose American System with its emphasis on nationalism and national growth had deeply impressed him as a teenager. Thus Blaine naturally identified with the concepts of nation and union. In 1854, during the storm over the Kansas-Nebraska Bill, he urged his readers to reject the Whig title and adopt the new one of Republican. As delegate and secretary to the first Republican convention in 1856, he was in a real sense one of the founders of that party. Later, he served as chairman of Maine's Republican state committee, a post he held until 1881 and from which he virtually dictated the appointments, platforms, and orientation of the state's Republican politics.

In 1863, in the midst of the Civil War, he entered Congress. For the next seventeen years he was caught up in the politics of Capitol Hill, as a member of the House until 1876, then as senator to 1881. In these years Blaine became a national figure, impressing his colleagues with his oratorical abilities and forming political friendships with an emerging group of young western Republican leaders, one of whom was James Abram Garfield. Blaine saw himself as a participant and a witness to a series of momentous events, a horrible war and a grand victory, which culminated in nationhood and unity. Unlike his Maine colleagues who preferred William H. Seward, Blaine supported Lincoln in 1860. Where the president articulated the concepts of union from the White House, Blaine nurtured a similar impulse in the House of Representatives. Elected Speaker of the House, Blaine promoted partisan measures with such zeal that observers compared his leadership with Clay's. (Occasionally his rhetorical abilities made enemies. Roscoe Conkling never forgave Blaine for a spirited verbal assault, and his home district in New York in 1884 went for Cleveland— who won the state and the election.)

On most Civil War issues Blaine faithfully adhered to Republican party dogma, though he never approached Reconstruction issues with the intractability of Thaddeus Stevens or the moral fervor of Charles Sumner and never held a central place in the tightly knit band of Radicals. A decade earlier, when Blaine matured in his politics, slavery had been for him the central issue in a great debate, and thus he matter-of-factly accepted emancipation and ultimately the enfranchisement of the black man. He voted for military reconstruction as a necessary concomitant to the salvation of the South and the uplifting of the ex-slave. When Republican policies moderated in the 1870s Blaine supported them, but he always believed abandonment of Southern Republicanism to be a mistake.

Blaine's first love was politics. Caught up in the presidential fever that affected Republicans in the seventies and eighties, his powers of leadership seemingly unmatched in Congress, Blaine appeared a logical choice for the kingmakers. His ablest biographer, David S. Muzzey, contends that Blaine really sought the nomination only once, in 1876, and that in subsequent conventions he merely deferred to movements in his behalf. His friendship with Garfield matured in the Grant years, and, as Garfield moved steadily from a solitary vote to the nomination in 1880, he did not forget Blaine's support. The president-elect spent four months dealing with the nerve-racking assignment of dispensing jobs to loyal Republicans. When Blaine got the nod for the State Department, the wheelhorses in Conkling's stable of Stalwarts called it a political payoff. It was, though Garfield had more choice in the matter than is commonly acknowledged.

The State Department of 1881 was not by any stretch of the imagination a hotbed of activism. Abroad the United States carried out its diplomatic missions through two dozen ministers plenipotentiary and resident, five chargés d'affaires, and about three hundred consuls. The schooling of most had been in politics and business, not international affairs. Of the regular ministers, the large majority were political appointees like Lew Wallace. (Garfield moved Wallace from Paraguay to Turkey because he had enjoyed reading *Ben Hur* and believed Wallace might follow with another work in a Near Eastern setting.) There were ministers of genuine ability, such as James Russell Lowell and Andrew D. White, sent to London and Berlin respectively, whose reputations had been acquired in literary or scholarly pursuits.

If 1881 represented the "nadir of American diplomacy," as later historians described the era, Blaine was certainly no example of the lethargic party faithful content to mark time as secretary of state. It is true that he and the president had not spent much time discussing foreign policy matters and that Blaine began his assignment with no detailed script for settling individual problems. Instead, he brought to the task only a sense of unflagging determination to make America respected by the other powers and to advance American interests in Latin America.

In Blaine's approach to foreign affairs in 1881 one can find numerous examples of the kind of thinking that Walter LaFeber has analyzed in detail in his prize winning work, *The New Empire*. Blaine easily grasped the fundamental arguments used by Seward and other foreign policy activists that the emergence of an industrial America dictated the pursuit of commerce and the extension of American interests southward into Latin America and westward across the Pacific. To Blaine, commercial expansion constituted only a part of the grand task; it must be matched with skilled diplomacy to bring peace to the Western Hemisphere, to assert American influence in the isthmian region, to block European intrusion in the hemisphere, and to advance American policies in the Pacific. Collectively these diplomatic efforts—partly economic, partly political—constituted Blaine's plan for demonstrating the strength of American nationality. The nation, having been tested in the Civil War, could now assert itself more vigorously in the Western Hemisphere. More than anything else, Blaine sought to prove to others, particularly to European governments, that the United States had arrived on the world scene and should be taken seriously. He challenged the British for Latin American markets, though he failed to convince Latin America that it should look to the United States, not Europe, for political and economic leadership.

Unfortunately, Garfield's death terminated Blaine's first tenure as secretary of state (he remained on under Arthur until December 1881), and subsequent investigations into his attempts to settle the War of the Pacific between Chile and Peru-Bolivia precipitated public criticism of his Latin American policies. Too much identified with intense partisan politics, Blaine was not yet taken seriously as an innovative and imaginative statesman.

While his friends promoted his candidacy for president in 1884, Blaine began work on his two-volume memoir, *Twenty Years of Congress*, the first volume of which appeared during the presidential campaign year. Though it will never rank with *The Diary of John Quincy Adams* or the *Memoirs of Cordell Hull*—one reason is that Blaine said little about foreign policy—*Twenty Years of Congress* reveals a remarkable mind at work and reflects Blaine's nationalism. If one dismisses those portions of the work that are frankly sustained Republican eulogies, one finds a superior intellect explaining the vitality and strength of the country.

In the 1884 campaign, haunted by vicious stories of political skullduggery and by charges of diplomatic ineptitude during his brief tenure as secretary of state, Blaine avoided foreign policy issues. The public had not embraced his ideas on the subject, and

indeed regarded his 1881 foray into Latin America with apprehen-
sion and suspicion.

Appointed secretary for the second time in the Benjamin
Harrison administration in 1889, Blaine found himself with aggressive associates, particularly Harrison and Secretary of the Navy
Benjamin Tracy. Ironically, in his second term Blaine turned out to
be somewhat out of touch with the rising tide of spread-eagle
diplomacy. In the Chilean imbroglio of 1891, he became the man
of moderation, so much so that Harrison himself seized the issue
and nearly took the country to war. The Pan-American Conference—planned for Blaine's first term but canceled by his successor, Frederick Frelinghuysen—convened in 1889, but Blaine got
little of what he wanted. In subsequent foreign policy matters he
seemed more restrained, more cautious, less certain of promoting
American interests than he had been in 1881. His failing health and
the loss of three children within a year contributed in part to this
decline in enthusiasm for a vigorous foreign policy.

The Blaine "style" in foreign policy was probably most
controversial in his dealings with Latin American problems.
Remembered principally for his efforts to call an international
American conference, Blaine saw in his Latin American involvements an unusual opportunity to bring peace to the southern half
of the hemisphere and to promote American political and economic interests. Perhaps no other Latin American venture of these
years precipitated more controversy than Blaine's interference in
the War of the Pacific (1879–83), a conflict between Chile on one
side and Peru and Bolivia on the other.

The war resulted from alleged Bolivian violations of the
Chilean-Bolivian settlement of a boundary dispute. In 1874 the
two countries had drawn up a treaty stipulating the division of
territory on the Pacific coast, in a desolate area called the Atacama
Desert. Chile, more economically aggressive than its neighbor,
began to develop the nitrate deposits of the Atacama. The 1874
treaty had stipulated that for twenty-five years neither government
could increase taxation rates in the region, but four years later, as
Chileans increased their exports of nitrate from the Atacama, the
Bolivian legislature authorized a new tax, to be paid into the

Bolivian treasury, on nitrates exported by Chile. The Chilean government not only refused to pay but unilaterally abrogated the treaty, landed troops in an area claimed by Bolivia, and seized control of the nitrate fields. Tensions erupted into hostilities, and Bolivia invoked its 1873 alliance with Peru.

Blaine viewed the Chilean-Bolivian-Peruvian conflict as potentially the most serious in a long list of Latin American boundary disputes. Other hemispheric nations looked for some kind of mediation by a friendly power, perhaps the United States or even a European government. In 1880 England, Italy, and France offered their services. Chile agreed, stipulating that Peru cede Tarapacá, also a nitrate province. When Peru and Bolivia objected and asked for United States mediation, the three European governments consented. The conferees met aboard a U.S. warship in October 1880, and agreed on nothing, principally because victorious Chile sought destruction of the Bolivian-Peruvian alliance and refused arbitral solutions.

The following March, Blaine became secretary of state. Though not the initiator of American efforts to end the war, he did go far beyond the policies of his predecessor William M. Evarts. In early 1881, Chile improved its military position, and by the time Blaine took office Chilean troops had occupied the Peruvian capital, Lima, and had installed a more pro-Chilean administration, headed by Francisco García Calderón. When Blaine received Calderón's representative in Washington, the Chileans must have believed that the United States had accepted Chile's basic demands.

Blaine had no such intention, however. He appointed new ministers to Lima and Santiago; to Peru he sent Stephen A. Hurlbut, formerly a Union officer and Illinois congressman whose most recent assignment was the command of the Grand Army of the Republic. Charges of financial mismanagement in the Union occupation of Louisiana had tainted Hurlbut's reputation, but those charges had not impeded his political advancement. To Chile, Blaine sent another ex-officer, Judson Kilpatrick, who had marched with Sherman and who had earlier served in Chile (1865–68) and had married a Chilean with important family connections in the church.

Blaine's instructions to both men showed that peace constituted his paramount consideration. Though recognizing that Chile deserved some form of territorial concession, he believed that the

Chileans should not make cession of territory a *sine qua non* for peace discussions and should, rather, honorably avoid popular pressures for territorial aggrandizement. Peru had a right to "orderly government" and national sovereignty in the provinces occupied by enemy troops that would allow the Peruvians to achieve a "just and reasonable" disposition of their case.[1]

Blaine saw in the Peruvian-Chilean dispute an excellent opportunity to convey to South American nations that a territorial cession wrung from one nation by another in war created continental strife and exacerbated efforts to achieve a general and lasting peace. As he explained in his instructions to the American minister in Santiago, Chile might have some claim to territory by reason of military conquest, but acquisitions obtained by force could never lead to permanent peace. In order to benefit all parties in the conflict, Chilean authorities should accept the referral of territorial questions to mediators. The first task, Blaine continued, was the restoration of a stable Peruvian government free of Chilean interference and military occupation.

Both the content and tone of Blaine's suggestion seem, in retrospect, reasonable, just, and fair; but two issues hampered any settlement along the lines he suggested. The first was the tremendous enthusiasm of the Chileans as their small army (2,400 troops against 13,200 Peruvian and 3,232 Bolivian soldiers) routed and humiliated the enemy. Moreover, the war furnished Chile with the opportunity to overcome the economic doldrums of the late seventies. The opening up of the nitrate fields to Chilean exploitation (financed in large part by English capital) offered to many Chileans the opportunity to modernize their society. To relinquish the grip over the northern lands just because an

1. Blaine was in effect asking Chile to repudiate territorial rights won by military conquest and he argued that international justice would be better served without Chilean interference in Peruvian affairs, even though Chilean troops were occupying key provinces and the capital of Peru. The issues, claims, and counterclaims in the dispute were extremely complex; they remained unresolved until 1929 when a treaty between Peru and Chile achieved a diplomatic solution. During the War of the Pacific, Chilean troops had occupied the provinces of Tacna and Arica in southern Peru, as well as its capital, Lima, and its principal port city, Callao. In 1882 Chile voluntarily withdrew from Lima and Callao but remained in the two provinces. After Blaine's repudiation in America, the two Latin American states negotiated an interim settlement that called for a plebiscite in the disputed provinces.

American secretary of state believed that Chilean expansionism hampered inter-American harmony seemed not only unacceptable but ludicrous. Secondly, Hurlbut and Kilpatrick interpreted their instructions loosely, almost working at cross-purposes.

Of the two, Hurlbut played the more crucial role, because he enjoyed Blaine's confidence and could act as intermediary between both Peruvian and Chilean officials in Lima. He advised Calderón to resist Chilean demands for territory and suggested a financial indemnity as the price for Chilean withdrawal. Hurlbut thought the United States must end the war. When the French broached the idea of a Franco-American statement on the war in the summer of 1881, Hurlbut killed the plan, knowing of course that Blaine feared European diplomatic intervention as much as a continuation of the conflict. Later, Hurlbut peremptorily notified the commander of Chile's occupation army that other countries would interpret the seizure of Peruvian territory as the initial step in a campaign of aggression. In Santiago, Kilpatrick adopted a pro-Chilean posture. The differing positions taken by the two American ministers led to a series of mutually acrimonious notes between Lima and Santiago. In November the exasperated Chileans finally arrested the Peruvian chief of state, Calderón, because, as Hurlbut wrote, he had refused Chile's peace terms. To both Hurlbut and Kilpatrick Blaine now sent reprimands, wording Kilpatrick's more strongly since he had misled the Chilean government by his misrepresentation of American policy.[2]

Besides the frustrations caused by the bunglings of his ministers, Blaine involved American policy in the affairs of foreign businesses in Peru. One of these, the Société Générale de Crédit Industriel et Commercial, distracted him from the Chilean-Peruvian settlement. The society was actually a holding company for European owners of Peruvian bonds whose management wanted to move into the nitrate and guano fields, using receipts to reimburse Chile, subsidize Peru, enhance the value of Peruvian

2. It should be remembered that by this time Blaine's days in the department were numbered. He had agreed to remain on after Garfield's death in September as a gesture of continuity, but he knew that Arthur wanted his own man. Blaine realized that he had only minimal time to salvage his entire Latin American program: the inter-American conference, the solution of boundary disputes, and the settlement of conflict. If he failed to mediate the War of the Pacific, he would fail everywhere in Latin America.

bonds, and enrich itself. Its president and lobbyist, Jacob Shipherd, a New York promoter, raised an old claim against Peru brought by Alexandre Cochet, a man who had allegedly discovered a scientific means of improving the commercial value of Peruvian guano. Shipherd estimated the Cochet claim at the stupendous price of one billion dollars. Another claimant was that of a U.S. citizen whose brother, Théophile Landreau, contended that Peru had wrongfully annulled a valid contract to exploit certain guano deposits. Blaine inherited the Landreau claim from the previous administration and gave it a nominal bureaucratic interest though he remained suspicious of both claims. Blaine had little respect for Shipherd, but in a series of widely publicized charges the latter convinced many people that he had received support from high officials in the Garfield administration. Naturally, Blaine's political enemies inferred the worst from such charges, though in 1882, during the congressional investigations of American involvement in the War of the Pacific, Blaine presented a spirited defense of his policies. As for Landreau, Blaine sought only to obtain for an American citizen a full and fair hearing in a Peruvian court. There is no evidence that Blaine gave these economic interests anything more than the attention they deserved; yet the cloud of suspicion that Blaine supported Peru because of American economic activities there—never disappeared, and Blaine suffered some ignominy in life and in death by the unforgettable sobriquet, the practitioner of "guano diplomacy."

Blaine's determination to salvage his Latin American policy, particularly his plans for the inter-American conference, before he left office prompted him to send a special envoy to South America. The new appointee, William Trescot, had assisted Blaine in developing a general Latin American policy earlier in the year. To assist Trescot, Blaine sent along his own son, Walker, third assistant secretary of state. On reaching his destination, Trescot was to convey to the Chilean government Blaine's belief that the Chilean-Peruvian imbroglio had been partly the fault of Hurlbut's indiscretions. If Chile remained recalcitrant, Trescot could suspend (not sever) diplomatic relations in hopes of bringing the Chilean government around to American reasoning. If that failed, then Trescot should tell the Santiago authorities that its policies of territorial acquisition would be discredited by the other American republics, whose governments would be asked to join the United States in an effort to preserve peace in the Western Hemisphere.

TRYING TO BULLY AND BROWBEAT EACH OTHER.

Mr. BLAINE (to Mr. BADGER BELMONT). "I hope you will treat me as a gentleman. I am not in a police court to be BADGERED."

Blaine's allusion to some form of multilateral intervention referred, of course, to his announced plans for the inter-American conference, though he denied that the proposed conference and the War of the Pacific were intimately related. As Russell H. Bastert demonstrated in his analysis of Blaine's Latin American policy, however, the timing of the Pan-American invitations (late November 1881) and the instructions to Trescot (early December) *were* closely related. In addition, Blaine sent most of the invitations to the neutral governments but allowed his envoy to carry the invitations for Chile, Peru, and Bolivia. Trescot's instructions had also included an unsubtle threat of American intentions to appeal to the other republics unless Chile moderated its demands.

Trescot's mission could not succeed, however. While he and Walker Blaine were en route to South America, the secretary of state resigned (19 December 1881); in Panama, the envoys learned of Kilpatrick's sudden death in Santiago; and soon found that Hurlbut was still promoting his own virulent anti-Chilean views among Peruvian officials. These men, assuming that such views were official policy, welcomed the new American envoys as heroes upon their arrival in Callao and Lima. In Chile, however, the Americans found an aroused and angry public, for in early January the new secretary of state, Frederick T. Frelinghuysen, had sent instructions that gave little hint of any softening of the American position vis-à-vis Chile. The envoys went to Santiago unaware that the Arthur administration was in the process of revising its approach to mediation efforts. In private conversations with Chilean authorities, Trescot conveyed the impression that the United States wanted only a peaceful solution fair to both sides (though he held in reserve Blaine's authorization to warn Chile that the United States was prepared to take its case to the other hemispheric governments).

Meanwhile, Frelinghuysen had publicized the diplomatic correspondence by sending it to the House Foreign Affairs Committee. While Trescot continued his negotiations with the Chileans, he privately expressed doubts about the possibility of an easy solution and thought a resort to force or an appeal to the other nations of the hemisphere might be necessary. For a time he debated withholding Chile's invitation to the conference, but learned that Hurlbut had already delivered an invitation to Peru (despite Blaine's instructions that only Trescot should give the invitations to Peru, Chile, and Bolivia). Trescot immediately decided to send the invitation to Chile, and at the same time he authorized the American minister in Bolivia to invite that country to the conference. When Trescot and Walker Blaine interviewed the Chilean foreign minister, Jorge Balamaceda, they were shocked to learn that the Chileans already knew of Frelinghuysen's revised instructions, which, while still blaming Chile for its unjust claims, vetoed any threats against the Santiago government. When, on 22 February 1882, the Chilean government finally received its invitation to the conference, it knew well that nothing would be done there to threaten its territorial claims. It had never officially accepted the invitation when the Arthur administration indefinitely postponed the proposed conference.

Trescot and his aide remained in Chile until late March, then returned to Peru. Before arriving there they learned of Hurlbut's death, and, because Trescot still hoped for a peace settlement under his guidance, when a modified peace proposal surfaced he personally carried it on a pack mule into the inhospitable interior to seek out the Peruvian vice-president's response. All efforts failed, however, and in April the secretary of state recalled his envoys.

Thus terminated ignominiously Blaine's dream of bringing peace to the western coast of South America. Forced to defend his policies in the 1882 congressional investigations of the affair, he never quite surmounted charges of "guano diplomacy." The young Democrat Perry Belmont, who left his account of these affairs in *An American Democrat*, occupied a principal role in the congressional hearings; he handled Blaine roughly in cross-examination. Blaine's defense of his policies never satisfied Belmont (and a later generation of textbook writers) because, for one reason, the former secretary spent much of his time portraying the war as a conspiracy of English capital, with Chile as the instrument of British commercial interests. The personal antagonism between Belmont and Blaine—the conflict between the chairman of the House Foreign Affairs Committee and the seasoned diplomatist— naturally generated public attention all the more, to the detriment of Blaine, whose support of the Landreau claim led inevitably to charges that economic motives explained his instructions to Hurlbut, Kilpatrick, and Trescot.

Blaine did defend the Landreau claim and he certainly displayed anti-English sentiments in his public utterances and in the congressional hearings; but for Blaine and a host of other late nineteenth-century politicians, a public wringing of the lion's tail was instinctive. In the privacy of his home, Blaine could lavish praise upon English culture and charm even the most skeptical English guest. Moreover, he did not neatly catalog separate issues. The prospect of unending conflict on the western coast of South America concerned him as much as the furtherance of American markets in Latin America. Economic expansionism was the hand-maiden of moral regeneration, and Latin Americans should look naturally to the United States for moral and economic leadership. To Blaine, the settlement of the War of the Pacific under United States auspices opened the way to stability, peace, and prosperity.

In his approach to the War of the Pacific, Blaine set a style that later policy makers sometimes followed. His appeal to the Peruvi-ans and especially to the Chileans rested on the notion that the United States possessed a special mission to settle intra–Latin American disputes. Though not the first secretary of state to mark out Latin America for special consideration, Blaine's meddling went beyond that of any of his predecessors.

In his first term, for example, he also involved American diplomacy in a controversial boundary dispute between Guate-mala and Mexico. Though he never became as irritated with Mexican demands for territorial concessions from Guatemala as he had with Chilean demands on Peru, Blaine encouraged the Guatemalan government to apply to Washington for a hearing. Rumors from Central America that Mexico planned a border war in order to make good its claim circulated in the State Department. Blaine saw in Guatemala the weaker disputant, and he involved American power to the point of preventing by diplomatic means an aggressive Mexican move. When the United States formally broached the idea of arbitration, both Guatemala and Mexico declined and later denounced Blaine's interference. The dispu-tants settled the problem in 1883, almost two years after Blaine left the Arthur cabinet. Mexico obtained a portion of the territory it had claimed, but neither country was satisfied completely with the outcome and neither appreciated Blaine's proposals.

Blaine really feared two related problems: an attempt by Mexico or Guatemala to use force to accomplish its goals and the possibility of European, particularly British, interference in the territorial quarrel. Such apprehensions were consistent with Blaine's approach to Latin American issues. As he had decried the threat to peace posed by the Chilean-Peruvian-Bolivian contest, so he condemned the harmful effects of the Guatemalan-Mexican quarrel. His meddling in that problem was, of course, less intensive than in the War of the Pacific, but he saw in it no less the potential for endless bickering and conflict. Blaine sincerely believed that the United States had a special mission to mediate disputes of this kind by the pursuit of a vigorous foreign policy short of armed intervention. Moreover, a more positive approach to the solution of intra–Latin American disputes would offer an opportunity for the United States to thwart European diplomatic interference in the hemisphere.

In some respects Blaine's participation in the Mexican-Guatemalan affair anticipated Elihu Root's Central American policies of 1906–7, which resulted in the 1907 treaties for the "normalization" of the often violent Central American political scene. Root's dilemma, of course, involved much more than territorial disputes; the Central American situation in 1906 displayed a chronic instability that endangered American interests (military and economic) and upset orderly political processes. Like Blaine, Root saw himself as a benevolent interventionist sincerely striving to show Central Americans how to model their political system on that of the United States. Blaine's intervention did not go as far as Root's because the United States established no Central American protectorates in Blaine's day, but his thinking led ultimately to such a conclusion. Like Root, Blaine also viewed himself as the champion of Latin America against European intrusion.

In his commitment to a more determined American policy in the hemisphere, Blaine laid the foundation for later policies, particularly the Olney and Roosevelt corollaries to the Monroe Doctrine. These amplifications of Monroe's principles rested squarely on moral and strategic doctrines. In the first Venezuelan boundary dispute of 1895, Secretary of State Olney proclaimed the Monroe Doctrine as hemispheric public law and challenged European powers to deal with Latin American nations according to American rules. Theodore Roosevelt's later proclamation of a hemispheric police power for the United States embodied prevailing assumptions that Latin Americans were culturally backward and incapable of straightening out their difficulties with European powers. This kind of reasoning had prompted Blaine to carry his mission of peacemaking to the western coast of South America and to Central America. He never contemplated a resort to "gunboat diplomacy"; yet his assessment of intra–Latin American conflicts led him logically to the idea that American policy had a special role in the hemisphere. Such an assessment constituted a fateful precedent.

Blaine's brusque rejection of a European guarantee for an isthmian canal is an example. After Ferdinand de Lesseps had initiated operations on the Panamanian isthmus, Colombia proposed a multilateral treaty guaranteeing the future canal's neutrality. To Blaine, such a treaty violated the special commitment the United States had made in the 1846 Bidlack Treaty with Bogotá to guarantee Colombian sovereignty and the right of free transit across Panama; it also challenged what Blaine considered to be American primacy in the isthmian region. The Colombian diplomatic venture prompted a note to the American minister in London, James Russell Lowell, stating that a multilateral guarantee of canal neutrality might lead to *political* dominance. Blaine not only decried the proposed scheme but broadened his diplomatic attack to a denunciation of the Clayton-Bulwer Treaty. Like most nineteenth-century politicians, he had learned well the art of baiting the British and thus joined numerous colleagues in his public outcries against the 1850 Anglo American isthmian agreement, condemning specifically its provisions for the neutrality of any future transisthmian route. He wanted the British to agree to the modification of the treaty allowing American political and military supervision over a future canal. In return, he pledged no American territorial acquisitions in Central America and, if the British wished, Blaine would acquiesce in the designation of free ports at each end of the canal. Such demands anticipated the concessions later obtained in the second Hay-Pauncefote Treaty of 1901, which freed the United States from the neutrality provisions of the Clayton-Bulwer Treaty and virtually assured American domination of any isthmian canal.

Blaine's most remembered contribution to Latin American affairs was his sponsorship of the first Pan-American Conference in 1889. In the eight-year interim between his abrupt departure from the Arthur cabinet and his return to the secretaryship of state in 1889, the idea of calling an international conference of the American states was not scrapped but merely shelved, and the Cleveland administration later played an important role in calling the conference. Blaine claimed that it would promote peace, rebuff European interference in the hemisphere, and advance American commerce in Latin America. The promotion of peace and furthering of commerce were in his mind distinct but related phenomena, each beneficial to the general attainment of a hemispheric harmony and the gradual rise of United States prestige in Latin America. During the Cleveland presidency, when Congress finally enacted enabling legislation, it followed closely Blaine's prescription, but with more emphasis on the economic benefits to be derived from a Pan-American meeting. Blaine in 1881 had given the attainment of peace high priority. In 1888, when Secretary of State Thomas Bayard dispatched the invitations, he followed the congressional mandate that the first business of the conference should be a discussion of measures to advance inter-American prosperity, to establish a customs union, to promote transportation and communication, and to provide a means of arbitration for disputes.

A later generation of diplomatic historians, analyzing the search for late nineteenth-century markets for America's industrial and agricultural surpluses, concluded that Blaine's economic expansionism inspired his Pan-Americanism. Blaine vigorously supported a search for markets, as did many of his contemporaries, and he perceived the close relationship between foreign policy and trade and investments; yet he was not single-minded in his approach. Recognizing the opportunity for promoting American commerce that the inter-American movement offered, he also saw in it an unprecedented chance to enhance American political prestige at the expense of Europe. Blaine was acutely conscious of the American-European rivalry in the hemisphere. At times the battle would be joined on commercial grounds, on other occasions, on political or diplomatic grounds; but always the end was the same: the enhancement of American prestige in the hemisphere. The conferees of 1889 did not adopt a customs union or the arbitral system Blaine had championed, though they did establish the International Bureau of American Republics, forerunner of the Pan-American Union.[3]

So much attention has been given to the economic aspects of

3. Since 1948 the union has become the permanent Secretariat for the Organization of American States.

Blaine's proposals that other, equally important results of the 1889 meeting have been deemphasized. In the first place, the fact that the conference finally met when Blaine was again secretary of state stood as symbolic testimony that his 1881 ideas had found more favorable public reception. In his first term, Blaine had to contend with the animosity stemming from his interference in the War of the Pacific. Public suspicion over the implications of his Latin American policies had done much to undermine what he had considered the principal goal of a Pan-American movement, the creation of a multilateral organization to settle intra-Latin American wars and boundary conflicts. Secondly, the fact that the first conference in the so-called new Pan-Americanism met in Washington had an important political legacy. It virtually assured that the United States would play the principal role in the Pan-American movement in later years; it meant that Washington could set the agenda for the meetings and be assured that no embarrassing criticisms of American policies in the hemisphere would be publicly aired in the conference sessions. In the first two decades of the twentieth century, when the United States became heavily involved in the internal affairs of a number of Latin American governments, Blaine's determination to preserve U.S. domination in the hemispheric system proved to be of immense political value to Washington. It prevented for years what American policy makers feared: a grand debate in the inter-American system on the Latin American policy of the United States. It should be noted, as did Alice Felt Tyler in her study of Blaine's foreign policy, that Blaine did not advance American control over Pan-American conferences to the exclusion of debate. He sincerely believed that Latin America deteriorated because of constant bickering and disputes and that the hemispheric nations might do well to follow his prescription for peaceful settlement of conflicts. The building blocks of true Pan-Americanism were goodwill and the recognition of common political and economic interests; but Blaine seemed not to realize that his presumptions of American cultural superiority, his grand design for the hemisphere, were interpreted by many Latin Americans as just another example of insufferable Yankee meddling. It was ironic, for Blaine saw in himself the true Pan-Americanist; yet his interference did much to advance the interests of one state over twenty others in a system that was ideally a partnership of equals, and it logically led to a

Pan-Americanism that two generations of Latin Americans would condemn as a front for American imperialism.

As he had done in Latin America, Blaine pursued assertive policies in the Pacific and the Far East. His policies were a logical continuation of the post–Civil War commercial expansionism typified by the foreign policies of William H. Seward; Blaine's approach constituted an important link in the evolution of Asian policy from Seward to John Hay. As Garfield's secretary of state, Blaine wrote the instructions to Commodore Robert Shufeldt, who opened Korea to American economic penetration. In his second term, Blaine encouraged the increasing Korean isolationism from China. New York investors interested in exploiting Korean mineral resources looked to Blaine for diplomatic assistance. He accepted matter-of-factly the 1878 treaty arrangement whereby the United States acquired rights to Pago Pago in Samoa and agreed to intercede in its behalf in disputes with other powers. When British and German interests began their encroachments into the islands, the American government interpreted their actions as a threat to Samoan autonomy. To ease tensions, Bayard called a conference in Washington in 1887, but it produced nothing more than a German suggestion that Samoa be transformed into a protectorate; Bayard insisted upon Samoan autonomy.

Harrison and Blaine inherited the unresolved dispute in March 1889. Already there had been trouble in the islands when German agents, rebuffed by the Samoan king, declared war and deported him. Their makeshift government fared no better at the hands of Samoan natives, and, in retaliation for an attack on German seamen, German ships shelled villages and proclaimed martial law. After these incidents, German, American, and British ships anchored in Apia harbor. News of the Samoan incidents, particularly the German counteroffensive against the native rebellion, filtered back to the United States. Journalistic embellishments of German wrongdoing inflamed American opinion against Germany, whose discriminatory decrees against allegedly diseased American pork exported to Europe had already aroused many people. In mid-March, Harrison named three commissioners, including John A. Kasson, to the Berlin Conference, called to settle the Samoan imbroglio. In a belligerent mood, Congress appropriated five hundred thousand dollars for protecting Americans in Samoa and another one hundred thousand for improving the harbor at Pago Pago. Before the conferees began their discussions, a hurricane slammed into Samoa, wrecking or sinking three American and three German ships in the harbor. The British fleet fared better. Most diplomatic historians point to the hurricane as a major factor in the peaceful resolution of the dispute, on the presumably unassailable grounds that it prevented any resort to force at the scene of action; but there is much evidence that neither Chancellor Bismarck nor the American government wanted to press the issue. Blaine wanted to preserve Samoan autonomy, a plan unsatisfactory to the British and Germans; Kasson tended to be pro-German, one of the other American commissioners, intensely anti-German. In the midst of such divided opinion it became difficult to achieve autonomy for Samoa. When the idea of a tripartite protectorate surfaced, no one found it very satisfactory but all accepted it as better than no agreement. Had Blaine been less insistent on autonomy, the British and Germans would have accepted the division of the islands on almost the same basis as the final settlement of 1899.

In the Samoan squabble Blaine revealed another trait in his approach to foreign policy: a suspicion of European power. In this he was of course very much in the tradition of the nineteenth century, where it was *de rigueur* to expatiate endlessly on the dangers of European embroilments. Where Samoa was concerned, he was not really expansionist but a man determined to preserve Samoan autonomy against European encroachment. When antagonisms with European countries involved areas closer to the Western Hemisphere, Blaine became much more assertive, invoking that spirited foreign policy with which his diplomacy has become associated. In his brief tenure in 1881, he had penned some thoughts on Hawaii that demonstrated clearly his belief that the islands were within the scope of the Monroe Doctrine. Later, in his post-1881 commentary on diplomatic and political affairs, Blaine revealed his deeper reflections on the future of the islands. Though Hawaii lay thousands of miles from the United States, it bore economic resemblance to Cuba, which controlled the Gulf trade, for the islands were the "key to the maritime dominion of the Pacific States." The United States rejected Cuban and Hawaiian annexation but forbade their acquisition by another European power lest they be "cut adrift from the American system, whereto they both indispensably belong." Blaine's analysis went beyond economic factors to incorporate his views of the destructive elements in Hawaiian society, by which he meant Oriental influence. The gradual rise of "Mongolian supremacy" he linked with Hawaii's future degradation. In the annexation crisis of 1893, for instance, some of the sugar planters were torn between the arguments against American absorption, which might mean the end of cheap Oriental labor, and the proposals for annexation, which among other things would thwart the antiforeign cultural nationalism of Queen Liliuokalani.

Blaine believed that ultimately Hawaii would be annexed. In 1889–90, he tried and failed to work out new treaty arrangements, sought as much by Hawaii as by the United States, that would have resolved the matter of reciprocity with the islands and, at the same time, laid the basis for a protectorate. In 1891, Queen Liliuokalani ascended the Hawaiian throne and launched her reactionary anti-American policies. John L. Stevens, Harrison's appointee to the Hawaiian post, was an avid annexationist. In the troublesome politics of the islands, Stevens encouraged and abetted the movement to overthrow the queen. He played a crucial role in the January 1893 revolution and in the drafting of an annexation treaty. Critics presumed that Stevens's precipitate maneuvers represented Blaine's policies. Both were annexation-ists; both feared the undermining of American influence in the islands; both sought to protect the interests of the sugar growers. Stevens and Blaine had known each other since their newspaper days in Maine in the 1850s; yet Blaine had never sent Stevens definite instructions, and there is no reason to believe that the resourceful Stevens required Blaine's inspiration to promote the usurpation of power. Had he lived, Blaine probably would have approved the annexation treaty, despite the embarrassing circum-stances of its birth, but this is not sufficient evidence to argue that he plotted Hawaiian annexation.

Blaine tried to resolve a number of other disputes: the Bering Sea controversy over pelagic sealing, the Chilean war crisis of 1891–92, the lynching of Italians in New Orleans in 1891. In one, the matter of pelagic sealing, Blaine assumed an intensely uncom-promising stance; in the others, he symbolized the model states-man, striving to moderate the bellicose sentiments of his associ-ates and at the same time to represent the position of his government.

Among the principal liabilities in studying Blaine's diplomacy is the problem of coping with several major interpretations of the man. Blaine's political career, stormy and controversial, confuses matters because he obviously sought the presidency and he aroused a loyal and dedicated following. Though lacking the moral firmness of Cleveland, Blaine operated by a higher code of ethics than most Gilded Age politicians; certainly he displayed more intellectual creativity and innovation than other late nineteenth-century secretaries of state.

In some respects, Blaine's intellectual energy hampered American policy and did his reputation no good. He brought to the Department of State no previous diplomatic experience, save journalistic and congressional discussions of foreign affairs. Though not unique in this matter, his lack of prior training was a hindrance, particularly in learning to deal with the day-to-day problems a policy maker encounters. Most of the other late nineteenth-century secretaries were men of meager preparation in diplomacy, but at least they did not attempt to chart crusading courses in foreign policy. Blaine did not suffer from that kind of self-doubt.

In the historiography of the period there exist several "Blaines." The first is the intellectual, the righteous Republican, the cultivated gentleman who appears in the biographies by Edwin Stanwood and Mary Abigail Dodge (Gail Hamilton). Except for the fact that both were intimates of the Blaine family, their accounts could be written off as campaign pieces; but the paucity of Blaine letters has compelled later historians to rely heavily on the two for details of Blaine's private life.

Then, there is Blaine the misunderstood thinker and diplomatic innovator and, if one stretches the logic sufficiently, the founder of the Good Neighbor policy. This Blaine was to a great extent the work of Alice Felt Tyler and David S. Muzzey, who wrote scholarly but sympathetic accounts of him. Tyler's study, originally published in 1927 but still the basic work on Blaine's foreign policy, portrays Blaine as a statesman striving to bring peace to the republics of Latin America by refurbishing the Pan-American dream of Simón Bolívar. Muzzey devotes more space to Blaine's life, particularly trying to defend his subject against the many charges of political and financial malfeasance. Blaine as the founder of the Good Neighbor policy is an interpretation derived by inference from the standard surveys of

the period. Obviously, he performed a critical role in the inter-
American conference of 1889; but the Good Neighbor policy of
the 1930s stood essentially for noninterference, nonintervention,
and a practical cooperation between the United States and the
republics of Latin America. Blaine's contributions to inter-Americanism promoted meddling, interference, and intervention, and in
the twentieth century gained few scholarly adherents north of the
Rio Grande and certainly none south of it. The value of the "Blaine
inter-Americanism," Luis Quintanilla wrote in *A Latin American
Speaks*, may be summed up in the phrase "Blah Blah Pan
Americanism." At least this view offers some alternative to the
diplomatic-history-text interpretation of Blaine who, according to
Thomas A. Bailey, was strong on oratory and short on common
sense. Even Samuel Flagg Bemis, ordinarily favorably inclined to
the more nationalistic secretaries of state, does not come to grips
with Blaine the thinker and innovator.

Actually, Blaine the thinker has been more the subject of the
less sympathetic accounts, particularly the revisionist diplomatic
studies focusing on the "new American empire" of the nineteenth
century. Walter LaFeber in his prize-winning *The New Empire* and
William Appleman Williams in *The Roots of the Modern American
Empire* depict Blaine as a major architect in the search for
industrial and agricultural markets. Both focus on Blaine's role in
the reciprocity debates of the Harrison years, wherein Blaine
apparently converted the staunchly protectionist McKinley to the
idea of lowering duties in order to expand agricultural markets.
Such an interpretation lends credence to the theory that a
"marketplace consensus" existed among politicians of the period;
but, as Paul Holbo has demonstrated in a recent essay, the
revisionist interpretations fail to take into account the bitter
emotional and political rivalries, particularly the Democratic
determination to lower the tariff, that affected economic aspects
of foreign policy. Moreover, revisionist students are inclined to
believe that nearly all policies dovetail into the economic. In
Blaine's case, this view sometimes illuminates, sometimes confuses. For instance, Blaine did promote American economic
expansionism in Latin America, in part because he correctly
observed a rising glut of agricultural and industrial products
without outside markets, but also in part because he believed that
the American and not the European political and economic system
was a better standard for Latin Americans.

Finally, there is Blaine the transitional figure. Too partisan to forget the antagonisms generated in the fifties and sixties, Blaine identified the destiny of the nation with that of Republicanism. Yet, in his intellectual repertory and in the policies of his two brief terms in the State Department, he displayed an imaginative and creative mind explaining the role of America in global affairs. He carried out, as far as possible, the foreign policy goals of Seward, and his Latin American ventures foreshadowed in intent if not execution the protectorate philosophy of the twentieth century.

BIBLIOGRAPHIC NOTE

Blaine was careless with his letters. There is a small collection of Blaine manuscripts in the Georgetown University archives, and three volumes and thirteen boxes are found in the Library of Congress Manuscripts Division. The letters of Garfield and Harrison contain numerous pieces to and from Blaine. Albert T. Volwiler has edited *The Correspondence between Benjamin Harrison and James G. Blaine, 1882–1893* (Philadelphia, 1940).

Blaine wrote a great deal. Among his many articles and several books the best insights into his thinking are *Twenty Years of Congress: From Lincoln to Garfield*, 2 vols. (Norwich, Conn., 1884–86), and *Political Discussions: Legislative, Diplomatic, and Popular, 1856–1886* (New York, 1887). For Blaine's official correspondence, of course, the interested student should consult the relevant *Foreign Relations* volumes for 1881 and 1889–92. The full State Department correspondence for these years is available on microfilm.

There are several biographies, mostly campaign pieces or works written by friends or distant relatives (for example, by Edwin Stanwood and Gail Hamilton). A sympathetic but scholarly treatment is David S. Muzzey, *James G. Blaine: A Political Idol of Other Days* (New York, 1934).

Still the best account of Blaine's foreign policy is Alice Felt Tyler, *The Foreign Policy of James G. Blaine* (Hamden, Conn., 1965; originally published in 1927), though it should be supplemented with more recent works, particularly Russell H. Bastert, "A New Approach to the Origins of Blaine's Pan American Policy," *Hispanic American Historical Review* 39 (August 1959), 375–412, David M. Pletcher, *The Awkward Years: American Foreign Relations under Garfield and Arthur* (Columbia, Mo., 1962), Walter LaFeber, *The New Empire: An Interpretation of American Expansionism, 1860–1898* (Ithaca, 1962), and Milton Plesur, *America's Outward Thrust: Approaches to Foreign Affairs, 1865–1890* (De Kalb, Ill., 1971). H. Wayne Morgan offers a synthesis of Gilded Age politics in *From Hayes to McKinley: National Party Politics, 1877–1893* (Syracuse, 1969).

Blaine has become more and more the subject of revisionist studies focusing on the economic background of late nineteenth-century foreign policy. For Blaine's role in these matters, see LaFeber, *The New Empire*, and William Appleman Williams, *The Roots of the Modern American Empire: A Study of the Growth and Shaping of Social Consciousness in a Marketplace Society* (New York, 1969). Recent dissertations that deal with Blaine's ideology are Richard C. Winchester, "James G. Blaine and the Ideology of American Expansionism," University of Rochester, 1966, who argues that Blaine's support for a rapidly expanding domestic economy before 1881 was transmuted logically into a vision of global empire; Allan B. Spetter, "Harrison and Blaine: Foreign Policy, 1889–1893," Rutgers University, 1967, who contends that Harrison and Secretary of the Navy Benjamin Tracy played the dominant roles in the Harrison administration's foreign policy; and Edward P. Crapol, " 'America for Americans': Economic Nationalism and Anglophobia, 1876–1896," University of Wisconsin, 1968, who shows that the nineteenth-century anti-English attitudes of Americans stemmed in large part from the power of English capital in the domestic economy, in Latin America, and in the Orient.

ALFRED THAYER MAHAN

Turning America Back to the Sea

Kenneth J. Hagan

Alfred Thayer Mahan, a naval officer who died in 1914, enjoys today a reputation and prominence unmatched by any other officer of the United States Navy. His most famous book, *The Influence of Sea Power upon History, 1660–1783*, was first published in 1890. In the introduction to the edition that is still in print Louis M. Hacker, a distinguished historian, compared Mahan to Darwin, noting that Mahan's book, "in its way and its place," had "as profound an effect on the world" as Darwin's *Origin of Species*. He found the lessons of Mahan still relevant and believed that the strategy of sea power enunciated in the book remained the key to American security and world peace, just as it was the secret of world peace while Britain was mistress of the seas.

Naval officers have joined historians in perpetuating Mahan's fame. Rear Admiral Stephen B. Luce, the founder of the Naval War College who convinced Mahan to join its first faculty, set the tone.

Deeply impressed by Mahan's lectures at the college, Luce hailed his colleague as a modern naval Jomini, a philosopher and strategist who at last had codified the principles of naval warfare and strategy. A half-century later, Captain William D. Puleston, U.S.N., repeated the theme in his biography of Mahan. He found his predecessor "an extraordinarily successful naval historian, naval biographer, and essayist. His historical studies were profound, his biographies illuminating, his essays timely and suggestive." Writing on the eve of World War II and in the midst of a hot debate over the relative merits of battleships, aircraft carriers, and submarines, Puleston attributed great influence to Mahan: "It is no exaggeration to assert that today, in the American Navy, every officer who prepares for or discusses war, follows the methods and invokes the ideas of Mahan." Much more recently, in October 1972, the president of the Naval War College justified sweeping changes in the curriculum of that institution with the observation: "There may be another Alfred Thayer Mahan in this year's class or the next. We cannot afford to miss him."

The man who has been the object of so much eulogy was in 1884 an obscure officer commanding the U.S.S. *Wachusett* off the west coast of South America. The United States was attempting to protect the investments of certain American corporations during a series of revolutions in 1884 and 1885, and the *Wachusett* was part of the minuscule but persuasive show of naval force used to dissuade revolutionaries from destroying American property. Mahan was bored with the assignment; sea duty generally had bored him throughout his career. Unexpected respite came in the form of a letter from Rear Admiral Stephen Luce, offering Mahan an appointment to the faculty of the newly formed Naval War College at Newport, Rhode Island.

Notwithstanding the tedium of shipboard life, Mahan expressed trepidation. He would "like the position, like it probably very much," but he thought Luce mistakenly gave him credit for knowing more than he did, and for "having given a special attention to the subject." Although Mahan had already written a study of the Civil War navy, *The Gulf and Inland Waters*, he otherwise had not displayed creative prowess. Many other officers by 1884 had contributed a great deal to the evolution of strategic and technological theory through the medium of the U.S. Naval Institute *Proceedings*, first published in 1874; Mahan had written only a single essay on naval education for that journal. Thus he had reason to doubt Luce's judgment in selecting him as the officer who could deliver decidedly didactic lectures on naval history to the classes at Newport. Unfortunately, Luce remained silent on the source of his inspiration, and all that is known is that the two officers had an acquaintanceship dating back more than twenty years to duty together at the U.S. Naval Academy and aboard the *Macedonian* during the Civil War.

Despite his initial doubts, Mahan proved equal to the task. Between 1885 and 1889 he composed the lectures that would be published in 1890 as *The Influence of Sea Power*, which contained the essence of all Mahan ever said on the subject of naval strategy.

The comments of Luce, Puleston, and Hacker suggest that there were at least two facets to Mahan's writing: history and propaganda. In the preface to his great work, Mahan readily admitted that he was "a naval officer in full sympathy with his profession." He was writing naval history because he believed "the study of the sea history of the past will be found instructive, by its illustration of the general principles of maritime war, notwithstanding the great changes that have been brought about in naval weapons by the scientific advances of the past half century, and by the introduction of steam as the motive power [of ships]."

Mahan was making a subtle but fundamental distinction that he repeated throughout the book. Naval history illustrates general, immutable principles of international relations and warfare at sea that are affected very little, if at all, by technological changes in weapons systems; put in other terms, Mahan distinguished between strategy and tactics. He contended that history illustrates unalterable strategic principles while tactical conditions vary to some extent with technology. The warrior's milieu is strategic before "hostile armies or fleets are brought into *contact*." Thereafter the environment is tactical; while history remains useful, it is a far less trustworthy guide.

Mahan's distinction is significant for two reasons. The first is that he clearly allowed for changes in naval warfare brought about by technological developments; thus those critics who have criticized Mahan's specifications for the ideal battleship have dealt with peripheral issues. More to the point is Puleston's argument

that Mahan would have welcomed aircraft carriers and submarines, but even here the essence is missed. Mahan was simply not
deeply concerned with—perhaps one ought to say he was
uninterested in—naval technology. The cursory manner in which
he passed over the millennial changes from oar to sail to steam
reflects this. "The best-planned schemes might fail through stress
of weather in the days of the galley and the sailing-ship; but this
difficulty has almost disappeared. The principles which should
direct great naval combinations have been applicable to all ages,
and are deducible from history; but the power to carry them out
with little regard to the weather is a recent gain."

The second significant aspect of Mahan's distinction between
strategy and tactics is its determinism. Mahan exposed himself as a
creature of the late nineteenth century, accepting change as
inevitable but believing that in every instance "deducible" laws
both limit and guide that transformation. War has unalterable
principles; "their existence is detected by the study of the past,
which reveals them in successes and in failures, the same from age
to age." Aware of the intellectual climate of his era, Mahan
concluded that the principles shaping strategy belonged "to the
Order of Nature, of whose stability so much is heard in our day;
whereas tactics, using as its instruments the weapons made by
man, shares in the change and progress of the race from
generation to generation."

Mahan's determinism was not limited to warfare; on the
contrary, it embraced the study of what today would be called
international relations. For Mahan the entering wedge was maritime trade. "The profound influence of sea commerce upon the
wealth and strength of countries was clearly seen long before the
true principles which governed its growth and prosperity were
detected." The enlightened age of the late nineteenth century had
mastered the underlying principles of national prosperity, which
Mahan set down in *The Influence of Sea Power*. "In these three
things—production, with the necessity of exchanging products,
shipping, whereby the exchange is carried on, and colonies, which
facilitate and enlarge the operations of shipping and tend to
protect it by multiplying points of safety—is to be found the key to
much of the history, as well as of the policy, of nations bordering
upon the sea."

The nation that continually increased its production, shipping, and colonies would maximize "its sea power in the broad

sense, which includes not only the military strength afloat, that rules the sea or any part of it by force of arms, but also the peaceful commerce and shipping from which alone a military fleet naturally and healthfully springs, and on which it securely rests." Regardless of their shrewdness and ambition, however, statesmen have less effect on the growth of a nation's sea power, and hence prosperity, than certain "natural conditions." Mahan enumerated these as geographical position, physical conformation, extent of territory, size of population, character of the people, and character of the government.

A favorable geographic position meant separation by sea from other nations, so that a country was "neither forced to defend itself by land nor induced to seek extension of its territory by way of land." The favorable geographic complement to isolation by sea was a series of deep harbors, especially if they were "outlets of navigable streams, which facilitate the concentration in them of a country's internal trade." The depth and quality of those harbors, together with the length of a nation's coastline, were more important to Mahan's calculation of sea power than the total area of a country. Likewise, the number of people in a nation was not nearly as important as "the number following the sea, or at least readily available for employment on ship-board and for the creation of naval material."

Aside from these physical and quantitative ingredients, Mahan stressed national and governmental character as determinants of a nation's maritime greatness. "If sea power be really based upon a peaceful and extensive commerce, aptitude for commercial pursuits must be a distinguishing feature of the nations that have at one time or another been great upon the sea." A taste for the sea and a benevolent geographic environment destined a people for "the most brilliant successes," so long as there was "intelligent direction" of their affairs "by a government fully imbued with the spirit of the people and conscious of its true general bent."

For Mahan, the ideal sea power was Great Britain, which had in profusion all of his essential "natural conditions." Alone among the powers of Europe, Britain was insulated from invasion by the all-encircling ocean; but what really made Britain a great sea power was the character of its people. Like the Dutch, the English "were by nature businessmen, traders, producers, negotiators." They surpassed the Dutch, however, in their ability to colonize.

"Successful colonization, with its consequent effect upon commerce and sea power, depends essentially upon national character; because colonies grow best when they grow of themselves."
To an unparalleled degree, Englishmen had been successful
colonizers because those who went abroad thoroughly identified
themselves with the colony where they resided, and they worked
for its economic development within the imperial system. Unlike
other colonists, Englishmen did not seek short-term, highly ex-
ploitative gains from their colonies.

Mahan was not perfectly lucid about what precisely made
colonies so valuable to the mother country. Certainly there was an
economic factor—colonies meant trade, and trade meant wealth—
but the naval aspect predominated in his extensive discussion of
the need to maintain "suitable naval stations, in those distant parts
of the world to which the armed shipping must follow the
peaceful vessels of commerce." He worried about protecting
far-off naval bases and concluded that the greatest security lay in
"a surrounding friendly population. . . . Such friendly surround-
ings and backing, joined to a reasonable military provision, are the
best defences, and when combined with decided preponderance
at sea, make a scattered and extensive empire, like that of England,
secure." Colonies, then, were shields of naval bases.

The United States, the real object of Mahan's interest, fared
less well. His own nation had enormous potential in each of the
"natural conditions," but that promise had yet to be realized. As
for geographical location, "the position of the United States upon
the two oceans would be either a source of weakness or a cause of
enormous expense, had it a large sea commerce on both coasts."
In other words, while the United States enjoyed internal lines of
communication, it suffered from inability to concentrate its naval
force because of its extended coastline.

Even more significant to Mahan was the distance of the
United States from the great trading centers of Europe. This
separation meant that the United States in the future could not
successfully employ its most popular form of naval warfare,
commerce raiding, "unless she finds bases in the ports of an ally."
Mahan saw one ray of hope to diminish American separation from
Europe: construction of an interoceanic canal in Central America.
Should that long-awaited event occur, the commerce of Europe
would be attracted to the Caribbean, which would then become
"one of the great highways of the world." European nations would

have interests "close along our shores, as they never have before." The United States would no longer be able "to stand aloof from international complications. The position of the United States with reference to this route will resemble that of England to the Channel, and of the Mediterranean countries to the Suez route." Then the geographical conditions would be perfect; the mainland would provide permanent primary bases of naval operations, and to guarantee complete American hegemony in those waters the United States would simply have to obtain secondary bases of operations in the Caribbean.

Should the canal not be constructed, Mahan saw little hope for realization of the American potential for maritime greatness. The people of the United States had the national character suitable for creation of power at sea—"The instinct for commerce, bold enterprise in the pursuit of gain, and a keen scent for the trails that lead to it, all exist"—but popular attention had been drawn inland, toward development of the continental resources. The government had contributed to the decline of a once prosperous merchant marine by refusing to subsidize domestic shipbuilding and by maintaining tariffs preventing American shippers from purchasing vessels built in European yards. Thus, of the three activities reflecting proper utilization of the "natural conditions," the United States had manifested genius only in production. Shipping continued to deteriorate as American goods were carried in foreign-owned ships, and colonies "the United States has not and is not likely to have." The only hope for creation of commercial and naval sea power lay in an isthmian canal that would rekindle the American mercantile spirit by competition close to home. It would also force the construction of a navy to defend those renewed interests.

Mahan wrote *The Influence of Sea Power* with full knowledge that reconstruction of the United States Navy in fact had already begun. In 1883 Congress had appropriated funds for new ship construction for the first time since the Civil War; thereafter appropriations came regularly. The "new navy" of steam power, steel hulls, and rifled breech-loading cannon was a reality before 1890.

It is true that no battleships had been constructed at the time

SHIPWRECKED PATRIOTISM.

UNCLE SAM AT SEA:—"It's Washington's Birthday, and I want to decorate, but—ahem—well—just lend me the loan of your mast, will you?"

Puck, 22 February 1882. Prints Division, The New York Public Library, Astor, Lenox and Tilden Foundations

Mahan wrote, but there were two excellent reasons for this failure. One was the technological immaturity of the American steel industry. Capacity to roll armor plate and forge heavy guns was only created during the 1880s as a result of experience gained by building small, very lightly armored warships. The United States could not have built a battleship in 1883. Secondly, when naval officers initially planned the vessels of the "new navy" they concluded that battleships did not meet "the necessities of *the present time.*" Rear Admiral John Rodgers and his fellow officers on the Naval Advisory Board of 1881 believed battleships would be *absolutely necessary for the defense of the country in time of war,*" but they thought war unlikely. In time of peace, they contended, the squadrons of the American navy were used for "surveying, deep sea sounding, the protection and advancement of American commerce, exploration, the protection of American life and property endangered by wars between foreign countries, and service in support of American policy in matters where foreign governments are concerned." Should the United States unexpectedly find itself at war, a fleet of cruisers and smaller ships could temporarily defend the American coast, carry out unspecified "offensive measures of possible vital importance, and hold a naval enemy in check until armored vessels can be supplied to perfect the defense and undertake offensive operations."

Rear Admiral Rodgers's statement demonstrates that some American naval officers had contemplated building battleships and had conceived a strategy of offensive warfare at sea before Mahan. In these crucial respects, and in several others, Mahan's thinking was not original; indeed, the keystone to his scheme of sea power, the interrelationship of production and shipping, previously had been described in great detail.

Before Mahan, the most eloquent naval spokesman for an American national policy of vigorous commercial expansion was Robert W. Shufeldt, the officer who commanded the U.S.S. *Ticonderoga* on a global cruise from 1878 to 1880. Shufeldt's purpose in making that voyage was to find new markets for American manufactured goods, especially cheap cotton fabrics. On the eve of departure Shufeldt explained his conception of the relationship between the navy and American commerce to Congressman Leopold Morse of the House Naval Affairs Committee.

Shufeldt advised Morse that commerce was important to a nation for two reasons. First, it served as an index of national

greatness. Secondly, foreign markets could absorb surplus industrial and agricultural production. China was an object lesson to be
studied. The absence of a substantial trade meant that even with a
population of four hundred million, China was "simply an
aggregation of people without external force." The United States
must take heed, for the American republic was recklessly abandoning to rivals its share of the transoceanic carrying trade. Such a
policy was "courting the contempt of nations and cultivating our
own insignificance." Before long this neglect would render the
United States "as formidable beyond her limits as China or as a
turtle in a shell."

Shufeldt used American history to document the proper
relationship of the navy and commerce. He reminded Congressman Morse that American naval operations historically had
been "interwoven with commercial enterprise upon the sea and
linked to every act which has made the nation great." Soon after
the birth of the United States the navy had eradicated piracy in the
Mediterranean Sea and West Indies. In the War of 1812 the navy
vindicated "the motto of 'free trade and sailor's rights.'" During
that war, said Shufeldt, Captain David Porter had "opened the
trade of the Pacific Ocean to the whaling fleet of America, and
incidentally to general American commerce." In mid-century
California was conquered, Japan awakened, South America pene-
trated, and the vast areas of ocean stretching from the equator to
the North Pole explored. "All this, while acting as the police of
every sea, the Navy has done in the aid and for the aggrandizement of American commerce."

Shufeldt advanced a naval-commercial argument that had all
the trappings of Mahan's thesis of sea power. He did not believe
that the interdependence of the navy and merchant marine was
restricted to periods of hostilities, either past or future; the
relationship was also that of protector and protected in time of
peace. "The Navy is, indeed, the pioneer of commerce." In his
search for new markets around the world, the merchant of every
Western nation needed "the constant protection of the flag and
the gun. He deals with barbarous tribes—with men who appreciate only the argument of physical force." Navies were the means
by which the searching trader could best be protected, and
Shufeldt even conceived of the naval role as one of pathfinder.
"The man-of-war precedes the merchantman and impresses rude

people with the sense of the power of the flag which covers the one and the other."

In addition to rebuilding the navy, Shufeldt advocated establishment of a worldwide network of American steamship lines to ensure access to foreign markets. Virtually every American naval officer of the 1870s and 1880s agreed with Shufeldt that the United States merchant marine must be revived; they disagreed on how to effect that revival. Some favored subsidies to American shipping companies carrying mail overseas. Others advocated reduction of the tariff to permit purchase of merchantmen built in Europe. Still others favored federal subsidies to domestic shipbuilders. Unable to agree and faced with congressional indifference toward the merchant marine, naval officers could only lament its decline and worry, as did Shufeldt and Mahan, that naval and national greatness might consequently escape the American grasp.

Some officers cut the Gordian knot by advocating naval construction regardless of the state of the merchant marine, and here they were bolder than Mahan. As Lieutenant Frederick Collins observed in the Naval Institute *Proceedings* of 1879, a recognition of the intimacy of commerce and the navy "should impel any nation discovering its commerce on the wane to redoubled efforts to maintain an efficient navy as one of the most important aids to its resuscitation." In other words, a nation should first build a great navy; a merchant marine and national greatness would then necessarily follow.

As noted previously, despite Mahan's citation of production and shipping as indexes of national strength, he discounted the historic American reliance on commerce raiding in time of war. Here again he was not breaking new ground. As early as 1874 Commodore Foxhall A. Parker had hinted that the United States should plan a strategy for the "encountering of a hostile force at sea." Parker would have exercised different classes of vessels— large gunships, torpedo boats, and rams—as units. "For at sea, as on land, 'war is nothing more than the art of concentrating a greater force than the enemy upon a given point.' " The commodore sensed the futility of discussing "the assembling of fleets when our flag scarcely floats from the mast-head of a merchantman upon the sea"; but he was looking to the future when "the great Republic will awaken from her lethargy . . . and once more put forth her strength upon the deep." If American mer-

chantmen again roamed the "remotest corners of the earth,"
Parker believed "that a navy will be created for its protection
worthy of a great people."

Half a decade later, Lieutenant Frederick Collins applauded
Parker's "perspicuity" which represented "in a general way, the
views of most of our officers" at that time. Collins wished to
augment the American "power of acting on the offensive." To do
so, he would build "as quickly as possible a fair number of
powerful ships, sufficiently alike in size, speed and armament to
form a homogeneous fleet." By 1890 senior flag officers like
Admiral David Dixon Porter and Rear Admiral Stephen B. Luce had
publicly espoused creation of a battleship fleet competent to
engage an enemy on the open seas.

Whether operating singly or in fleets, steam-driven warships
must refuel. Mahan had admired Great Britain because it had
woven a network of colonies to shelter the naval bases supporting
the global fleets and squadrons of the Royal Navy; in 1890 Mahan
could envy the British their colonial system, but he could not
believe the United States would acquire overseas colonies. Thus
he satisfied himself with a rather ill-defined hope that his country
at least would "provide resting places" for its warships, "where
they can coal and repair." In this modest expectation also he had
been anticipated.

In 1883 Secretary of the Navy William E. Chandler recommended establishment of "coaling and naval stations" in the
Caribbean, Brazil, the Strait of Magellan, El Salvador or Honduras,
Madagascar, the island of Fernando Po off the west coast of Africa,
the coastal islands of Korea, and on both sides of the Panamanian
isthmus. During war, Chandler believed, American cruisers would
"require frequent supplies of coal at distant points. If they
attempt, in default of the necessary coaling stations, to cruise
under sail alone, their offensive power will be reduced to the
lowest limit." They would "become the prey of vessels one-third
their size, approaching under steam." Despite this strongly
worded recommendation, by 1889 the United States Navy had
stacks of coal only at Honolulu, Samoa, and Pichilinque in Lower
California, and an old hulk, the *Monongahela*, had been outfitted
to store one thousand tons of coal at Callao, Peru.

The hesitancy of naval officers to dispute the traditional
American reluctance to expand overseas accounts in part for the
absence of coaling stations. Before 1889 only a handful of officers

counseled a break with the past. In 1880 Lieutenant Charles Belknap hoped that the question of coaling stations would be studied at the highest levels. His essay on naval policy was awarded the Naval Institute's first prize by the judges, Secretary of State William M. Evarts and Secretary of the Navy Richard W. Thompson. Six years later, when nothing had come of Secretary Chandler's proposal, Lieutenant Commander F. M. Barber angrily complained that "general usefulness in *time of war,* for a *man-of-war* . . . is a question of coal-piles and not of canvas . . . for no man-of-war would dare go to sea in time of war under sail with any expectation of reaching port, let alone of capturing or protecting anything." He thought naval officers should make Congress aware of what American warships would have to do if deployed "away from home when a war broke out and coal is still contraband of war—viz. *Stay in port,* and in case of a long war dismantle ships and send crew and officers home."

Belknap and Barber were lonely voices in a wilderness of complacency and might have remained so had there not been a crisis over Samoa in 1888 and 1889. At issue was control of the fine natural harbor of Pago Pago. Britain was nominally a participant in the dispute, but Germany and the United States were the principal contenders. In the late fall of 1888 and early months of 1889 each of the three countries gradually increased the number of its warships in Samoan waters while the diplomats devised arguments to justify exclusive rights over the islands. Berlin and Washington made the strongest claims against each other, and the diplomatic gulf widened ominously. Fortunately for international peace, a hurricane struck Samoa in March of 1889, blowing several ships ashore and figuratively cooling the tempers of statesmen half a world away, who hastily negotiated a tripartite sharing of Samoa.

American naval officers drew their own conclusions from this first real brush with a determined European power in an area long thought to be an American preserve. Some, such as Rear Admiral Stephen Luce, simply reaffirmed their dedication to battleships without altering their conviction that cruisers must have sails. Others, notably Commander T. F. Jewell, reassessed American naval strategy in light of the new technological and political environments. Jewell was willing to keep some sailing vessels as training ships because indoctrination aboard square-riggers produced officers with quick wits and seamen with strong bodies; but he did not think the United States Navy should "take a step backward in order to develop the muscles of our men." He advocated removing all sails from every class of warship, and he preferred the most direct solution to the lack of overseas refueling depots: "Our country should establish coaling stations abroad." It might not be possible to acquire them "peacefully to any great extent, but it certainly could be done in the Pacific, and not improbably in the West Indies, without resort to force." Jewell thought Hawaii the best location in the Pacific, and he urged the government to establish a regular naval station there and to stop "wasting a golden opportunity" to ensure American hegemony in the Pacific.

The Pacific Ocean, an isthmian canal, the Caribbean Sea, and commerce were all interrelated in the minds of Mahan's predecessors. Writing in the *Journal of the American Geographical Society of New York* in 1886, Commander Henry C. Taylor pointed to the Caribbean and Gulf of Mexico as natural destinations for the industrial and agricultural products of the Mississippi Valley. The United States must dominate both bodies of water. "It is more than a consequent [*sic*] of greatness, it is greatness itself; it is part of the definition—we cannot be a nation of the first rank while lacking control of the seas and coasts immediately south of us."

Lieutenant Commander Charles H. Stockton chose to elaborate on the implications of a canal for trade with the Pacific. No island or country bordering that ocean would be immune to accelerated economic growth once a canal cut Central America. As an example of the potential of Pacific commerce, Stockton referred to New Zealand. Geographically analogous to the British Isles, it was peculiarly fitted "for colonization by whites of Anglo-Saxon origin." It was endowed with abundant coal deposits, splendid agricultural resources, and spacious harbors, and was already a leading producer of wheat and wool. In time it should become as well "a maritime and manufacturing country, and an important element in the commerce of the world." Without question, Stockton asserted, "New Zealand belongs to the domain of the American canal, both with regards to the United States and Europe."

Naval officers of the generation before Mahan also agreed on the strategic significance of the Caribbean Sea. Toward the end of the 1880s, in a confidential letter to Secretary of the Navy William C. Whitney, Rear Admiral Stephen Luce assumed a posture that Commander Taylor and others writing for publication could not then hold. Luce predicted early completion of an isthmian canal, "and those maritime people who have the gift of foresight are making timely provision to protect and control the stream of ocean commerce that must pour through one or more of the openings in the cordon of islands that enclose the Caribbean Sea." Specifically, he espied French plans for a protectorate over Haiti. If successful, "St. Domingo will certainly follow, when the whole island [of Hispaniola] will become French to the discomfiture of the English." Even if France governed the island, however, England still would have Jamaica and Bermuda. "The latter is at our very front door, as it were; a standing menace to any complications that might arise between this country and Great Britain." From a naval viewpoint, Bermuda was second in strength only to Malta "in the long line of England's outposts."

Luce understood American repugnance to overseas territorial aggrandizement. To prevent European encirclement of the eastern access to a canal, he proposed an American protectorate over the Virgin Islands. Denmark should be induced "for a consideration . . . to surrender her claim to the islands." Local autonomy should be preserved, while the people could "decide to pass under the protection of the American flag" by plebiscite. Luce hoped thereby to acquire a strategic toehold in the eastern Caribbean without entailing "certain embarrassing features inseparable from actual possession."

Mahan was strangely quiet about Hawaii in *The Influence of Sea Power*, but other officers were quite vociferous. In 1876 Admiral of the Navy David Dixon Porter raised the specter of English domination of the Hawaiian Islands. Congressman Fernando Wood of the Ways and Means Committee had charge of a bill to implement the Hawaiian Reciprocity Treaty of 1875, and he had asked Porter's opinion. The admiral warned that the islands were geographically analogous to Bermuda. Porter brooded that the British "have long had their eyes upon them" as "a principal outpost on our coast where they could launch forth their ships of war upon us with perfect impunity." Bases on the North American continent were always vulnerable to attack by the American army, but islands were relatively secure. To Porter it almost seemed as if Her Majesty's government had a grand design for Pacific power. The British had recently acquired a base in the Fiji Islands, an action that could only be viewed as "the preparatory step to the occupation of Hawaii." Porter did not fear territorial or cultural alienation of Hawaii from America; his concern was mercantile. Believing that acquisition of Hawaii would enable England to complete a chain of naval stations across the Pacific, he saw danger in such an arrangement, for it would allow a foreign power to dominate American commerce in that ocean.

Behind Britain loomed another dangerous power with similar ambitions. Writing thirteen years before the Samoan crisis of 1889, Porter noted that Germany had quickly risen as a naval power and in a decade would be "second only to England and France." Berlin sought island bases in the West Indies and in the Pacific "for the same reason as England, namely, the extension of her commerce." Porter was convinced that other European powers also eyed Hawaii avariciously, and growth of "the foreign element in the population of the islands" meant that in fifteen years they would easily fall "into the hands of some other power." The remedy was simple: tie the islands to the United States through reciprocal trade and reiterate the Tyler Doctrine of 1842 which denounced European acquisition of the islands as inimical to the interests of the United States.

Congressman Wood accepted the navalist's emphasis on commerce when reporting the bill. He concluded that the Hawaiian Islands could "do but little in promoting their prosperity, without more intimate relations with this or some other commercial authority." Observing briefly that Hawaiian civilization and religion were "modeled after our own," he passed on to the heart of the matter. "The Pacific Ocean is an American Ocean, destined to hold a far higher place in the future history of the world than the Atlantic." Significantly, he placed the commercial consideration first when describing the Pacific as "the future great highway between ourselves and the hundreds of millions of Asiatics who look to us for commerce, civilization, and Christianity." The Hawaiian Islands lay "midway between us and them as the necessary post provided by the Great Ruler of the universe as points of observation, rest, supply, military strategy, and command, to enable each other to unite in protecting both hemispheres from European assault, aggression, and avarice."

Mahan caught up with Porter and Wood in 1893, when the *Forum* published his article "Hawaii and Our Future Sea Power."

The Hawaiian revolution of that year posed the question of American annexation of the islands in unmistakable terms, and Mahan elaborated on his "natural conditions" in arguing for acquisition. Geography determined the islands' significance and the American responsibility. Hawaii was twenty-one hundred miles from San Francisco and from the archipelagoes of the western Pacific. An enemy warship could not reach the west coast of the United States and return home without refueling at Hawaii. Equally important was the commercially central position the islands would occupy once an isthmian canal was opened. China and Japan, regarded by Americans of the late nineteenth century as highly promising outlets for their industrial goods, would be most directly reached from the canal by a route passing near Hawaii. The islands would be at a crossroads of trade between the consuming Orient and the producing east coast of the United States.

As always, Mahan dealt in absolutes when contending that for naval and commercial reasons Hawaii must be under the domination of the United States. "Let us start from the fundamental truth, warranted by history, that the control of the seas, and especially along the great lines drawn by national interest or national commerce, is the chief among the merely material elements in the power and prosperity of nations." From that axiom "necessarily follows the principle that, as subsidiary to such control, it is imperative to take possession, when it can be done righteously, of such maritime positions as contribute to secure command." This principle "has its application also to the present case of Hawaii."

If the Hawaiian revolution seemed to have created that "golden opportunity" of which Commander Jewell dreamed, other events in the Pacific during the last decade of the century added the negative impetus of threat. The Samoan crisis of 1889 marked the beginning, as Mahan tersely observed in the *Atlantic Monthly* of December 1890. "The incident of the Samoa Islands, trivial apparently, was nevertheless eminently suggestive of European ambitions. America then roused from sleep as to interests concerning her future." Mahan interpreted the dispute as symbolic of "the conflict between German control and American interests in the islands of the western Pacific," and he brooded over "the alleged progress of German influence in Central and South America."

What made German-American competition especially explosive was the character of the two peoples. While Germany's moves into the Pacific were "sustained with the aggressive military spirit characteristic of the German Empire," Mahan thought the expansion arose "from the national temper more than from the deliberate policy of the government, which in this matter does not lead, but follows, the feeling of the people,—a condition much more formidable." The American people, especially those on the west coast, were assured, energetic, and determined in assertion of United States preeminence in the Pacific. Mahan's nation was "by far the greatest, in numbers, interests, and power, of the communities bordering upon the eastern shores of the North Pacific."

Other nations, notably Japan, were manifesting expansionist tendencies in the 1890s. Japan's ambitions were directed largely against China, which seemed helpless; yet Mahan did not rule out the possibility that the "racially homogeneous" and rapidly multiplying Chinese might somehow "obtain the organization by which alone potential force receives adequate military development." If the "teeming multitudes of central and northern Asia" should expand, there was no doubt in Mahan's mind that their direction would be eastward to the islands of the Pacific and perhaps even to the North American continent itself. In that case, "the only barrier will be the warlike spirit of the representatives of civilization." Then naval power would play "the leading part which it has in all history, and the United States by her geographical position must be one of the frontiers from which, as from a base of operations, the Sea Power of the civilized world will energize."

As the decade of the 1890s advanced, Mahan became increasingly insistent that the large standing armies of Europe would be indispensable in any future conflict between Christian European civilization and the barbarism of the East. Moreover, he found in the armies of Europe a testament to the superiority of Western civilization. Informed by the Social Darwinism of the era, Mahan could write in seriousness: "Conflict is the condition of all life, material and spiritual; and it is to the soldier's experience that the spiritual life goes for its most vivid metaphors and loftiest inspirations. Whatever else the twentieth century may bring us, it will not, from anything now current in the thought of the nineteenth, receive a nobler ideal."

Such a militaristic conclusion stamped Mahan's outlook as

decidedly more aggressive than that of his naval predecessors; yet his definitions of civilization and barbarism differed very little from those held by the officers of the 1870s and 1880s. Mahan concisely defined "our not unjustly vaunted European and American civilization" in the *North American Review* of November 1894. It was an "oasis set in the midst of a desert of barbarism, rent with many intestine troubles, and ultimately dependent, not upon its mere elaboration of organization, but upon the power of that organization to express itself in a menacing and efficient attitude of physical force sufficient to resist the numerically overwhelming, but inadequately organized hosts of outsiders." The only difference between this definition and the descriptions of the world accepted by officers like Luce, Porter, and Shufeldt was a slight one of tone. Mahan apparently felt threatened by the possible expansion of Asian peoples, whereas his forerunners conceived only of the use of naval and military force for the extension of American commerce.

Mahan had composed a conundrum he could not solve. Germany in Samoa in 1889 and Britain in Venezuela in 1895 showed that European policies impinged on American interests. The civilized nations were obviously divided among themselves. Still, if Asia should awaken, European and American interests would be equally threatened. As the decade wore on, Mahan warned against both dangers without ever questioning the ostensible superiority of Western civilization. "The seat and scene of the loftiest culture, of the highest intellectual activities, it is not in them so much that it has exceeded the rest of the world as in the political development and material prosperity which it has owed to the virile energies of its sons, alike in commerce and in war."

A variety of forces determined the expression of this manly vigor, and in Mahan's explanation of late nineteenth-century European expansion several themes neatly intermingled and reinforced one another. Manifest Destiny, racism, and Darwinism blended smoothly with a pre-Hobsonian analysis of the results of industrial surpluses. "It is because so much of the world still remains in the possession of the savage, or of states whose imperfect development, political or economical, does not enable them to realize for the general use nearly the result of which the territory is capable, while at the same time the redundant energies of civilized states, both government and peoples, are finding lack of openings and scantiness of livelihood at home, that there now obtains a condition of aggressive restlessness with which all have to reckon."

It was "entirely evident" to Mahan that the United States did "not now share this tendency"; but by the Monroe Doctrine the United States had long before accepted "the necessity, recognized with practical unanimity by her people, of insuring to the weaker states of America, although of racial and political antecedents different from her own, freedom to develop politically along their own lines and according to their own capacities, without interference from governments foreign to these continents." The United States had voluntarily assumed this duty. Since it rested "not upon political philanthropy, but simply upon our own proximate interests as affected by such foreign interference, [it] has towards others rather the nature of a right than a duty."

Nowhere was the duty of the United States more clearly defined by history and interest than in the Gulf of Mexico and Caribbean, and as the 1890s closed Mahan again embroidered the theme of necessary American domination of those waters. He compared them with the Mediterranean, and he drew conclusions from the analogy of Suez. "Wherever situated, whether at Panama or at Nicaragua, the fundamental meaning of the canal will be that it advances by thousands of miles the frontiers of European civilization in general, and of the United States in particular; that it knits together the whole system of American states enjoying that civilization as in no other way they can be bound." The Caribbean was "the very domain of sea power . . . and centre of those influences by which such a maritime highway as a canal must be controlled, even as control of the Suez Canal rests in the Mediterranean."

There were two ways by which to dominate the canal itself. One was to exercise political and military power in and around the isthmus. Mahan preferred indirect control by means of "a distinctly preponderant navy." He believed the mobility of naval force always gave it an advantage over fixed installations. To be truly preponderant in the Caribbean and Gulf of Mexico, however, and thus to be certain of controlling the canal's eastern approaches, a naval power ought to secure certain outlying geographical points. By 1897 Mahan was willing to be quite specific, and in an article published in the October issue of *Harper's* he forecast the direction American imperialism would take in the

Caribbean within the next three years. He observed that "the phenomenon of the long, narrow peninsula of Florida, with its strait, is reproduced successively in Cuba, Haiti, and Puerto Rico, with the passages dividing them. The whole together forms one long barrier, the strategic significance of which cannot be over-looked in its effect upon the Caribbean; while the Gulf of Mexico is assigned to absolute seclusion by it, if the passages are in hostile control." One result of the Spanish-American War was that the United States acquired the right to naval bases in two of the three critical islands Mahan named, thereby ensuring that the adjacent waterways would never be "in hostile control."

Neither the outcome of that war, nor its inception, nor any major American diplomatic event of the late nineteenth or early twentieth centuries can be directly attributed to Mahan. He was not a Richard Olney, who as secretary of state in 1895 bluntly informed the British government that in matters concerning the Western Hemisphere the decree of the United States was "law." He was not a John Hay, whose Open Door notes moved the United States to center stage in the dramatic confrontation of Western powers over helpless China. In fact, he was not even the independent commanding officer of a ship whose men might precipitate a war scare between Chile and the United States by brawling in Valparaiso or ensure the triumph of Hawaiian revolution by landing in Honolulu.

In 1890, at the time of publication of *The Influence of Sea Power upon History*, Alfred Mahan was merely a captain in the United States Navy with thirty-four years of continuous service. His senior status was primarily a function of longevity. In the navy of that era a line officer could reasonably expect to advance to rear admiral if he lived long enough. Mahan was on his way to flag rank, which was customarily followed by retirement and oblivion. Instead, seven years later, Captain Mahan was an international celebrity who had discussed naval strategy with Queen Victoria and received honorary degrees from Oxford, Cambridge, Harvard, and Yale. He published almost a book a year, and his articles in such popular journals as the *North American Review*, *Atlantic Monthly*, and *Harper's* earned five hundred dollars apiece.

With the exception of a short stint on the Naval War Board

during the Spanish-American War and membership in the American delegation to the first Hague Peace Conference of 1899, Mahan had no direct formal access to American policy makers in the 1890s. He spent the first two years of the decade awaiting reconvening of classes at the Naval War College and writing his second major interpretive history, *The Influence of Sea Power upon the French Revolution and Empire, 1793–1812.* In 1893 he was ordered to sea as commanding officer of the U.S.S. *Chicago,* much against his will and over the protests of influential friends like Theodore Roosevelt and Henry Cabot Lodge. His extended cruise in European waters was both gratifying and frustrating. During stops in England in 1893 and 1894 the British lionized him, but the rear admiral aboard the *Chicago* found public adulation of his flag captain increasingly distasteful and irksome. He used pettifogging irritants, those timeless and ineffectual remedies of minor tyrants, to make Mahan pay the piper, but he did not drive him to insubordination.

When the *Chicago* returned to the United States, Mahan retired from active duty in order to devote all his energy to writing. He soon produced *The Life of Nelson,* which was extremely well received in England. Mahan's immortality was assured, and for the rest of his life he enjoyed the delightful *fin de siècle* existence of a gentleman of letters. He kept in touch with the powerful men of his times through essays, letters, and conversations and with the great men of history through research and books.

William D. Puleston, Mahan's biographer, believed that as a member of the Naval War Board Mahan's "direct responsibility for the major decisions of the war was scarcely less than McKinley's." There is little if any evidence to support this conclusion, and Puleston's very next sentence is a far more accurate appraisal. "But it was through his writings that he exerted the greatest influence on the course of events." Lodge, Roosevelt, and other expansionists on this side of the Atlantic imbibed Mahan along with Strong, Fiske, and Burgess. On the other side of the ocean, British commentators credited Mahan's works with greatly facilitating parliamentary approval of appropriations for the naval expansion of the 1890s. In a Nelson Day editorial of 1893 the *Times* of London took the broadest view by comparing Mahan to the great scientific lawmakers of history. "By his pregnant conception of sea-power and his masterly exposition of its influence upon the history of the

British Isles, Captain Mahan may almost be said to have effected a revolution in the study of naval history similar in kind to that effected by Copernicus in the domain of astronomy."

The comparison with Copernicus is suggestive. In his brilliant historical novel, *The French Lieutenant's Woman*, John Fowles vividly depicted the foundation of Victorian thought as science, particularly the Darwinian hypothesis. By the close of the century British and American thinkers had converted Darwin's biological analysis into a scheme of social theory known as Social Darwinism. Liberal reformers and die-hard conservatives alike accepted the postulates of this interpretation. Basically it held that competition in the marketplace resulted in the triumph of the men most fit to hold wealth and exercise power as trustees for the less well-endowed mass of mankind. With a few exceptions, Social Darwinists believed that governmental interference with the economy must be at an absolute minimum if the competitive process was to function properly. Ignoring the embarrassing contradictions of imperial preferences and protective tariffs, they concluded that by virtue of their efficient industrial production Great Britain and the United States had proven themselves most in harmony with natural law. The British and American economic, political, and social systems therefore represented the highest step thus far attained on the evolutionary ladder. To these theorists, Anglo-American civilization should envelop the world, and most of them were willing to help spread the gospel.

Alfred Thayer Mahan fitted perfectly into this environment. He stressed the importance of industrial production and commerce to the United States and any nation seeking greatness. He very obviously believed that Anglo-American civilization was superior to all others, and he was anxious to extend that culture into regions of barbarism. In these respects, however, he differed little if any from a host of other American naval officers.

What made Mahan's writing unique and so thoroughly harmonious with the intellectual milieu of his time was his injection of science into history. Stephen Luce had described naval warfare as a science and had hoped to find someone who could deduce principles of naval strategy from history; Mahan did precisely that. Nowhere is his success more evident than in the first chapter of *The Influence of Sea Power*, where he discussed with apparent detachment five elements, or "natural conditions," that had "determined" the "history of seaboard nations." In all of

his subsequent narratives he never abandoned those determinants, and in his topical, analytical essays on contemporary events
he artfully employed them to enhance the case for American naval
and political expansion overseas.

It was Mahan's great fortune to be writing in a decade when
certain changes in national and international conditions made
imperialism increasingly popular with large numbers of Americans. Domestically, beginning in 1893, there was a serious depression that did not moderate and revert to a period of boom in the
usual cyclical manner. The depression of 1877 had first given rise
to serious consideration of the need for overseas outlets for
surplus American industrial products by politicians like Secretary
of State William M. Evarts and Secretary of the Navy Richard W.
Thompson, as well as by naval officers like Robert W. Shufeldt.
Increased exports would mean fuller employment of factory
workers at home and thus reduction of social discontent and the
chances of upheaval and revolution. With the more extended and
far more serious depression of the 1890s these ideas were revived,
but markets were less accessible abroad. In the 1880s and
increasingly in the 1890s the European powers colonized Africa
and Asia and levied heavy or prohibitive duties upon importation
of American goods into the new dependencies. Thus the United
States seemed to have two choices: increase its exports to those
areas not yet closed or acquire protected markets of its own. In
both cases colonies would be essential, either as bases from which
the navy could protect the lives and property of American
merchants in distant places, or as markets.

The colonies and overseas naval bases Mahan desired came
with the Spanish-American War. Almost simultaneously Mahan's
friend Theodore Roosevelt was elevated to the presidency. That
vigorous exponent of American expansion built the canal in
Central America that Mahan and other navalists had long expected. Through energetic use of naval power Roosevelt assured
American hegemony in the Caribbean, as the naval officers of the
last decades of the nineteenth century had insisted would be
necessary once the canal became a reality. By showing the fleet to
countries as far away as Australia and Japan Roosevelt thrust the
American naval frontier far into the Pacific, something naval
officers had been urging for a quarter of a century. The former
assistant secretary of the navy did not neglect shipbuilding when
president. He consistently urged and won congressional approval

for bigger warships with greater range, heavier guns, and thicker armor.

In most aspects, Roosevelt's naval and diplomatic policies represented fruition for the naval officers of the late nineteenth century. Mahan was one of those men, and it was his writing that most forcefully and effectively summarized their position. In present-day terms, he was a highly successful propagandist for a policy of "realism" by which American statesmen pursued power through judicious use of the stupendous geopolitical resources of the United States.

BIBLIOGRAPHIC NOTE

Any study of nineteenth-century American naval history must begin with Harold and Margaret Sprout, *The Rise of American Naval Power, 1776–1918* (Princeton, 1939), who roundly praise Mahan. A recent dissenter is Peter Karsten, *The Naval Aristocracy: The Golden Age of Annapolis and the Emergence of Modern American Navalism* (New York, 1972), who concludes that Mahan's views were outdated when first expressed. The most well-balanced biography is still [Captain] William D. Puleston, *Mahan: The Life and Work of Captain Alfred Thayer Mahan, U.S.N.* (New Haven, 1939).

Robert Seager II analyzes the ideas of navalists in Congress and in uniform during the decade preceding Mahan in "Ten Years before Mahan: The Unofficial Case for the New Navy, 1880–1890," *Mississippi Valley Historical Review* 40 (December 1953), as does Kenneth J. Hagan in *American Gunboat Diplomacy and the Old Navy, 1877–1889* (Westport, Conn., 1973). Benjamin Franklin Cooling, *Benjamin Franklin Tracy: Father of the American Fighting Navy* (Hamden, Conn. 1973), carefully reassesses Mahan's immediate impact on American naval policy and concludes that it was less than believed by Walter R. Herrick, Jr., *The American Naval Revolution* (Baton Rouge, 1967). John A. S. Grenville and George B. Young, *Politics, Strategy, and American Diplomacy: Studies in Foreign Policy, 1873–1917* (New Haven, 1966), argue that Luce was the great innovator and Mahan the popularizer.

The final answer to the riddle of whether Luce or Mahan more heavily influenced Secretary of the Navy Tracy and his successors must be sought in the annual reports of the secretaries of the navy, the *Congressional Record*, and the hearings of the Senate and House appropriations and naval committees. The indispensable guide to the documentary history of the nineteenth-century American navy is Robert W. Neeser, *Statistical and Chronological History of the United States Navy, 1775–1907* (New York, 1909).

Walter LaFeber, *The New Empire: An Interpretation of American Expansion, 1860–1898* (Ithaca, 1963), deftly sketches the intellectual, political, and economic environment that shaped Mahan's "strategic formulation." Harold U. Faulkner discusses the domestic and international turmoil of the 1890s in *Politics, Reform, and Expansion, 1890–1900* (New York, 1959); but the essay by Marilyn B. Young in Barton J. Bernstein, ed., *Towards a New Past: Dissenting Essays in American History* (New York, 1968), most succinctly captures the flavor of disruptive imperialism that made Mahan's ideas popular after 1893.

Charles C. Taylor, *The Life of Admiral Mahan* (London, 1920), reflects Mahan's continuing popularity in England. William E. Livezey, *Mahan on Sea Power* (Norman, Okla., 1947), catalogs the effect of Mahan's thinking on American domestic and foreign policy. More limited in chronological scope, but deeply researched and finely balanced, is Richard D. Challener, *Admirals, Generals, and American Foreign Policy, 1898–1914* (Princeton, 1973). Harold and Margaret Sprout describe an apparent decline in the influence of Mahan's ideas after 1918 in *Toward a New Order of Sea Power* (Princeton, 1940). During the interwar period Louis Hacker condemned nineteenth-century imperialism by exaggerating Mahan's influence and criticizing his views in "The Incendiary Mahan," *Scribner's Magazine* (April 1934).

The U.S. Naval Institute *Proceedings* and the *Naval War College Review*, the two most prestigious professional American naval journals, frequently carry articles extolling Mahan and arguing that his work remains relevant to contemporary American policies. The most intelligent of these is [Commander] James A. Barber, "Mahan and Naval Strategy in the Nuclear Age," *Naval War College Review* 24 (March 1972). Other examples are [Captain] Carl H. Amme, "Seapower and the Superpowers," U.S. Naval Institute *Proceedings* 95 (October 1968), and [Captain] Jack E. Godfrey, "Mahan: The Man, His Writings and Philosophy," *Naval War College Review* 21 (March 1969).

The striking similarity between the analyses of twentieth-century "realists" and Mahan's ideas is evident in Hans J. Morgenthau, *Politics among Nations: The Struggle for Power and Peace* (New York, 1948). George F. Kennan interprets Mahan from the realist's perspective in *American Diplomacy, 1900–1950* (Chicago, 1951).

Mahan's prolific pen made any interpreter's task congenial. His most important works are *The Influence of Sea Power upon History, 1660–1783* (Boston, 1890), *The Life of Nelson: The Embodiment of the Sea Power of Great Britain* (Boston, 1897), and *The Interest of America in Sea Power, Present and Future* (Boston, 1897). The historical method and political viewpoint introduced in these three books were simply amplified in Mahan's other writings.

NOTES ON THE CONTRIBUTORS

James B. Chapin, assistant professor of history at University College, Rutgers University, studied with Walter LaFeber at Cornell, where he received his Ph.D. in 1971. He is now at work on a study of Rhode Island politics from 1776 to 1865 and is revising his doctoral thesis, "Hamilton Fish and American Expansion," for publication.

Cecil B. Currey, professor of history at the University of South Florida, studied with W. Stitt Robinson at the University of Kansas, where he received his Ph.D. in 1964. His publications include *The Road to Revolution: Benjamin Franklin in England, 1765–1775* (New York, 1968) and *Code Number 72: Ben Franklin, Patriot or Spy* (Englewood Cliffs, N.J., 1972).

Norman A. Graebner, Edward R. Stettinius Professor of History at the University of Virginia, holds a Ph.D. from the University of Chicago. Among his many works in American history are *Empire on the Pacific* (New York, 1955), *The New Isolationism* (New York, 1956), *Cold War Diplomacy* (Princeton, 1962), and *Ideas and Diplomacy* (New York, 1964); his latest book is *Recent United States History* (New York, 1972). In addition, he has edited a number of important collections of documents and essays in the field of American diplomacy, including *An Uncertain Tradition: American Secretaries of State in the Twentieth Century* (New York, 1961). Professor Graebner is also a past president of the Society for Historians of American Foreign Relations.

Kenneth J. Hagan, assistant professor of history at the U.S. Naval Academy, studied with Charles S. Campbell at the Claremont Graduate School, where he received his Ph.D. in 1970. He has recently published *American Gunboat Diplomacy and the Old Navy, 1877–1889* (Westport, Conn., 1973), and is compiling a bibliography of nineteenth-century American naval history.

Lawrence S. Kaplan, professor of history at Kent State University, studied with Samuel Flagg Bemis at Yale, where he received his Ph.D. in 1951. He has published extensively on the diplomacy of the early national period, as well as on twentieth-century American foreign policy; his works include *Jefferson and France* (New Haven, 1967) and *Colonies into Nation: American Diplomacy, 1763–1801* (New York, 1972). He is currently at work on a cultural history of American foreign relations.

Lester D. Langley, associate professor of history at the University of Georgia, studied with Charles Stansifer at the University of Kansas, where he received his Ph.D. in 1965. Among other works he has published *The Cuban Policy of the United States* (New York, 1968), and he has edited *The United States, Cuba, and the Cold War* (Lexington, Mass., 1970) and *The United States and Latin America* (Reading, Mass., 1971). Professor Langley is currently at work on a book-length study, *Andrew Jackson and the World.*

Frank J. Merli, associate professor of history at Queens College of The City University of New York, studied with Robert H. Ferrell at Indiana University, where he received his Ph.D. in 1964. He has written *Great Britain and the Confederate Navy, 1861–1865* (Bloomington, 1970), and is currently preparing a book on nineteenth-century neutrality from 1819 to 1919.

Ian Mugridge, assistant professor of history and assistant vice-president for academic affairs at Simon Fraser University, studied with Alexander DeConde at the University of California, Santa Barbara, where he received his Ph.D. in 1969. He is currently working on an analysis of foreign influences on the making of the U.S. Constitution; in addition, he is editing the American correspondence of Sir Robert Liston and is preparing a monograph on William Randolph Hearst and American foreign policy.

David M. Pletcher, professor of history at Indiana University, studied with J. Fred Rippy at the University of Chicago, where he received his Ph.D. in 1946. Among his many publications are *Rails, Mines, and Progress: Seven American Promoters in Mexico, 1867–1911* (Ithaca, 1958), *The Awkward Years: American Foreign Relations under Garfield and Arthur* (Columbia, Mo., 1962), and *The Diplomacy of Annexation: Texas, Oregon, and the Mexican War* (Columbia, Mo., 1973).

Geoffrey S. Smith, associate professor of history at Queen's University, Ontario, studied with Alexander DeConde at the University of California, Santa Barbara, where he received his Ph.D. in 1969. In addition to a number of articles on Latin American history, he has written *To Save a Nation: American Countersubversives, the New Deal, and the Coming of World War II* (New York, 1973). He is currently working on a full-length biography of Charles Wilkes and a study tentatively entitled *The Bifocal Vision in American Foreign Relations: A Study of American Images of Europe and Asia.*

Gordon H. Warren, assistant professor of history at Central Washington State College, studied with Robert H. Ferrell at Indiana University, where he received his Ph.D. in 1969. He is currently preparing his doctoral thesis on the *Trent* affair for publication and is working on a soon-to-be-published study of American entry into wars, *Firing the First Shot.*

Patrick C. T. White, professor of history at the University of Toronto, did graduate work at Cambridge University and received his doctorate from the University of Minnesota in 1953. A specialist in Canadian and American diplomacy, he is preparing a history of Canadian American relations from 1815 to 1846. His publications include *A Nation on Trial: America and the War of 1812* (New York, 1965), and he has edited (with an introduction) *Lord Selkirk's Diary, 1803–1804* (Toronto, 1958), *The Critical Years: American Foreign Policy, 1793–1823* (New York, 1970), and (with an introduction) *Conducting the Diplomacy of The New Nation, 1793–1815* (New York, 1971).

Theodore A. Wilson, professor of history at the University of Kansas, studied with Robert H. Ferrell at Indiana University, where he received his Ph.D. in 1966. He has published *The First Summit: Roosevelt and Churchill at Placentia Bay, 1941* (Boston, 1969), which was awarded the Francis Parkman Prize. Professor Wilson has served as senior research associate at the Harry S. Truman Library Institute and has received fellowships from the National Endowment for the Humanities and the Guggenheim Foundation. He is currently completing a study of the origins of foreign aid, 1943–53 (with Richard McKinzie), and preparing a biography of Henry A. Wallace.

INDEX

Aberdeen, earl of, 169–70, 172, 177, 181
Abolitionist movement, 176
Adams, Charles Francis, 204–5, 211–12
Adams, Henry, 209, 234, 248
Adams, John, 12–13, 62, 84, 105, 115–16
Adams, John Quincy, 105–33; advocates naval exploration, 138, 140; attitude of, toward partisanship, 110; background of, 105; characteristics of, 107–8, 110; early career of, 106–7; and embargo, 95; as expansionist, 112; and Federalists, 106, 110; and fishing rights, 117; and Florida purchase, 120–21; and Holy Alliance, 114; and intervention in Greece, 129; and Jackson, 119; Latin American policy of, 122–25, 127, 130; and Louisiana, 118–21; and military preparedness, 112; and Monroe Doctrine, 20, 127, 128–30; and neutrality, 106, 111–12; and relations with England, 115, 116–18, 149 n; and relations with France,

115; and relations with Monroe, 108; and relations with Russia, 115, 126–27, 128, 130–31; and relations with Spain, 120, 126; as secretary of state, 108–9; Seward as disciple of, 200
Adams, Samuel, 2, 3–4
Adams-Onís Treaty, 119–21
Adet, Pierre, 75
Aix-la-Chapelle, Conference of, 123, 125
Alabama, C.S.S., 155, 231 n
Alabama claims, 212, 231, 232–42
Albany Plan of Union, 21
Alexander I, 110, 114, 115
Alien and Sedition Acts, 90
American Plan of 1776, 23
Articles of Confederation, 32
Ashburton, Lord, 148

Balamaceda, Jorge, 266
Bancroft, Edward, 7, 8, 12
Bancroft, George, 167, 172
Barber, F. M., 291
Bayard, Thomas, 270
Baynes, John, 21
Bear Flag Republic, 180
Beaumarchais, 10, 19
Beckwith, George, 47, 48